THE COMPLETE GUIDE TO BOLT-ON PERFORMANCE
EDITED AND DESIGNED BY LARRY SCHREIB

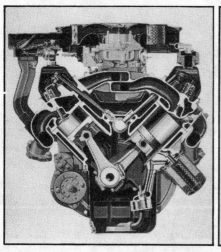

THE COMPLETE GUIDE TO BOLT-ON PERFORMANCE

S-A DESIGN PUBLISHING COMPANY
11801 E. SLAUSON BLVD. BLDG E
SANTA FE SPRINGS, CALIFORNIA 90670

The information contained in this publication is intended as general guidelines for replacing components with suitable OEM or Specialty replacement parts. In all cases manufacturer recommendations, procedures, and instructions supersede and take precedence over descriptions herein. Specific component design and mechanical procedures vary considerably in every case and are beyond the control of the publisher, therefore the publisher disclaims all liability incurred in connection with the use of information contained in this publication.

ISBN 0-931472-04-0

TABLE OF CONTENTS

INTRODUCTION

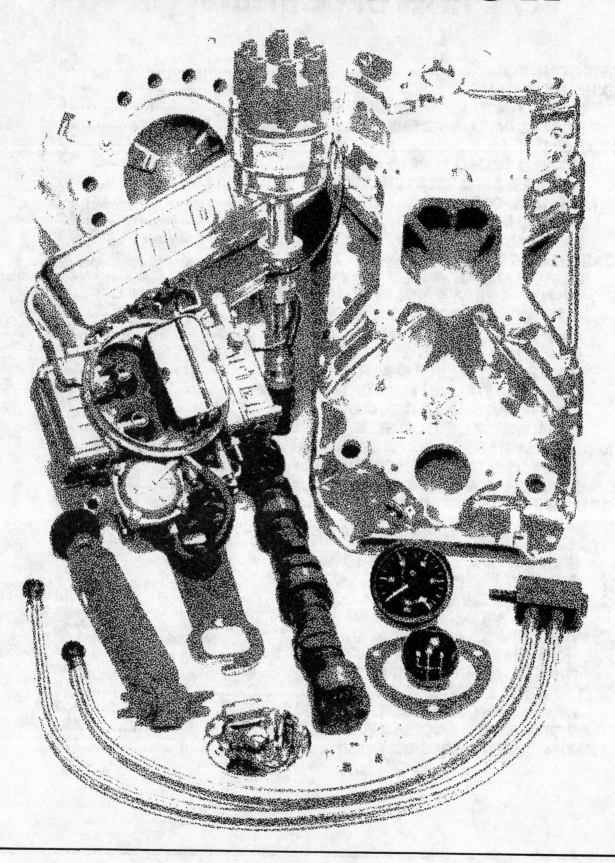

The contrast between a stock, late-model "smog-ified" engine and a high-performance street machine is more than just the addition of a few pieces of chrome. The best street machine engines today feature parts inside and out that are designed to gain the most performance per dollar while retaining good fuel economy and a sensible emissions level. The proper selection of bolt-on equipment is an important factor when building performance and reliability.

Everyone would like to have a finely-tuned, responsive engine. This is true regardless of whether we're speaking of the "bench racer" at the local hamburger stand or the businessman who drives a Seville or a Cordoba. Unfortunately, you can no longer buy a car from a dealership that offers what most of us would consider an "acceptable" level of performance. (If your checkbook can cover the payments on a $28,000 Porsche Turbo-Carrera, or some similar exotic automotive jewel, and the high-buck German or Italian mechanic you will need to keep it running, you're wasting your money on this book.) It is, however, possible for anyone with a small understanding of automotive mechanics and a modest investment of time and money to significantly improve the performance of nearly any automobile! This book is intended as a basic "do-it-yourself" guide to help the average person recapture engine "performance," while at the same time it eliminates common misconceptions about "racing" and "super-high-performance" techniques that are totally inappropriate for day-to-day driving.

Glancing through the various sections of this book, you may have the impression that this is another automotive publication that's going to talk about expensive, esoteric engine-building techniques. It's not. We've covered just about every facet of what it takes to build a performance-type street machine using easily-understood "bolt-on" procedures and using modestly priced and easily obtained replacement parts. By boiling down the feedback we've gathered from most of the well-known speed equipment manufacturers, engine builders, and dyno technicians, we hope to help you avoid the most common mistakes made by enthusiastic (but inexperienced) backyard mechanics. In the long run this will help you save a considerable amount of money.

What is a "Street" Engine?

Looking at auto magazines, browsing in speed equipment supply shops, and wandering through the pits at a race track can give you a heady impression of what a performance engine is supposed to look like. But when you mentally add up the cost of all the neat doodads, there is a considerable financial argument to leave your newly acquired Mustang or Camaro or Barracuda totally stock. Unfortunately, many enthusiasts are introduced to street performance as a minor variation of all-out racing—nothing could be further from the truth.

The overriding concern for any and all street engines must be *practicality*. This is undoubtedly a difficult quality to define in exact terms because each of us probably has a different view of what is practical or not practical. However, there are some generally accepted guidelines for an engine subjected to the very high demands of daily driving. What it *should not* do is overheat in traffic, stumble or hesitate upon acceleration across every intersection, require frequent tuning or adjustments, or cost a fortune to build and run. What, on the other hand, it *should* exhibit is a reasonable combination of good fuel economy, low emissions and, of course, good performance. This seems a lot to ask of an engine but such a combination is feasible today more than ever, thanks in large part to the efforts of conscientious equipment manufacturers who have kept pace with our rapidly changing times. Spurred on by the ever-increasing cost of gasoline and the need to contribute to cleaning up our polluted air, their research has shown that the *right combination of equipment* provides benefits in all three areas: emissions, economy and better street performance.

If you can restrain your impulse to buy equipment based solely on "hairy" looks or what so-and-so has on his car, you'll probably have a better chance of success. The ancient Greeks had an advanced civilization ruled by the wise philosophy "moderation in all things," and you'll find as you read on that their sage advice applies as much to street engine building as it does to social philosophy. The bonus in the offing is that your "practical" street engine will also be affordable, both to build and to run.

Emission Concerns

Certainly a lot of very different kinds of people will be reading this book, but if we can make one safe assumption about all of them, it is that they all breathe AIR. We're not going to go into a long diatribe about air

The "dyno tune," when performed by a conscientious expert, may be the best performance investment for your dollar. If you plan to add other equipment (which might negate the "blueprinting" of the stock carburetion and ignition) dyno tune the engine after the new equipment is installed.

The speed shop is where you will probably buy most of your bolt-on performance equipment, so you can *see* what you're buying. Fast communication between small speed shops and warehouse wholesalers has made an ever-widening array of products available to every local area.

pollution here, we all should know by now what kind of mistakes Man has made with his environment, the air, the water and the earth. What we will say, that isn't often said in performance automotive publications, is that hot rodders have been just as guilty in their own way as the industrial giants we curse whenever we pass a billowy cloud over a factory's smokestack. Back when hot rodding was in its infancy (when our public image couldn't have been worse even if we had known about emissions) the steps to engine performance were simple. You bought a set of high-compression finned-aluminum heads, a dual exhaust system and a fancy intake manifold with as many carburetors as possible and topped it off with all the ignition advance the

Though add-on equipment can substantially increase the power output of your engine you will also have to keep it properly tuned. There are many excellent manufacturer manuals with performance tuneup specs.

engine could take. If a hot rodder had suggested back then that perhaps we were wasting fuel and adding too much CO, HC and NOX to the air, he would have been laughed out of the drive-in parking lot. Obviously, times have changed.

Things have gotten to the point where in the not-too-distant future the exhaust pipes of new cars will be welded shut in order to comply with federal emissions regulations, and the hood will be locked from the factory and only your congressman will have the key. Fortunately, we aren't there yet, and in most states you are still free to modify or tune your own car. But California, where so many automotive trends have their start, has become increasingly strict in the past five years, and when it comes to legislation about automobiles, there's some truth to the political slogan "As California goes...so goes the nation." Every state will sooner or later have strict emissions laws and annual, semi-annual or spot roadside emissions checks of your vehicle's tailpipe. So it behooves hot rodders to understand what produces emissions and what lowers them so we can tune our high-performance street machines properly.

Many experts, if pressed, would agree that the hot rodders (who make up no more than 1% of the drivers on the road) make far less of a contribution to our dirty air than the 30% or 40% of the "average" drivers who don't keep their cars tuned. Ditto for fuel efficiency. Be that as it may, let's keep our collective noses clean for the sake of the continued enjoyment of our hobby without harassment, and maybe we'll all breathe a little easier for it.

Budgeting a Street Engine

In today's inflated economy, few of us have money to burn. Everything costs more than it did yesterday, but less than it's going to cost tomorrow. While replacement parts have increased in cost, the cost of skilled labor has gone up even more. You'll find that even building a fairly basic street machine can become prohibitively expensive if you have to farm out all of the work to professional shops. If you are just starting, our best advice to you is to take advantage of the automotive courses offered at trade schools and night schools. The adult education classes at most high schools are practically free. This could be the most important advice we could impart about getting started in hot rodding. Even if you never make a single modification, an auto shop course could save you thousands of dollars over the years on just simple do-it-yourself maintenance. Doing all of the work yourself can save you even more when you're dealing with hot-rod modifications. If you have to go to a professional shop for a camshaft installation, for instance, *the labor could cost you twice what the cam and kit cost.*

Even when armed with the practical knowledge to do most of your own work, it still costs money to improve your car's performance. The old adage you used to see on speed shop walls was "Speed costs money. How fast do you want to go?" The cost chart in this chapter should give you a clue as to the relative costs of common specialty equipment.

Most of the personnel you'll find in the speed shop will be helpful and knowledgeable about the equipment they sell. Their expertise can be a big help when planning a "driveway" engine project and they will know what items or brands have given other customers the best power and reliability.

The modern speed shop has everything for the performance fan, with fully-stocked shelves and neat displays, a far cry from the "barn" atmosphere of 15-20 years ago. From sway bars to superchargers, shops today carry more equipment and better quality merchandise than ever before.

Obviously, you can't afford to run out and buy everything on that list (unless you happen to be pretty wealthy). In fact, you should hold back your buying impulses *until* you have read this book thoroughly and understand exactly what each component will contribute toward your performance goals. If you can't afford to buy everything, then you'll have to do like most of us and budget your engine modifications by planning for "stages" in its performance development. Once you have read each chapter, you should have a good idea which pieces will best suit your purpose.

We've designed this book with a progressive table of contents, that is, the chapters are arranged in what we believe is their order of relative importance. The first chapters cover those areas of performance development that will give you the most results for your money, continuing on to those areas which are more expensive or complicated to follow. Thus, you may have only a certain amount to spend on your first *stage,* and you may only need to carry out the how-to's in the first or second chapter, leaving the later modifications for when you can afford them. In other words, don't read through this book and then blow your first budget allotment on a camshaft and kit.

Quite possibly, there's a first step we haven't discussed in this book about performance bolt-on's—the so-called dyno tune. A good dyno tune at a professional shop with a chassis dynamometer can work wonders for your street driveability and performance without you buying a single piece of specialty equipment. You

might think that $50 or so is a lot of money for a "tuneup" when new parts aren't included, but the dyno tune is not your garden variety "clean-and-gap" routine. While the standard type of tuneup is designed to eliminate hard starts, poor driveability and wasted gas, or get rid of an annoying miss at idle, the dyno tune is a method of gaining more power without adding any new equipment.

Most professional dyno tune shops begin by testing your car on their dyno to accurately assess its existing power level, and then they work to improve the power by modifying and adjusting the ignition and carburetion systems. You can think of it as a kind of "blueprinting" for the top of the engine just like decking and align-boring are blueprinting steps for the lower end. A conscientious dyno operator will play with various combinations of carburetor jetting, ignition lead and distributor advance curves to achieve the best possible performance for your specific engine, your specific driving style, your specific gasoline (an important "variable" these days), and your specific altitude and climate.

As a first step in your quest for performance, the dyno tune could be a valuable stage in your development. However, "good" dyno tune shops are not found on every street corner and there are some chassis dyno operators who use the instruments more as an advertising gimmick than as a useful tool. We would suggest that if you do plan to make some of the engine modifications outlined in this book, have the dyno tune done *last* so you'll have the benefit of knowing the best "topside blueprinting" for your modi-

fied engine. Otherwise, the dyno tune is perfect for the guy who will be making minimal changes, but would like to have his stock setup deliver its maximum capabilities.

So enter here the wide world of bolt-on performance equipment. You won't find any superchargers, radical race parts, or "atomic catalytic combustion sparker" gimmicks here. What you will find, hopefully, is a clear path through the maze of dazzling equipment to be found on the walls of your local speed shop or the pages of those mail order catalogs scattered around the garage. More power to you!

COMPARATIVE EQUIPMENT COSTS

PART	COST	INSTALLATION LABOR
Dual exhausts and mufflers	$120	$35
Headers	$75	$30-$150
Free-flow air cleaner	$15	n/c
Aluminum intake manifold	$100	$40
4-barrel carburetor	$75	$10-$25
Camshaft and kit	$130	$175
Dual-point ignition	$50	$15
Breakerless CD ignition	$30-$300	$30
Heavy-duty clutch	$75	$30-$50
Heavy-duty shocks	$60	$15
Traction bars	$50	$25

Buying and installing high-performance (or "specialty") equipment never has been a particularly cheap deal. However, the home mechanic can easily obtain a very respectable level of performance if he buys wisely, installs the equipment carefully, and follows a well thought out plan (levels of 400-500 horsepower are possible).

EXHAUST SYSTEMS

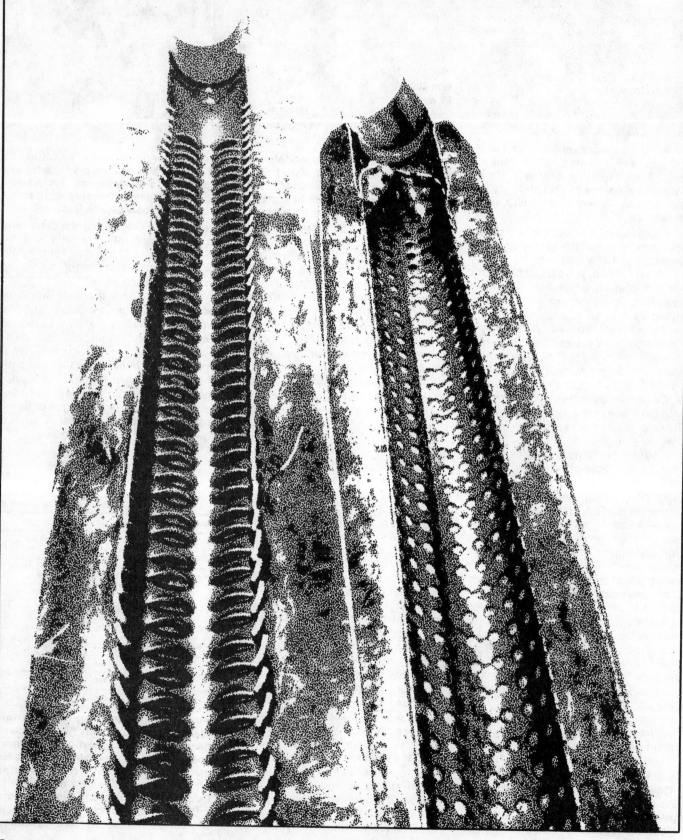

The further you dig into the world of high performance, the more you will realize that most modifications involve a *compromise* of some sort. You generally can't get the maximum improvement in power without some sacrifice in another direction. But one area where this doesn't quite hold true is your exhaust system, a major reason we are discussing the exhaust system before we get into other bolt-on modifications. No other area of modification will yield as much horsepower-per-dollar-spent as reducing exhaust restriction, and it's the only performance avenue that doesn't have some drawback. The usual sacrifices in the quest for power are driveability and fuel economy, not traditional characteristics of a strong hot rod, but improvements in the engine's exhaling have no effect on the former and can substantially improve the latter!

Most cars as they come from the factory have a single-exhaust system. On a V-8 engine, the exhaust paths from each bank of four cylinders start out equally enough—they both have a single cast-iron exhaust manifold. The manifold connects directly to the exhaust ports in the heads and funnels the gasses and noise from each of the four ports into one large pipe.

The stock manifolds are made of cast iron because this material resists the corrosive effects of exhaust gasses and moisture and it is a relatively cheap material that lends itself to inexpensive sand casting techniques. Stock manifolds come in a bewildering variety of shapes and sizes. Most of them are designed to fit the engine and chassis with the least interference and they are generally quite heavy and bulky to dampen the noise generated by the "tail end" of combustion rushing into the head ports. Very few, however, are designed to provide maximum flow.

From this inauspicious beginning the stock exhaust system goes downhill in efficiency. Each exhaust manifold connects to a steel pipe, which hugs the engine as it drops down under the pan. The two pipes join into one and run back toward the muffler. This is where the biggest problems begin. The exhaust from all eight cylinders is now going into a single pipe with a diameter barely sufficient to accommodate a healthy sneeze! This single pipe usually goes back to the middle of the car, taking numerous twists and bends to clear crossmembers and driveline parts, and dumps into the stock muffler. Here we find another engineering marvel filled with baffles and chambers and weighing a ton. It does only one thing well, it keeps your car as quiet as a graveyard. From the muffler on back, the little tailpipe makes several more bends to clear the rear axle and on some cars there may be a second muffler, or "resonator," to slow things up some more.

Dual Exhausts

Beginning with the assumption that you have a minimum amount of money to spend on your street machine project, let's begin with the easiest step in exhaust system development, a switch to a dual-exhaust system. We've seen what type of restrictions are imposed by the stock system, luckily these are easily improved

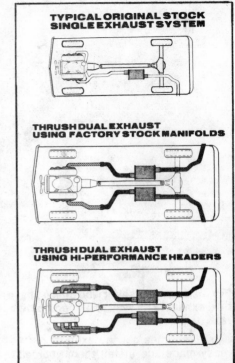

Dual exhausts will do as much for improving low-rpm engine response as any other modification you can make, without sacrificing economy.

upon. Switching to a dual-exhaust system has long been one of the favorite routes to better performance.

If you have a welding set, you can purchase the U-bends, straight exhaust tubing and mufflers and do the work at home. This can save a few dollars here and there, but it can be grubby work (we won't use the tired old pun and say that the work is exhausting), and most enthusiasts would rather not do it at home unless they happen to have a ramp, work pit or hoist. Welding overhead beneath the car is usually no picnic either, but you

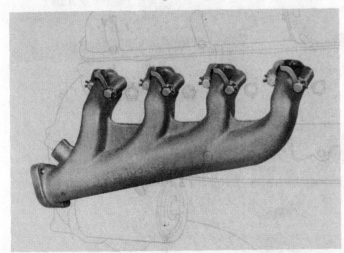

Often you can find high-performance cast-iron manifolds in your dealer's parts book, like these 428 Cobra-Jet manifolds for big-block Fords, and the 271-hp 289 models for smallblocks.

A stock single-exhaust system chokes the engine with restrictive manifolds hooked to an inefficient pair of pipes joined into a single small-diameter pipe.

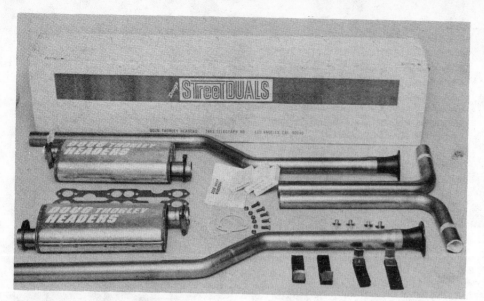

For the do-it-yourselfer who doesn't have a muffler shop handy, there are complete dual exhaust kits available to go from your manifolds or headers all the way to the rear.

can sometimes get the exhaust parts ready-made and install them yourself without welding. Until the coming of the expensive catalytic converter, almost every car manufacturer offered dual exhaust on a few of their models as an option. Some parts are still listed in dealer's catalogs waiting for you or you could purchase specialty pipes, clamps, hangers and mufflers at an auto parts store, speed shop or muffler shop.

The easiest and least expensive way to convert is to leave one side of your stock single system (the side that has the muffler and tailpipe) alone and just add the necessary pieces to give the other bank equal treatment. You'll

have to cut off the pipe from one side where it crosses over and joins the main pipe going to the muffler. The crossover stub that is left can be welded up, leaving a complete system on one side. New parts will be needed to make a complete system for the other bank, and you only have to buy one muffler.

Performance Duals

While this is the *easiest* method, it isn't the recommended route if real performance is your goal. To really overcome the restrictions on your engine's breathing, you're going to need: two better-than-stock mufflers;

pipes with fewer restrictive bends in them than stock; and perhaps most important, a set of pipes of *larger diameter* than your stockers.

Depending on displacement, your stock engine probably had an exhaust pipe diameter of 1½-1¾ inches, unless it is a special high-performance model. When you build your own system, the experts tell us the pipes should be a minimum of 2 inches in diameter for a high-performance street machine. A system built of 2¼-inch pipes would be even more desirable, and 2½-inch pipes are best. The larger the engine's displacement, the larger the pipes should be, so if you're running a motor of over 400 cubic inches, 2¼- to 2½-inch pipes would become the minimum size.

You also want to remove as many bends as possible. Unnecessary bends can be as restrictive as small-diameter pipes, especially if these bends occur before the mufflers. However, "straightening" the exhaust system of a street machine generally involves some compromises. The factory puts the bends in your pipes for two reasons: to provide better service access to some undercar components; and to provide clearance from moving parts such as the driveshaft and rearend (so the pipes aren't squashed during suspension travel). When you try to straighten out the system, you may make your car harder to work on (a sacrifice most enthusiasts are willing to make for the promise of extra power), further, rear axle interference is likely unless most of the stock after-muffler contours are maintained to provide for

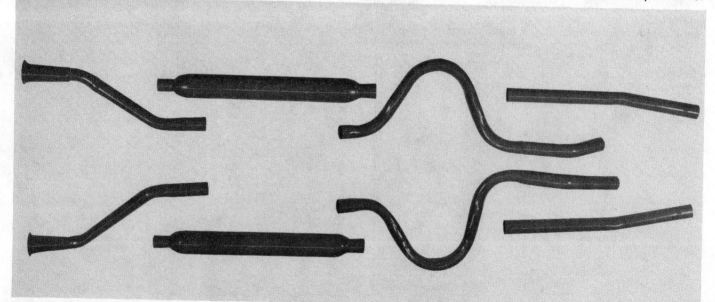

A complete high-performance exhaust system will include large diameter header pipes leading from the exhaust manifolds (or headers) back to low-restriction mufflers with equally-large exhaust tubes leading back to the rear bumpers. A simplified system may end at the rear axle but the best setup is to route the pipes over the top of the axle (allowing for axle movement) and back to the bumper.

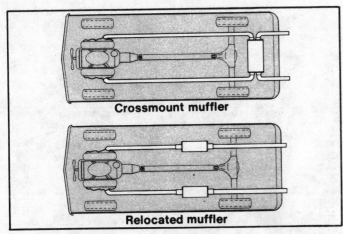

Crossmount muffler

Relocated muffler

If you choose to run straight-through duals on one of the crossmount-type cars, you'll have to use skinny mufflers because such cars don't have much ground clearance, but a straight system should reduce back pressure.

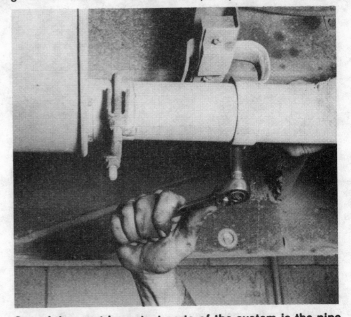

Large diameter pipes are important to a free-flowing system. If you plan to add headers later, the large pipes can hook directly to the collectors for a straight-through system all the way to the mufflers.

axle movement.

Dual Exhaust Routing

Your stock system probably extended all the way to the rear of the chassis where the gasses exited the tailpipe somewhere under the rear bumper. If you are purchasing a ready-made dual exhaust set, you won't have much choice about routing, but you can shop for the system that provides the least restrictions.

Generally, the pipe leaving the exhaust manifolds will be the most restrictive part of your system, since the larger-than-stock headpipe (exhaust tubing is called headpipe in *front* of the muffler and tailpipe from the muffler back) will have to clear the starter, oil pan, steering gear and other engine compartment necessities. From here back to the rear axle, you can usually keep the pipes straight (although this may be a problem if there is a transmission crossmember in the way) as long as ground clearance is not a problem. However, if you route the pipes to clear under-chassis members, the pipes may be lower than stock as they parallel the driveline. Also, try not to run the pipes too close to the floor or you could be giving yourself and your passengers a hot foot! In fact, custom muffler shops generally go by the simple rule of allowing one inch of clearance along the whole length of the exhaust system, since the pipes do move somewhat as the engine vibrates.

Your new mufflers should be mounted in the straight sections of pipe between the transmission and the rear axle, because there is usually more room to install them just ahead of the axle. The floor is often "dimpled" upward to provide clearance. Exhaust system manufacturers recommend that there be at least three hangers and clamps on each side of your dual setup. One should be up front near the transmission crossmember, one near the muffler (where the support is really needed) and one at the end of the system. Also, choose your hangers carefully—cheap ones are not usually worth the cost savings. Look for strongly-built hanger assemblies that use rubber reinforced with cord and utilize two rivets on each end of the rubber strip. These heavy-duty brackets are often sold through dealer-part outlets and "quality" auto stores.

Here's an unusual system for dual exhausts on a van. There was plenty of room for a conventional system, but the owner preferred to have both pipes exit at the left. This is a true performance system, with headers, 2½-inch pipes, turbo mufflers and balance tube (arrow).

One of the most important parts of the system is the pipe hanger. Look for hangers that have heavy gauge metal straps and always insist that they be rubber cushioned with fiber-reinforced material.

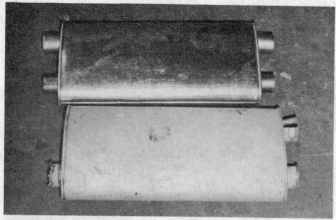

Most of the popular "pony" cars have a crossflow muffler mounted at the rear axle. The stock one for a single exhaust has only one inlet, while the performance replacement (above) has two, so that dual pipes can be utilized with dual outlets, too.

Whatever your pleasure in type of exhaust tip, your local speed shop or muffler shop has a variety of round, square, long, short, curved and straight tips to choose from. The curved ones are helpful in ducting away from bumpers.

Exactly where you end your system is up to you. For many years it has been popular to end the exhaust system just in front of the rear axle. Usually, simple turned-down chrome tips were the only tailpipes beyond the mufflers. The prevailing street theory held that the shorter the system was, the less restrictive it would be, and stopping just short of the rear axle neatly avoided the bends necessary to clear rear axle movement. The only flaw to this design, as most hot rodders found out, was the induced low-frequency vibration and noise. Not only was there not enough pipe after the mufflers to dampen the vibrations, but also the expanse of sheetmetal flooring over the exhaust outlets acted as a sounding board.

Sometimes it was quieter outside the car than inside!

Though there was some merit to ending a system just ahead of the rear axle, this is no longer a necessity in the design of a modern low-restriction exhaust system. We now have better-flowing mufflers that are usable on the street, and if the system has large-diameter tubing with a free-flowing

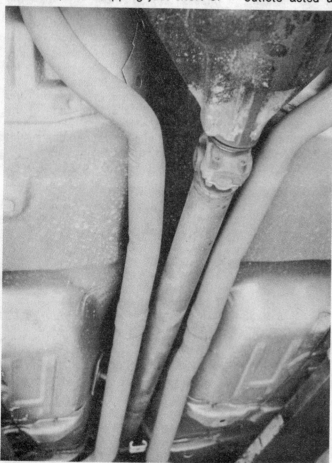

With the low floorpans on many cars, running the exhaust pipes parallel and close to the driveshaft is the only way to run free-flowing pipes and still have sufficient ground clearance.

Avoiding the inevitable bends required to make the system route up and over the rear axle is easy if you can build a side-exit system like this, but this may produce more low-tone noise than full-length pipes.

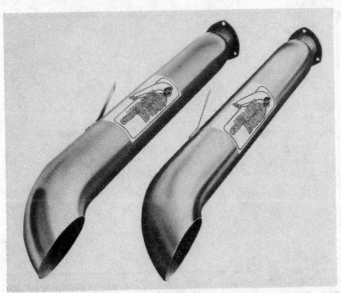

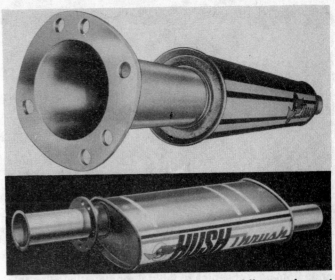

Sort of like a header-muffler and sidepipe all in one, this Cyclone model is 4 inches in diameter and contains a 26-inch muffler.

If you're installing headers and have no welding equipment to hook up the mufflers yourself, you can use special header-mufflers like these Thrush models that bolt right up to the header collector flange.

headpipe, the gentle curve needed to clear the axle will not affect flow. Having the system go the full distance to the rear bumper can often make the difference between an unbearable and a pleasant exhaust note.

A compromise of sorts that used to be "in" in the mid-1960's was a side-exit exhaust. In this case, the system doesn't end ahead of the axle, nor does it extend over the axle to the rear bumper, instead, the tailpipes turn outward after leaving the mufflers and exit under the rocker panels just ahead of each rear tire. This affords a "racey" look to a street machine because Nascar stockers and SCCA sedan racers generally had such a system (although without mufflers), and it was this type of low-restriction system that came as standard equipment on the 1965 Shelby GT-350 Mustangs.

The side-exit system has some drawbacks, of course (Shelby owners can attest). The noise and pollutants can be a problem to the driver if there is a straight side exit, to say nothing of the annoyance caused to other motorists. Have you ever been stuck in traffic next to a guy with side pipes who insisted on "clearing out the gunk" by revving his engine (just your luck it's an oil burner, too) every ten seconds? If you do go for the side-exit style, at least use a tip that points the exhaust rearward and not straight out the side. A side-exit system with tips that point downward is even better, and you'll find that most specialty sidepipe systems are meant to be installed this way.

High-Performance Mufflers

Mufflers have always been viewed as a "necessary evil" by the hot rod fraternity. However, the increasing amount of noise legislation directed against automobiles in the past ten years has made them even more important than ever. The "experts" are making us more aware every day of the noise pollution around us, and it seems that someday we'll have to apply for a license to play the radio in our vehicles outside of our own garages. Seriously, the state and federal governments have displayed an increasingly harsh attitude toward exhaust noise. In turn, the specialty part manufacturers have taken a serious look at their products and their advertising campaigns. In the past, many high-performance mufflers were advertised with "macho" names and the copy did everything but come out and say that

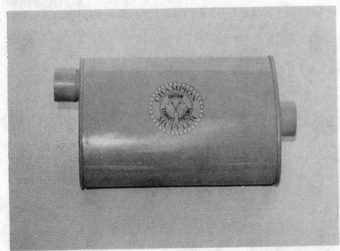

A well-designed performance muffler will not restrict the exhaust flow and will greatly increase driving enjoyment. Spending several hours in a car with a deafening muffler will convince you.

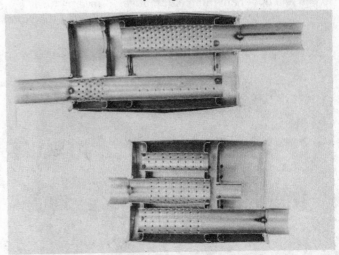

The interior design of a "reverse-flow" muffler is important. Here the very efficient original "Turbo" muffler (bottom) is compared to a similar copy. The flow path in the turbo is efficient (low restriction) and quiet.

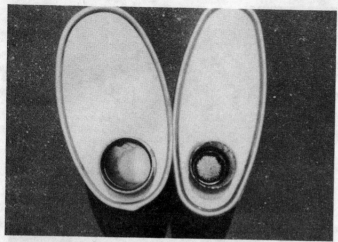

The original turbocharged Corvair muffler was one of the best performance units made. Copies available today range from poor cheapies to faithful reproductions like this one from Walker (left). Compare the internal core size to the cheapie turbo (right).

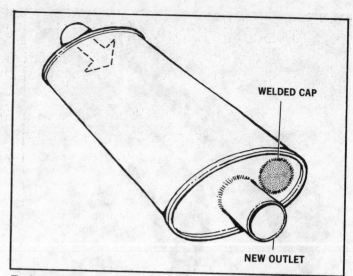

WELDED CAP

NEW OUTLET

Turbo mufflers or any oval-type muffler with the outlet off to one side can be improved slightly by capping the original outlet and welding in a new one in the center.

these mufflers, i.e., the Purple Hornies, Cherry Bombs, etc., were the loudest you could buy. As times have changed and the authorities have become more "aware," muffler manufacturers have taken a new approach. Now their products have names like "Quiet Power" and their ads emphasize not noise but efficiency.

The ideal muffler would pose no restriction to the engine and keep the tailpipe sounds to a whisper. As in most things, the ideal is never realized, but there are a variety of mufflers today that strike a reasonable compromise between power and quietness.

The foremost muffler type on everyone's lips these days is the "turbo muffler." Turbocharging has become such a popular mode of increasing power, without sacrificing other attributes, that even Detroit is getting behind it, and the word "turbo" is used to sell just about anything automotive. In the hot rod muffler business

it's very fashionable to offer a "turbo muffler" as a high-efficiency street part. What the moniker means is that such a muffler is "similar" to the design of the original GM muffler built for the turbocharged Corvair Spyders.

The original turbo mufflers were the result of extensive testing by Chevrolet engineers to find a muffler that wouldn't restrict the supercharged engines, yet would have a decibel level no higher than other production cars. The engineers not only did a good job for the Spyders, they also created about the best high-performance muffler ever built. The Corvair is gone today, but the muffler design lives on in the form of many aftermarket copies. The originals aren't in the GM parts bins anymore, but Walker and other muffler companies make fine replacements.

The Corvair design uses the reverse-flow concept, formerly considered the worst from a performance

standpoint, but it has the virtue of a healthy inlet size (2½ inches) and an equally large core and exit. Other car manufacturers have had their own high-efficiency mufflers hidden in their parts catalogs for years, but they achieved lesser notoriety among performance buffs without the romantic connection with turbocharging. Looking for these other mufflers may have you walking into dealerships that don't normally see too many hot rodders, so go easy with the counter men.

Late-model fullsize Cadillacs, for instance, have a good-flowing muffler, and you know they have to be quiet to silence those monster motors to Cadillac standards. Another unlikely source is your local International Harvester dealer. Ask him for part #376607-C1 and he won't ask you for very much money. You'll be getting a muffler with virtually the same dimensions as the Covair unit. If you're looking for a stock replacement muffler

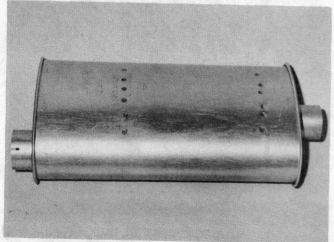

This International-Harvester muffler features a 2½-inch inlet and 2½-inch core all the way through. It's even better for quiet performance than the Chevrolet L-88 type!

The Chrysler Street Hemi muffler measures 4 inches by 10½ inches by 21½ inches and has a healthy enough core to be suitable for just about any performance street engine. It's oval design allows it to replace most stock mufflers.

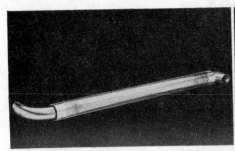
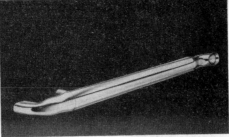

Sidepipes come in a wide variety of styles. They're often installed as "dummies" without being hooked to the exhaust system, but the type with long mufflers inside them can be an effective substitute for a full-length under-the-car system.

for some other make, just ask for the police-car units, since the black-and-whites usually have the biggest engine and the most free-flowing exhaust in the line, for keeping up with hot rodders. The police units can also be found in the parts books by looking up numbers for the top-of-the-line super-cars of yesterday. The Chevrolet L-88, Chrysler Street Hemi, Ford 428 Cobra-Jet, etc., all came with large-core mufflers.

If you don't want to restrict yourself to factory mufflers, there are a host of specialty designs, both copies and originals. Some of the designs seen today are rather poor copies of the Corvair unit, with the only similarity being the general shape and the name "turbo."

The well-known "glass-pack" muffler field is even more wide open. Glass-pack mufflers are available in just about every length from short one-foot resonators to yard-long super-mufflers for big engines. Look for quality construction in a muffler, rather than a catchy name. It's safe to say as a general rule that the longer a glass-pack muffler is, the quieter it will operate. Almost all glass-pack mufflers are of the straight-through design with a round body and welded end

caps, but differences in core construction will determine efficiency and reliability.

While a stock-type muffler may achieve its sound reduction by forcing the exhaust and sound waves to go through chambers and around corners or large baffles, the straight-through glass-pack design can only scrub the sound off with friction. Generally, the shell of the muffler is filled with an insulating material such as fiberglass packing and the core is designed to divert some of the sound waves into this packing, which is not always effective at all frequencies.

There are several ways to divert the sound waves into the fiberglass, either with holes drilled in the core metal, louvers or saw cuts in the core, or punched holes. The punched holes leave a lip on one side of the holes that acts like a scoop, and most glass-packs either have the punched holes or the saw cuts. The specialty muffler manufacturers have a good time with their advertising literature, telling you their system is the best way, but each design has its own merits. The punched holes with the lips are probably the best at limiting high-frequency waves, but the saw-core design is said to offer the least amount

of restriction. "You pay your money and take your choice," because if you choose the less-restrictive core design, you'll have to have a longer muffler to maintain the same low noise level. Further, almost all glass-pack mufflers have a smaller inside diameter through the core than at the inlet. These mufflers can actually *increase* exhaust restriction and have a *louder* note. However, the previously mentioned supercar mufflers and some of the "turbo" designs will provide the highest system efficiency at an "acceptable" noise level.

Having a low noise level isn't only a consideration for your neighbors or passengers, it may soon become a legal necessity. Few aspects of a high-performance car attract the attention of the local constabulary quicker than a loud exhaust system. In California, legislation has been enacted that makes it illegal for any muffler shop to install an exhaust system that is louder than what came on the car originally. This stellar piece of law-making means that every muffler shop has to buy a decibel meter and other sound-testing equipment to evaluate every job they do. Also, if they install a standard set of mufflers off their shelf and don't test the system, the car owner may get a ticket and the muffler shop may get a healthy fine if the exhaust note is a little too loud to suit the California Highway Patrol.

Eventually, California will resolve its decibel legislation problem with a workable plan, but when it does, you can be sure that many other states will follow in their "model legislation" footsteps. Now's the time to make your system a good one (read, quiet one), so future laws don't negate your time and investment.

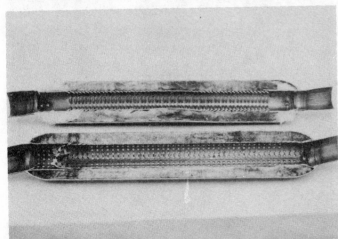

Glasspack manufacturers use a variety of ways to duct the sound and gasses into the packing around the central core, including holes, louvers and saw-cuts. The latter type is the least restrictive.

Whether you're running headers or not, a crossover or balance tube (arrow) between the two exhaust pipes *before* the mufflers can aid low-end torque and help reduce resonant noise.

HOW TO INSTALL DUAL EXHAUST PIPES

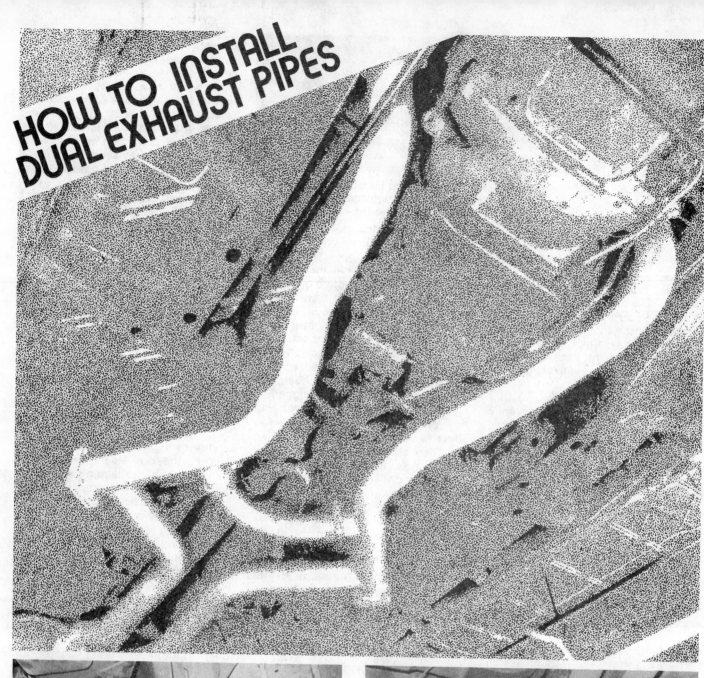

Not exactly a free-flowing setup. Our subject is a 350 Firebird with a single exhaust, catalytic converter and transverse muffler just behind the rear axle. Camaros and Firebirds often have dual *tailpipes* without really having an efficient system.

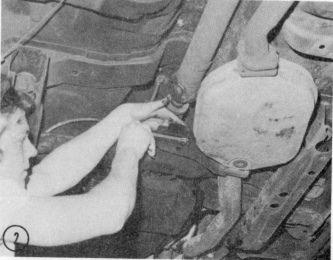

The stock single system is cut off right behind the "Y," and the support unbolted at the converter. In some states it may be illegal to remove the converter for street use, so check local regulations before starting.

Being careful to support the pipe at the center where the weight of the converter is, you can cut through the rear pipe just ahead of the rear end, as is being done here by the experts at Champion Muffler, Whittier, CA.

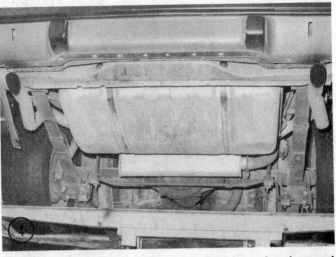

At the rear, the Firebird's *single* exhaust pipe twisted around the rear axle to enter this large crossflow muffler, which features two tailpipes for a deceptive appearance of performance.

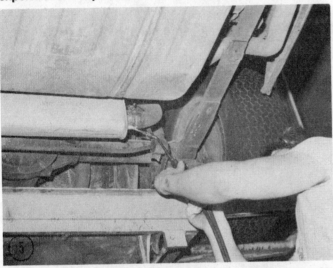

The upper clamps may be difficult to get at when removing the stock tailpipes, but the old *exhaust* pipe can simply be cut or chiseled off. You can save the tailpipes if they aren't rusted.

With the muffler clamps and hangers undone, it's still difficult to get the transverse muffler down if rust has formed on the pipe joints. Squirt penetrating oil at the tailpipe joints and work the pipes back and forth to pull them free.

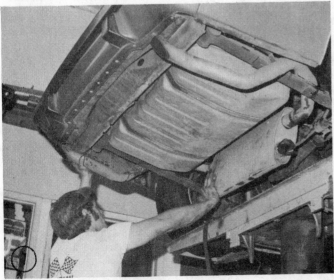

When you can get the muffler down this far, you should have room to swing a rubber hammer against the pipes to free them from the muffler.

There isn't much room under the floorpan of a Camaro or Firebird for two regular mufflers, so you may want to retain the transverse muffler concept, but you can order a new one with *four* inlet/outlets for a true dual exhaust and dual tailpipe system.

17

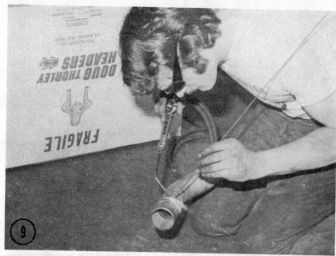

Our tailpipes were stubborn and we had to *cut* them off, so Kenny Anema welds short lengths of pipe onto the tailpipes to make up for the section cut off at the muffler. The alternative is to buy a new pair of tailpipes.

The tailpipes are meant to slip right over the muffler inlets, so they need to be expanded slightly to fit easily. Assuming you don't have one of these neat machines, you can also pound the end of the pipes with an expander cone.

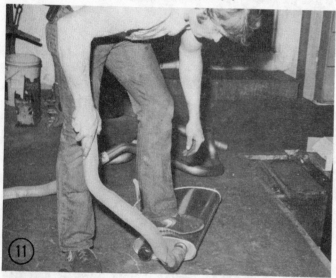

The rubber mallet is used again, this time to get one of the tailpipes started onto the muffler, before the muffler is fitted to the car.

Getting the heavy muffler and both pipes installed isn't easy! One pipe (the left one here) is put into place and rested on the axle while the right pipe and muffler are jockeyed into place.

The lower two outlets in this new Walker muffler are for the exhaust pipes, which were standard off-the-shelf items. Here Kenny groans to twist them over the muffler inlets. The muffler is held in place by the tailpipe clamps and brackets.

The "store-bought" pipes lead over the rear axle and bend in toward the driveshaft tunnel. Here they are held to the desired height for alignment.

All that remained for our custom installation was to hook the newly-installed headers to the exhaust pipes. If you retain stock exhaust manifolds, the entire dual system can often be purchased as a bolt-on set with no welding or tube-bending required.

After a quick measurement, Kenny takes a length of 2¼-inch pipe and applies a simple bend and expands the front end (arrow) to fit header cones.

The bend was put in to bring the pipes in toward the driveshaft tunnel, where there was more room for the pipes. Note how the pipe fits neatly over the adaptor cone bolted to the collector.

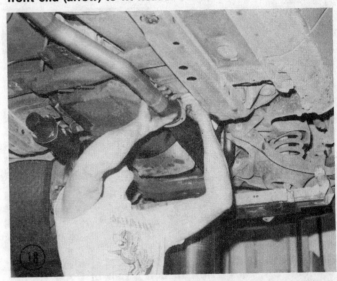

The pipe was removed for a second bend to straighten out its path toward the rear, and new gaskets were installed at the collector.

Champion Muffler always welds their connections for a leak-proof fit, but you could use clamps instead. You could have the two middle pipes bent up at a muffler shop and you could install them at home without any welding, or have them welded later at a shop.

The final step in any professional job is to give all the new piping a shot of heat-resistant exhaust paint to protect against early rustout. This Firebird is now ready to deliver better mileage and free-flowing performance.

HOW TO INSTALL SIDEPIPES

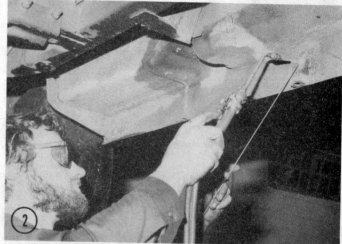

Kenny Anema of Champion Muffler, 14426 E. Whittier Blvd., Whittier, CA, shows how to bolt a pair of Doug Thorley Showtubes onto a Chevy van. If you plan to make your sidepipes functional, you'll need the type with mufflers inside.

The Doug Thorley Showtubes have brackets on them already. Hold the sidepipes in the desired position under the rocker panel and mark where the chassis brackets need to be located. Champion Muffler welds them on, but you could just as easily bolt them in place.

To keep exhaust system vibrations to a minimum, the sidepipe is bolted to the chassis bracket with a rubber grommet on either side of the bracket.

This is only part of the sidepipe installation that is even remotely difficult, making correct measurements of the pipe and bends you'll need to match the sidepipe to the stock head pipe.

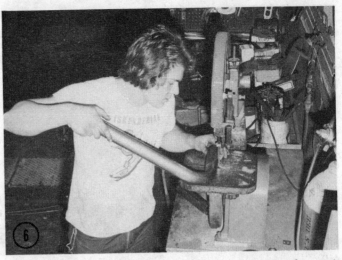

A beautiful tube-bender makes it easy for pro shops, but you could make your connecting tube by joining straight lengths and pre-shaped bends, or take your measurements to a shop and have them custom form one for you.

The old philosophy of exhaust work is "measure twice, cut once!" And the cleaner and closer you make your cuts, the easier your components will be to weld together with leak-proof joints.

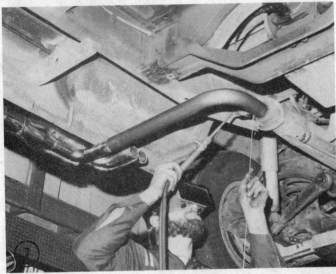

With the connector pipe shaped and cut to size, you can hook everything up. Connections can be made with clamps, but welding makes for a quiet and positive (safe) seal.

Welding the collector to the sidepipe will hold the latter permanently in position. If the pipes are of different sizes, use reducers or adapters.

In some sidepipes, all but one of the tubes is blocked off inside, like these Show-Tubes. In other pipes, use engine "freeze" plugs to block them off so all of the exhaust is forced through the sidepipe muffler.

As a final touch, a coat of heat-resistant paint will retard rust and add to the appearance of the complete system.

HEADERS

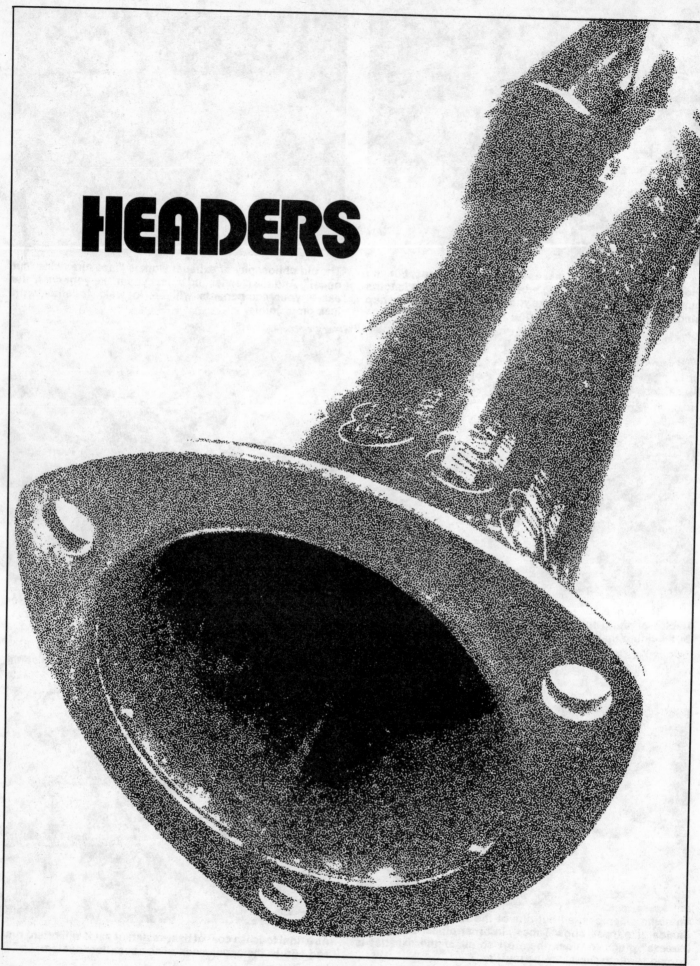

We've already explained what a performance exhaust system is and why it's important to your street machine, but there's an important part of the total exhaust picture we haven't talked about—*headers*. Talk to the man behind the counter at your local speed shop for a short time and you'll find that the perennial sales favorite in engine bolt-on equipment is a set of steel tube exhaust headers.

Ever since the "energy crisis" of 1974 all motorists have been conscious of the need to cut fuel consumption. Hot rodders have fallen under this new awareness, too, and most of us think twice now before buying a piece of equipment for our car that might burn a little more of the Arab gold. But no other piece of bolt-on equipment has a better reputation for fairness in this area than tubing headers, and rightly so. Improvements in engine breathing will not only increase power but improve mileage, and whatever gains your street machine made when you followed our exhaust system advice, you can expect to *nearly double* that improvement when you complete the system with a set of headers.

Reducing engine "backpressure" obviously does good things, but how do tube headers make a contribution? Drag racers discovered long ago that, paradoxically, the least restrictive systems didn't necessarily make the most power. At first, they would route the exhaust straight out of the head ports into a set of short, straight pipes, one for each port. Later, they found that grouping the pipes together and making them longer produced more power, especially at the lower end.

Installing tube headers to reduce backpressure is one of the best ways to improve a street machine because you gain economy as well as power. Almost anyone can do the installation at home and then have the connection to the system done at a muffler shop.

As the builders of specialty exhaust components became more scientific in their approach, they discovered that efficiency was not maximized by just allowing the engine to breathe in an unrestricted manner, further improvements could be gained by building in a certain kind of restriction. The proper size of "primary" pipes, the right length, and the correct grouping or "collecting" of these pipes into one large pipe produced substantial power gains. This effect is now called "scavenging." Headers are designed to make each exhaust pulse travel down the primary pipe and join the common pipe, called a collector, at a time in the engine firing order when it creates a drafting effect, causing the exhaust from the subsequent combustion cycle to literally be sucked out rather than just released.

The exhaust gas released into the port creates a pressure wave that travels over 1500 feet per second, with the gasses themselves moving about 250 feet per second. However, it is not a continuous flow, but is a periodic pulse. When the pulse gets to the end of the primary tube, it creates a suction on the other end of the pipe (the port end) which helps to draw out the residual exhaust gasses from the cylinder. If the pulse timing is correct, this rapid exit flow can create a partial suction that will aid intake flow before the movement of the piston produces full effect on the intake charge. Thus, proper scavenging *aids both in emptying and filling* cylinders.

Header manufacturers over the years have taken a variety of approaches to achieve maximum scavenging. Of course, those headers manufactured for strictly racing applications were designed with no compromises, and this led to some wild "bundles of snakes." There isn't a wealth of hard scientific data in header research, and each manufacturer has his own pet theories. The interesting thing is that most of their ideas seem to work. But if any generalities can safely be made, the two most impor-

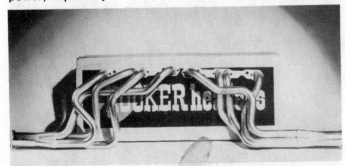

Most manufacturers try to make their headers of equal length, but due to chassis design and expediency in manufacturing, this isn't always possible. These Hooker headers for a Chevelle are an example of how the rearmost pipes have to go through several extra bends to make them the same length as the pipes at front.

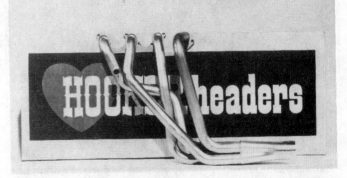

Because four-cylinder engines have a lot of inherent vibration, choose only the heaviest-duty header you can find for such applications. In some cases, a support strap from the collector to the transmission is advisable.

tant factors in header design are primary and collector tube *diameter* and *length*.

If you make any investigation about headers, you'll quickly learn that the most advertised header feature is that they are "equal length." This is generally accepted as meaning that all of the primary pipes are the same length. Everyone agrees this is important to get maximum power from the engine. What is unfortunate is that precisely equal-length pipes are seldom possible in a production header. This is due to the confining space of the engine compartment and chassis of the average passenger car.

Obviously, the pipes at the front of the car, coming from the front cylinders, will become the criterion for building the rearward pipes. The rearward pipes have a shorter distance to the collector, and to make them the same length as the front pipes, they have many extra bends and twists. Finding the room for these extra bends isn't easy, at least not without making the lower part of the engine difficult to work on and the headers difficult to install. Racers are willing to put up with these problems. However, most of the production headers sold in speed shops for street use exhibit some compromises in order to make installation easier and to fit around various street accessories such as power steering or air conditioning.

One approach to the equal-length problem used in some headers is to design the pipes for ease of installation, without regard to length, and to equalize them by letting them extend to different depths in the collector. In other words, the front pipes would dump out at the beginning of the collector, and the rear pipes would continue inside the collector until they are the required length. This necessitates a fairly long collector, and many manufacturers would disagree with

For the do-it-yourselfer with an unusual engine/chassis combination, several exhaust manufacturers make all the pieces to build your own set of headers. Flanges may come without tubes (right), with formed tubes (center), or with the tubes already welded to the flange.

this approach, saying that some of the true scavenging effect is lost if the pipes don't enter the collector area at the same point. Collector length will also be affected and this may be important because overall collector length is also a design factor to be considered; the collector is an important part of the overall header length that the engine "feels."

In general, long overall lengths are useful for cars that need low-end torque, while the shorter lengths are "tuned" to aid high-rpm output. It's easy to see why equal-length pipes are important, since all cylinders will reach their peak power at the same time. Luckily, a difference of a half-inch here or there won't make much difference, even in a race car, and a street header can be off by as much as two inches in tube lengths and not substantially hurt performance. Likewise, a difference in collector length of a few inches will not make a noticeable difference in performance on a street engine. Most

conventional headers have primary pipes that fall into a range of 30 to 36 inches in length and join in collectors 12 to 30 inches long.

In the past, the makers of race-car headers have looked askance at makers of street headers for using small diameter primary pipes simply to make the headers easier to install. But during that time headers were mostly used for all-out performance or semi-racing engines. The average bargain header sold in practically every speed shop probably is too small for an all-out engine, however, today this type of rompin'-stompin' street engine is something like a dinosaur. The day of the "street/strip" car is practically gone (the fuel crunch and the ever increasing professionalism of drag racing have almost eliminated this approach). With the typical street engine of today, built in moderation, the headers now on the market are just about the right tube size and length. A modern street engine must exhibit

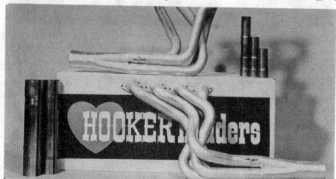

Because primary length plays such an important part in how much power a set of headers produces and at what rpm, some racing headers like these Hookers are adjustable, with a variety of different intermediate section lengths available to "tune" the exhaust to the requirements of the car and track.

Sometimes the configuration of the chassis precludes using what might be the optimum tube size and primary length, as is the case with these short headers for the Corvette. A longer header would provide more low-end torque for street driving.

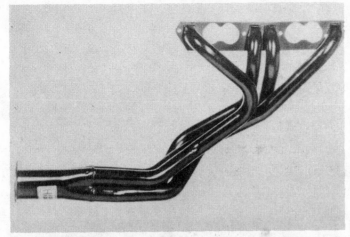

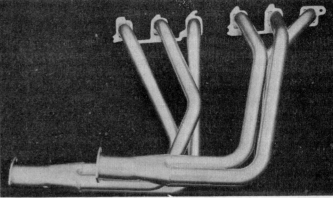

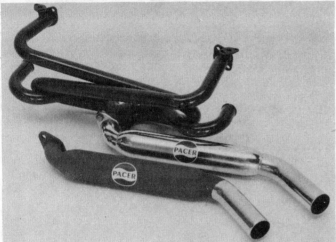

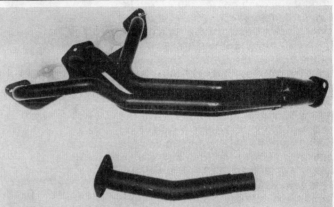

Headers are available to fit nearly any type of engine: (clockwise from upper left) a typical V-8 header; a set for a 6-cylinder engine (two groups of three tubes); a single header for an inline four; and tuned-length tubes with muffler for a flat-four VW.

good fuel economy and tractability, and should be built for the lower speed ranges and crisp throttle response. These engines really need a smaller-than-optimum tube size to maintain exhaust velocity at lower engine speeds.

While we're on the subject of what makes a good street header, we must mention an alternate design to the standard four-tube type, the so-called tri-Y. This design, in which the four pipes are paired off into two pipes before joining the collector, was popular in the late Fifties and early Sixties. In fact, when Carroll Shelby was developing the famous GT-350 Shelby Mustang, he studied a variety of header designs before deciding that the tri-Y style gave the best all-around response on the 289 Ford engine. Although he realized that the four-tube design gave better peak results at high rpm, he knew most of his cars would spend very little street time at 6000 rpm or more, and if someone wanted to race a Shelby, they could put on a set of four-into-one headers.

The standard four-tube header sacrifices velocity to have the least possible restriction at high rpm. Increasing tube size in a four-tube design allows higher horsepower at high rpm,

but to the detriment of low and mid-range power. The tri-Y headers can't offer the same peak horsepower at 6000 rpm (although nearly), but they are less "peaky" and offer the broadest torque curve of any header design. Even increasing the tube size in a tri-Y doesn't seem to hurt the low end, so they appear to be the perfect street

header. Unfortunately, they are more complex and expensive to build and most young performance enthusiasts want the same type headers their racing heroes use. As a consequence, there are few tri-Y sets available today.

There is a third type of header that we should mention, the factory cast-iron header. Back during the muscle-

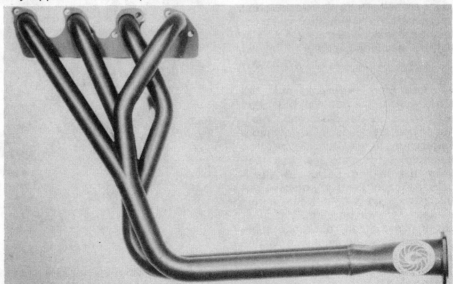

Although the tri-Y header design is uncommon today, Cyclone has applied the principle to their header for the Vega four. They call it a Bi-Y and it features four pipes into two and those two into the collector.

car era when performance was considered a sales tool in Detroit, the automobile manufacturers came up with some neat free-flowing cast-iron manifolds for their police and high-performance models. Many of these designs may still be available from your dealer's parts books. In the Ford line, for instance, there were units for the hi-po 289 (271-hp) that would be good for any smallblock Ford, and the CZAE-9430-B beauties for the big-blocks in the 390-427-428 family. The Cobra-Jet 428 manifolds are almost as good if you can't get the old 427-style. Mopar fanciers can utilize the 340 smallblock Duster type manifolds (#3614367, left, and #2863545, right), while most of the B-block fans would be wise to use the 383-440 "Road Runner-GTX" castings. Chevrolet has its own goodies. The cast-iron "rams horns" found on mid-Sixties Corvettes and featuring three-inch header pipe flanges are the best factory manifolds but they are now very rare and are no longer available from GM parts outlets. The advantages of using the factory free-flow manifolds compared to buying a set of headers are lower cost, less noise, ease of installation, and extended life—they will usually last as long as the car. Of course, the disadvantages are that the cast-iron manifolds are much heavier and don't produce as much power as tube headers.

Those last items we mentioned bring up a good point; there are a few disadvantages to tubing headers, despite their overwhelming popularity. Being made of steel tube, they are prone to rust. This is a big problem in areas that have severe winters or lots of rain, especially those where winter roads are salted with chemicals. Most hot rodders thoroughly clean and paint their headers with heat-resistant paint before installation, and with regular care they should last as long as any other part of your exhaust system.

Two other drawbacks that are attributable to the thin-wall tube used in headers are the heat and noise. Tube headers expose a lot more surface area to the air than a cast-iron manifold, thus some feel that they keep the engine cooler by dissipating exhaust heat very quickly, but this also means that your engine compartment will be warmer. In most cases, it's difficult to change spark plugs on a header-equipped engine when it is still hot. Fortunately, tube headers cool quickly, so you don't have to wait all day.

The noise factor is interesting. Header experts are often asked by beginning hot rodders, "Won't install-

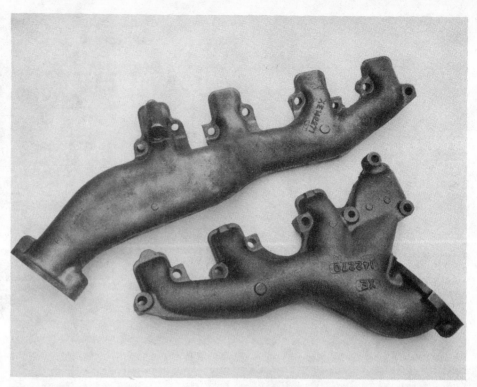

High-performance tube headers are the best choice if top power is required but many of the factory hi-po cast-iron manifolds work adequate for a mildly-modified street engine. Factory manifolds are cheap, quiet and allow the engine compartment to remain somewhat cooler, but they will cost about 15-25 horses.

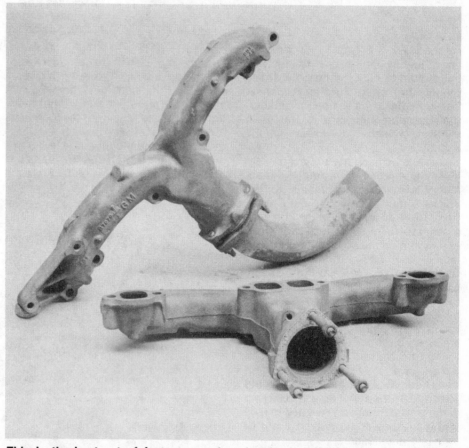

This is the best set of factory cast iron header manifolds ever made for the smallblock Chevy. Note the full three-inch header pipe flange. These "ram's horn" manifolds were used on hi-po Vette engines in the early-mid 60's and are now rare, but they would be suitable for engine swaps or engines fitted into extremely tight compartments.

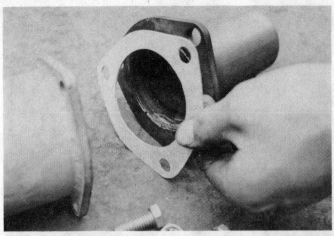

Gaskets are a hassle when installing headers. They fall out or will not line up with the bolt holes. This type of header gasket with slots at each end make it much easier. You just install the header loosely with the two end bolts and then the gasket can be slipped in behind the flange and lined up.

The gasket between the header collector flange and the head pipe adapter should be of high quality. Pull the collector bolts up tightly to insure against leaks, and carry an extra pair if you plan to uncork the pipes at the drags (they tear easily).

ing a set of headers make my car louder?" The yes-and-no answer they get sounds confusing at first. The headers by themselves don't really change the exhaust note from the tailpipe substantially, but the thinwall tubing does generate some resonant vibes in the engine compartment. This isn't enough to attract the attention of the gendarmes, but gives your engine a slightly "tinny" sound that knowledgeable performance buffs will recognize immediately.

The "leaky exhaust" sound you hear from some street machines running headers is usually due to loose header bolts or blown header gaskets. Since most header bolts fit into cramped spots right next to one of the pipes, there's seldom room for lockwashers or anti-vibration tabs (like stock exhaust manifolds usually have) and the repeated expansion and contraction of the steel-plate flanges means that frequent retightening of the header bolts is necessary to maintain a good seal. Also, if the bolts are allowed to loosen during normal driving, this can ruin the header gaskets as the gasses find an easier way out. Most of these problems can be eliminated, however, if your choice in headers is carefully made. Thick port flanges, sometimes incorporating a raised-bead weld around the tube entrance for added gasket compression, can greatly reduce leakage problems. It also pays to check the "flatness" of the flange with a straight-edge *before* you buy. For further hints refer to the accompanying selection guide.

Depending on the brand, size, header style and the engine you put them on, some headers may pose installation problems. We'll assume you have taken our advice from the exhaust system chapter and already have a dynamite system of low-restriction pipes and mufflers, in which case you only need hook the collectors to your pipes. However, in some particularly tight engine/chassis fits, such as the big-block Mustangs, the entire engine will have to be unbolted from the car and jacked up in the air a few inches in order to slip the headers into place from beneath the chassis. In a lot of stick-shift cars, the clutch linkage passes between the left-side primary pipes, and the cross-shaft and linkage must be removed to install the header. It may be wise for you to purchase a set of spark plug wire looms or holders at the same time as your headers, to keep the ignition wires from touching the pipes, and a set of heat-resistant silicone wires wouldn't be a bad idea, either.

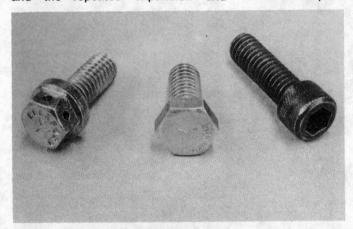

There are three choices when it comes to choosing header bolts. The standard bolt (center) needs a longer wrench and may not fit when the header pipes are near the bolt location. The "header bolt" at left is handier because it takes a smaller wrench. The Allen bolt (right) requires the least amount of side clearance to the pipes, but you need a straight shot at the face to use the Allen wrench.

After initial installation of new headers, you'll have to go back and retighten all the bolts after the first few hundred miles. Thereafter, periodically inspect and tighten the header bolts until they take a set.

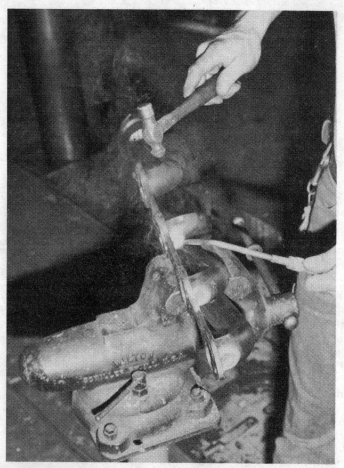

One potential installation headache of some header designs is that the bend of the pipes makes it difficult to get a wrench on the bolts. Experienced installers often heat the area next to the problem bolt with a torch and use a small ball-peen hammer to dimple the pipes for better bolt and wrench clearance.

Most header tubes are welded to the flanges on the *inside* edge, which leaves a weld bead that can cause exhaust leakage if the weld is uneven. Most professional header installers use a body grinder on the flanges to smooth them out for a better gasket seal.

The manufacturers' catalog should give you information on what modifications, if any, are required to install their headers on your car, and with which accessories they are designed to be compatible. One of the "accessories" you should be concerned with is the much-maligned smog pump. The smog, or A.I.R. pump, directs air into the exhaust manifolds to help oxidize unburned exhaust gasses, and contrary to popular opinion, they don't really hurt performance by more than the few horsepower it takes to drive the pump. In many states, in order to stay legal you'll have to retain the pump when you switch to headers. This means you need to purchase headers with the A.I.R. fittings on them. Most speed shops also sell a set of nipples and tubing (for weld-them-yourself installations) to make non-smog-fitting headers legal.

Two other minor inconveniences are related to the carburetor. It might seem like the carb has no connection with the exhaust system, but on some models there is a heat riser tube that goes to the choke. You'll have to make

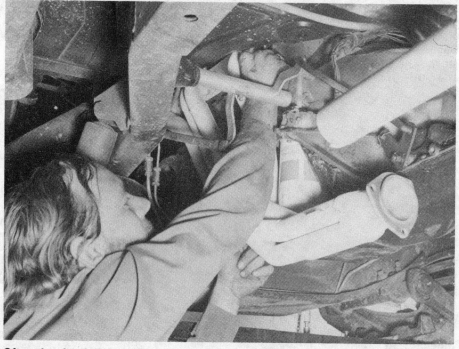

Often the clutch linkage or the transmission shift linkage needs to be modified or removed temporarily for installation of headers. You may want to check the manufacturers' catalogs to find the header that fits with the fewest number of modifications.

some new provision for supplying heat to the choke element now that your stock exhaust manifolds have found their way to the trash bin. Luckily, header makers sell "choke stove kits" that clamp a small heat box to one of the header pipes and duct the heat to the choke. If you are contemplating a carburetor change along with the headers (refer to the carburetor chapter first), consider buying one with an electric choke element. This will eliminate the need for stove kits and provide a more reliable, "sano" installation.

Another concern relating to your carburetor is the possible need for a jet change. When you install a set of headers and a good exhaust system, you've increased the efficiency of the engine, and the improved scavenging effect can make the stock carburetion a little *lean*. If left alone, this could shorten the life of exhaust valves and seats, so remember it might be necessary to rejet slightly richer after your headers are installed (see carburetor chapter). In fact, it wouldn't hurt to make your intake system as efficient as your new exhaust, which leads us into the upcoming chapters.

Header Selection Hints

1) Design and selection should be based on intended use—large and/or adjustable primary and collector tube diameter for high-output race engines, while smaller (2-inch or less) should be used for street (provides better low-end response and easier installation).
2) Thicker tubing and flanges (both port and collector) will provide longer life and better sealing.
3) Make sure that the headers you are buying will allow the use of the accessory equipment you wish to retain (air conditioning, power steering, etc.). Also verify that the mandatory smog equipment connections are provided.
4) If an occasional sojourn down the quarter mile is foreseen, the style and ease of disconnecting the collector flanges should be considered.
5) Use only "quality" brand-name header gaskets. The cheap ones just aren't worth the minor cost savings.
6) Realize that almost all headers will reduce ground clearance and can be somewhat of a "nuisance" for street driving.
7) For maximum life with minimum maintenance, headers should be thoroughly cleaned and painted (or aluminized—although expensive the ultimate in rust prevention) before being installed.
8) Special mufflers made just for headers are more of an off-road installation than a street set-up. They are usually too loud and are not normally designed for to-the-rear-bumper connection.
9) Always use a crossover tube in the exhaust system before the mufflers as this will result in *less* noise and *more* power.

Most headers are painted with inexpensive paint at the factory in order to prevent rust. This is usually not heat-resistant paint. For maximum durability have the headers sand blasted and repaint them with Sperex or some similar quality heat-resistant paint.

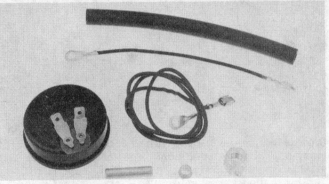

Installing tube headers may prevent the stock carb choke system from operating correctly. This Holley electric choke kit will restore full choke functioning to Holley two- and four-barrel carbs.

If yours is a machine of recent vintage and you need to keep all the smog equipment to stay legal, then buy headers that have the screw fittings to attach the pipes from your air injection pump. Headers can be retrofitted with weld-in fittings.

Racing engines can use larger-diameter tubes than street engines. This 454-inch engine uses 2¼-inch tubes but in a street chassis with muffler a 2-inch pipe will give increased low-end torque.

HOW TO INSTALL TUBE HEADERS

1

Crowded engine compartment of this 350 Firebird is typical of smog-era working conditions. You can't even *see* the exhaust manifolds. Here a new Carter 4-bbl and Doug Thorley headers are being installed by the crew at Champion Muffler.

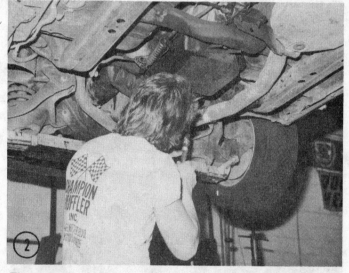

2

The stock Firebird system is two short headpipes going into a single pipe. The "Y" is cut off here and the single exhaust system removed.

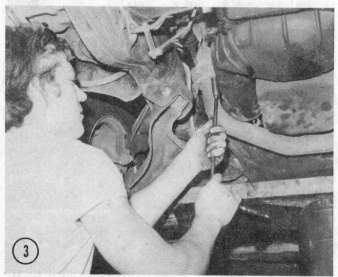

3

Penetrating oil will be a big help to loosen the nuts holding the Y-pipes to the manifolds. A long extension and a flex socket make it easier to get at all three nuts on each manifold.

4

With the flanges unbolted from each exhaust manifold, the crossover can be removed and discarded.

30

Back topside, the sheetmetal covers that collect hot air for the air cleaner can be removed, to provide easier access to the exhaust manifold bolts.

We couldn't have picked a tougher example for a header installation than a 350 Pontiac. A long set of extensions is necessary to get at the six stubborn bolts on each manifold. Most can only be reached from underneath.

The job can be made easier if the front wheels are removed, as the two center bolts on each side are easily reached through the fenderwells.

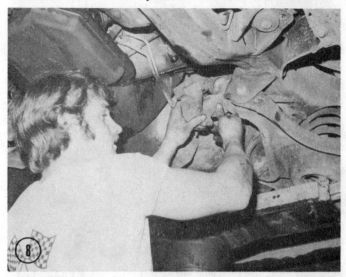

After exhausting your supply of curses, you'll have all the bolts out and can remove the heavy cast-iron exhaust manifolds from underneath.

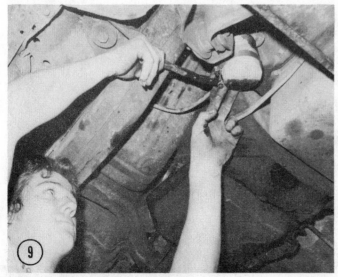

Doug Thorley suggests you remove the oil filter (and the oil filter adapter on the block) from the right side in preparation for fitting the headers.

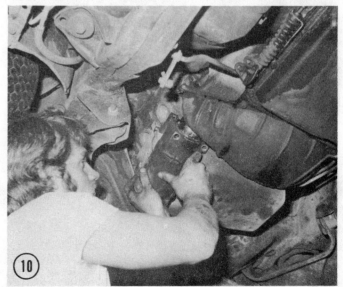

Things are tight on the driver's side, too, so there the starter motor must be removed before the tube headers go into place.

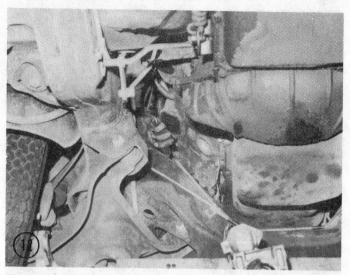

On some cars there may be either brake or fuel lines that need to be relocated for clearance. This fuel line must be bent down along the crossmember.

The brake line here must also be moved down, away from the headers. It attaches to the crossmember with a bolt at the brake block, which must be relocated along with the tubing.

Most commercial headers are well made, but even the best require little "blueprinting" touches. Here a grinder is used to smooth out the welds on the inside of the flange to make a good seal.

After the grinding operation, lay the new gasket in place and check for complete sealing around the pipes.

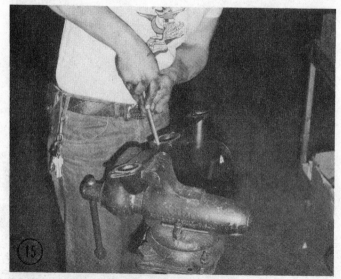

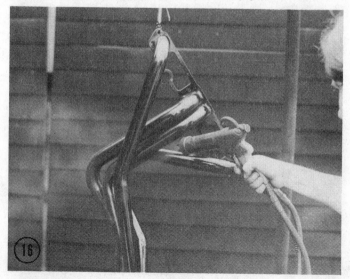

The gasket can also show if all the bolt holes are properly drilled. You may need to file them to clean out the burrs from grinding.

Before the headers are bolted in place they should be sprayed with a high-quality heat-resistant paint. Have a commercial sand blaster remove the old paint if possible.

It may not be easy "sneaking" the headers in place, but it's more fun than installing the stock exhaust manifolds. Gaskets are often most easily installed from the topside.

After the right-side header is fully bolted up, install the filter adapter back on the engine block.

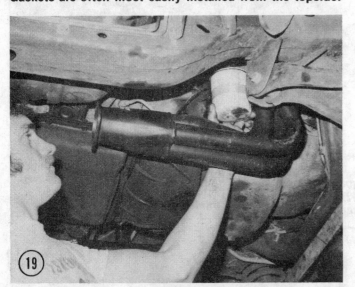

The filter can now be installed, but it's advisable to use as short a filter as possible to make removal easier and to keep exhaust heat away from the filter.

When the left-side header is in place, but loose, reinstall starter and then install the header bolts. Don't tighten any header bolts until all of them are started.

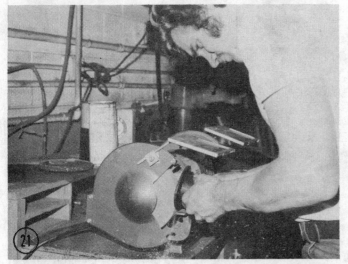

The header collectors are usually connected to the exhaust system by reducer cones. Since they are welded on a production line it won't hurt to reweld the reducers for a tighter seal.

The reducer cones are bolted up with new gaskets, ready for hookup to the exhaust system. Some bending of the clutch or shifter mechanism may be necessary to clear the headers (do it carefully).

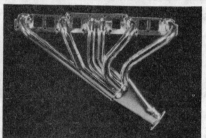

ADVANCE ADAPTERS is well-known for four-wheel-drive engine and trans adapters, but they also manufacture a complete line of performance headers for off-road machines.

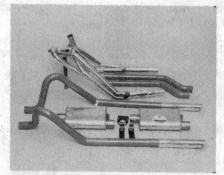

CANNON INDUSTRIES is ready for the V-6 revolution in performance with their line of equipment such as headers and dual kits. This one is for the Capri/Mustang II V-6.

CASLER PERFORMANCE pioneered the low-cost "economy" header. Today they offer four-tube headers for better fuel economy and performance from the most popular American V-8's.

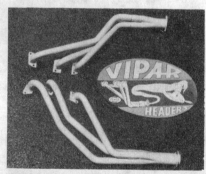

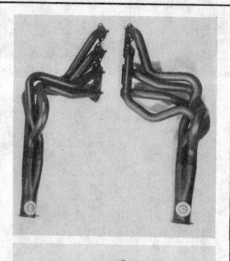

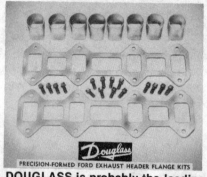

DOUGLASS is probably the leading company in the making of exhaust bends, flange kits, glasspacks, and stock mufflers and dual exhaust kits.

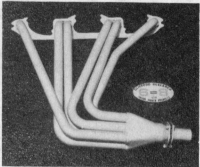

CLIFFORD RESEARCH concentrate their effort on the inline engine. Their line of Vipar headers includes this pair for the GM V-6 and a set for the Toyota Land Cruiser inline six-cylinder.

CYCLONE AUTOMOTIVE has a complete catalog of custom exhaust products, including headers for all popular applications, mufflers and dual-pipe kits, header mufflers and even header "kits."

EAGLE SPECIALTY PRODUCTS are making a name for themselves with their rugged line of headers, mufflers, sidepipes and universal dual kits. They feature heavy-wall tubing for extended durability in street use.

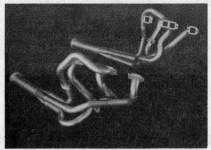

HEADERS by ED are built for many unique applications. The company offers supplies for the do-it-yourself header builder and complete headers for street, strip, and even tractor pullers and boats.

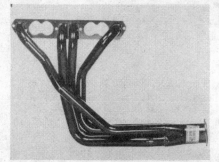

HEDMAN HEDDERS has been making hot rod exhaust system parts for many years, being one of the first to offer ready-made headers. Today their lineup includes street, racer, RV, and off-road models.

HERBERT AUTOMOTIVE is known as a leading source for engine swap kits, and most of their kits include a special set of headers to make the installation possible.

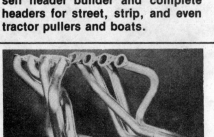

HOOKER makes a complete line of headers for race cars and street use. In addition to their main line of headers, they also offer special header mufflers and even a V-8 Vega engine/custom-header swap kit.

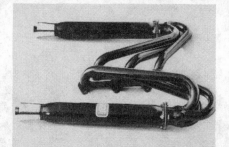

IECO's reputation rests on their fine line of specialty products for the Pinto, Vega, and Corvair, which includes quality exhaust systems like this Corvair dual header.

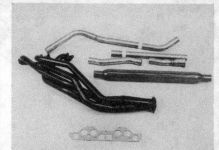

INTERPART is known for their line of products for the imported and compact-car field, including headers and complete exhaust systems for small cars and mini-trucks, such as this Datsun kit for 510's and pickups.

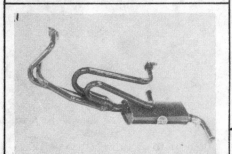

PACER PERFORMANCE PRODUCT has a line of exhaust products for Volkswagens, including this "Turbo Quiet" extractor and muffler, designed to meet the strict California noise level standards.

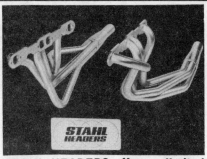

STAHL HEADERS offers a limited selection of dyno-proven headers designed almost exclusively for racing use, with true equal-length, adjustable, primary pipes.

DOUG THORLEY has been a famous name in performance exhaust products for fifteen years. Not only do they offer a full line of headers, they also manufacture attractive and functional sidepipes and dual kits.

THRUSH PERFORMANCE, a Canada-based company, is familiar to most hot rodders through their colorful advertising. They offer a full line of mufflers, dual exhaust kits, and their famous sidepipes.

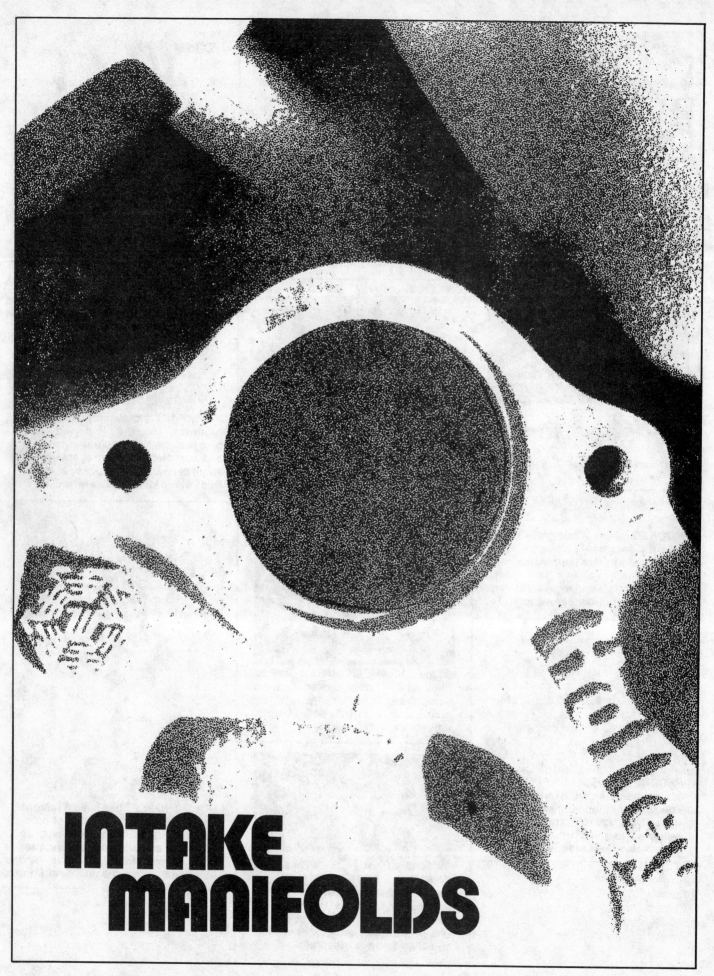

INTAKE MANIFOLDS

While headers are touted as the most popular pieces of speed equipment and perhaps the most cost effective, the carburetion of a street engine greatly influences both performance and appearance. If you've been following us so far, it should make sense to you when we stress again that a good street engine is a combination of carefully selected parts, all working together. Even if you never open up the inside of your engine, the parts you bolt on the outside should be as carefully matched as a set of pistons or bearings.

Now that you have a free-flowing exhaust system installed, it's about time to do the same for intake flow. Unfortunately, many enthusiasts make their biggest mistakes when choosing intake and carburetion parts, usually by buying for "looks" rather than considering function. Nothing makes a street engine look more like a "real racer" than a giant tunnel-ram manifold sporting two huge Holleys. On the other hand, few combinations could be less practical. What is hard for many beginners to understand (particularly when they have been exposed to "street freaks" in magazines and the exotic engines seen at the local dragstrip) is that what works on a race car at high rpm doesn't always work on the street.

The design requirements of the internal combustion engine are so complex that you can't really "have your cake and eat it too." Therefore, the choices of street speed equipment must of necessity be engineering compromises. The basic compromise is between the needs of an engine producing maximum power at high rpm (such as a racing engine) and the needs of a street engine that must perform smoothly, economically and produce its most usable power in the lower rpm ranges.

Let's look at the racing induction first. We have already seen how high exhaust gas velocity will facilitate exhaust system tuning and create a scavenging effect on the cylinders. The same physics govern the intake charge and creating the right kind of intake and carburetion "tuning" can induce a "ram" effect. That is, the intake charge has enough velocity to more completely fill the cylinders on the intake stroke than would be allowed by the simple pressure differ-

There is an almost endless number of manifold choices available for the street runner. Major manufacturers make two-barrel, four-barrel, dual-quad and triple two-barrel manifolds for nearly every engine family. However, the four-barrel type manifold is undoubtedly the most economical and most practical choice for day-to-day driving.

A typical high-performance street engine will probably feature a specialty ignition, a set of tube headers, and a good single four-barrel intake system. Well chosen bolt-on equipment can increase performance and high-rpm reliability. It is difficult to obtain better economy when all-out performance is the main goal, but with careful attention to equipment selection a flexible compromise is possible.

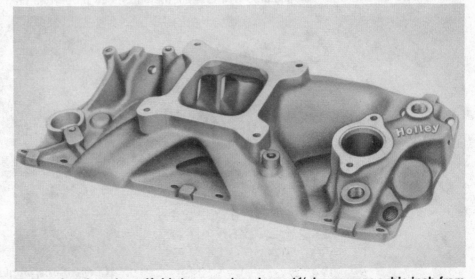

Modern four-barrel manifolds have produced over 1½ horses-per-cubic inch from race-modified 355-inch engines. On mildly-modified street engines they can easily produce 1-1¼ horses-per-inch with respectable economy.

The most successful type of high-rpm carburetion is that which provides a separate throat for each intake port, such as this manifold for mounting four Weber two-barrels on a Chevy V-8. Note the direct equal-length of the runners, but this often isn't practical for street use because of cost.

The single-throat-per-cylinder theory has been used on many small four-cylinder engines with considerable success, but such engines are rpm-sensitive and fitting such a setup under the hood of a street machine could be a real headache.

ential.

Just as with the exhaust system, the ideal intake system would pose the least restriction to the cylinders and allow them to fill as quickly and completely as possible. One of the improvements provided by a set of headers over stock exhaust system is that right after leaving the ports the exhaust pulses aren't forced to fight each other inside a common chamber. The intake system "likes" this same treatment at high rpm, and consequently most racing engine inductions offer a separate feed for every cylinder.

In those engines that are equipped with fuel injection, there is a separate fuel supply jet, air tube (velocity stack) and throttle butterfly for each cylinder (each intake port). The same holds true for carbureted racing engines, and you may have noted that Ferraris, Formula Fords and other exotica also

have a separate carburetor throat for each cylinder. If it's an eight-cylinder engine, then it has eight individual carbs or feeds from four two-barrel carbs, and a four-cylinder engine runs with four carbs or two two-barrels. This way every cylinder will receive the same amount of fuel and air.

Unfortunately, what holds true for the racing engine doesn't necessarily work for a street engine, and the individual-feed approach usually performs sluggishly in the low-rpm ranges. If the system can supply enough fuel-air for high rpm, then it usually also supplies *too much* for lower engine speeds. Such an engine may not be able to idle long without fouling the plugs because of over-rich black carbon buildup. A clean, crisp idle and smooth transition to the higher engine speeds are features you want in your street engine and these properties are

not often necessary in a racing engine or found in an individual-port manifold.

From the early days of the flathead Ford through the period of overhead V-8 development, specialty intake manifolds have been a mainstay of the speed equipment business. These parts will probably be just as popular in the future as the smaller inlines and V-6's become the prime movers of Detroit machinery. Probably 99% of the engines on the street today use some form of single-carburetor induction. We'll get back to the idea of multiple carburetion later on, but, for now, let's say that there are two basic types of intake manifolds available to us today—the single-plane and the dual-plane. Each of these types usually mounts a single two-barrel or four-barrel carburetor in the center and have air passages that lead from the carb to the various intake ports on the

The GM and Ford V-6 engines, which are touted as being the designs of the future, already have a variety of specialty manifolds available for performance and economy.

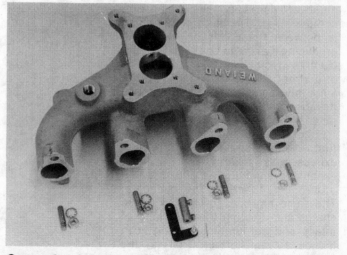

Conventional single- and dual-plane manifolds are available for many six- and four-cylinder engines. This is also an excellent way to adapt a US-built carb (such as the Holley 500-cfm 2-barrel) to an import car engine.

engine.

We'll discuss the dual-plane manifold first. It's been around longer and has been the style used almost without exception by Detroit since the V-8 engine was introduced.

Dual-Plane Manifolds

In the dual-plane design the two- or four-barrel carburetor is essentially divided in two halves by the manifold with each half of the carb feeding half of the engine cylinders. The dual-plane designation comes from the fact that these two halves of the manifold are built on different planes, that is one half is routed over the other. On a V-8 each half of the carburetor feeds two ports on each side of the block. Every other cylinder in the firing order is tied together, so that successive firings don't feed from the same manifold plane or carburetor throat. In a typical Chevy V-8, with a 1-8-4-3-6-5-7-2 firing order, cylinders 1-4-6-7 are fed from one plane, while the second plane feeds 8-3-5-2. This is the design most used by auto manufacturers and is sometimes referred to as the 180-degree design. By dividing the air-fuel mixture into two chambers like this, the dual-plane manifold exposes each cylinder to a smaller volume when the intake valve opens for that port. This volume can then respond quickly to fill the cylinder and since air-fuel mix is inducted *every other firing* from this volume, intake restriction is minimized.

In theory this sounds like a great design but, as we know, practice is a little different. The dual-plane design is used as original equipment because the high runner velocity provides smooth low-speed operation, good torque and throttle response. Despite the good runner velocity the dual-plane

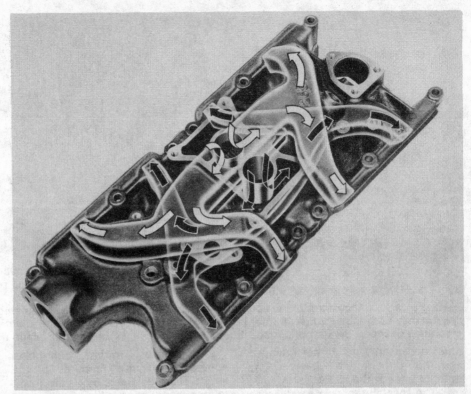

This phantom view clearly shows how the standard dual-plane intake manifold groups the left and right carburetor venturis over passages that each feed four cylinders, two on each bank for each carb throat.

falls short in the upper rpm ranges and has limited (albeit good) potential for high-rpm, high-performance use. Just as a good set of headers equalizes the exhaust flow for each cylinder a good intake manifold does the same, providing each intake port with an equal charge and velocity. But the over-and-under nature of the dual-plane manifold always requires compromise in the routing of each runner, and some cylinders have a longer or "more crooked" intake passage than others. This unequal distribution may sometimes lead to mixture problems that can only be solved by "cross jetting." Even in some stock OEM installations,

one side of the carburetor has to be jetted differently than the other to keep both banks at roughly the same air-fuel ratio.

The so-called "high-rise" manifold, so popular in the Sixties, was a variation on the 180-degree, dual-plane design. One of the features that the OEM manufacturers have designed into their dual-plane manifolds is good hood-to-air cleaner clearance. In fact, in an effort to clear the hood on late-model cars and for emission reasons, most OEM manifolds are built as "low-risers," sacrificing good performance as a result. When manifold profile is kept low, the runner design

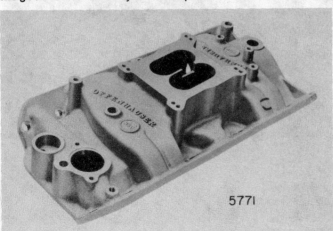

5771

In the past, a typical hot rod four-barrel manifold was similar to an optional stock dual-plane design, except for having longer runners that gave it the "high-rise" name.

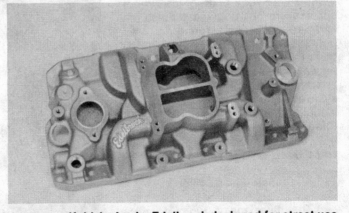

A new manifold design by Edelbrock designed for street use is the SP2P, which is a cross between the single-plane and dual-plane. Long runners that keep mixture velocity up are said to be especially helpful to cars that are equipped with very high rear end gears (lazy) and weigh over 4000 lbs.

Adding a performance manifold to your street machine may require the use of a low-profile air filter if you have minimum clearance between the carburetor and hood.

Occasionally spacers are used to raise the carb above the normal mounting pad. This is a race trick used to increase high-rpm power. The effect is slight and may create hood clearance problems on a street machine. Note this spacer has a plenum divider which also increases low-end response in a single-plane manifold.

must necessarily get rather cramped and the runners don't have a very straight shot at the intake ports.

The specialty (and in some cases factory high-performance) approach was the high-rise manifold in which the two planes of intake channels were raised up enough to provide a more direct shot at the ports. The carburetor base was also raised (to the detriment of hood clearance and often requiring a hood scoop or at least a special low-profile air cleaner), in an effort to provide a longer "ram" channel for the air-fuel mixture.

Unfortunately, enthusiasts began to confuse a raised carburetor pad with the true high-rise design and there were some manifolds which capitalized on this confusion, featuring higher carburetor pads without the higher-angle runners that increase mixture velocity. These manifolds with, in effect, built-in carburetor spacers are no longer manufactured and are only rarely found in used outlets. Also, hot rodders often bolted thick carburetor adapters and spacers between their carb and manifold in an effort to have a high-rise design. While a correctly designed spacer can occasionally create better high-rpm flow, this is seldom accomplished without the runners being straightened out somewhat.

Single-Plane Design

The other major type of specialty intake manifold design is the single-plane. This has become the state-of-the-art manifold for the Seventies.

In contrast to the dual-plane approach, all the runners in the single-plane design are on one level, joining a common plenum chamber under the carburetor. Until the problems of fuel economy and exhaust emissions became concerns of the specialty manifold engineers, this was thought to be a race-only design that lacked low-rpm response and torque. While studying existing manifold designs for the one best approach to the emissions-economy-power problems, these engineers discovered how to build single-plane manifolds that *managed high mixture velocity even at lower speeds.* Even more important the overriding concern was found to be *even cylinder-to-cylinder distribution,* something the unequal-length runners of the dual-plane didn't provide. In the single-plane manifold, all of the runners are kept as short, straight and as direct to the ports as possible. However, considerable research has been devoted to plenum chamber and runner-to-plenum entry designs in order to obtain optimum cylinder filling.

The beauty of this approach is that

The single-plane manifold design pioneered by Edelbrock's Tarantula manifold has become the accepted standard where high performance at higher-than-normal engine speeds is desired. A proper manifold and carburetor combination will give a considerable power increase throughout the rpm range.

Most manufacturers offer both street and racing versions of their single-plane manifolds. This Holley Strip Dominator is designed for drag and circle racing. The tip off is the separate valley cover that keeps hot oil off the bottom of the runners. Lack of carb preheat crossover make such manifolds troublesome during cold startup.

by giving each cylinder an equal share of the mixture at an equal velocity, the overall emissions and economy picture is brightened along with the performance potential. Obviously, if two cylinders get a lean share of the total mixture due to poor manifold design, then not even cross-jetting can substantially improve things. Jetting richer to bring the two lean cylinders up to the desired air-fuel ratio would only make the remaining cylinders rich and worsen the economy and overall tailpipe emissions. Conversely, jetting down to correct the air-fuel for the majority of cylinders could result in those two lean cylinders getting even leaner, perhaps to the point of engine

damage and certainly to the detriment of emissions.

The modern single-plane specialty manifold is designed to solve most of these interrelated problems by minimizing the length variation between the runners and keeping low-rpm mixture velocity high. These manifolds allow more precise jetting by delivering more equal air-fuel mixtures to each cylinder. It may seem incongruous that a performance manifold can be good for fuel economy but this even distribution means that jetting can be as lean as practical because you don't have to worry about burning pistons in "problem" cylinders, and the best use is made of the fuel and air the engine

takes in. It follows that emissions can be reduced for the same reasons—by making the most of the minimum amount of fuel.

Multiple Carburetion

Carburetion has always occupied a glamour role in hot rodding, perhaps because the carburetor and manifold are the most visible pieces of speed equipment. Those hot rodders who visit drag races frequently see all manner of exotic intakes sprouting huge carburetors on exotic manifolds and it is easy to succumb to the unwise but typically American philosophy that what they've got isn't enough and "more is better and too much is just right." This has given rise to some pretty elaborate induction systems, including homemade and specialty "log" manifolds with as many as eight two-barrel carbs.

On the more practical level, the most popular multiple carburetion setups for street use have been the three two-barrel (3x2) and the dual four-barrel (2x4). Although largely supplanted on the street by the very efficient single four-barrel manifolds we have today, these multiple carburetion systems bear some looking into, if only to discourage their use for some engines.

Carburetion has to be tuned to the displacement of the engine. That is, the larger an engine, the more air-fuel it needs, and vice versa. Back when Detroit was interested in performance, a host of optional multiple carburetion inductions were available, from the first dual-quad manifold for the '56 Corvette to the 3x2 combinations for the big-block Fords, Chevies, Oldsmobiles, Pontiacs, and Mopars and the four one-barrel setup that was optional

These ridges inside the ports are what Edelbrock calls "reversion dams," designed for street manifolds to prevent combustion pulses from going back up toward the carburetor, hurting low-rpm velocities.

The two passages connecting to the plenum on this street single-plane manifold are for the hookup of late-model stock EGR, or exhaust gas recirculation, to remain emission legal.

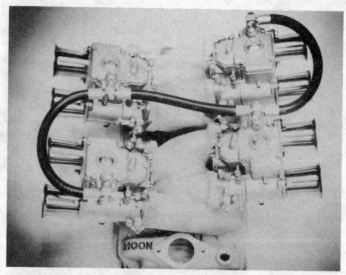

Dual-quad carb setups are not common these days. Modern single four-barrel inductions can provide equal power at any throttle setting short of wide open but, on the other hand, nothing has the eye appeal of a sharp multiple-carb induction.

The ultimate in multiple carburetion was developed during the heyday of factory Trans-Am racing. This smallblock Chevy with four Weber two-throat carbs works fine at 9500 rpm but it has limited practicality.

on the Corvairs.

With the exceptions of those hot smallblock Corvettes of the Fifties and early Sixties, the dual-quad or 2x4 setup was reserved for the larger displacement engines. At first, the 2x4 seems like the ideal setup. Since there are eight butterflies for the eight cylinders it coincides with what we described earlier as being the ideal high-performance situation. However, placement of the two carburetors unfortunately leads to some manifolding problems.

To simplify linkage and air cleaner design most 2x4 setups mount one four-barrel carb in front of the other, but for efficient engine operation at low speeds, we can't have all eight barrels opening at the same time. This would cause severe low-to-high speed tran-

sition problems—commonly called bog. On the other hand, for maximum performance at high rpm, we want them all to reach wide-open throttle at the same time. This problem is neatly solved through the use of a *progressive* throttle linkage. The progressive linkage uses a set of sliding links and stopscrews to allow the engine to operate on only two barrels of *one* of the carburetors through most of the rpm range, but "kicking in" the other barrels near full throttle. Further, this allows reasonable economy of operation around town, since the engine is being fed, for all intents and purposes, by a two-barrel carburetor. But progressive linkage by itself won't solve the transition problem caused by *rapid* throttle opening—which occurs when the throttle is "stomped" during engine

idle. To overcome this problem, most four-barrels have vacuum secondary dashpots or airflaps that delay air flow through the secondary venturis until the engine has built up sufficient speed to utilize the additional flow (more on this in the carburetor chapter).

In most designs the front half of the rear carburetor is used as the "primary" carburetion, and is equipped with a full idle circuit and choke system for easy starting. The other carburetor need not have any restrictive choke mechanism, since it is only used for "pedal-to-the-metal" bursts.

The manifolding problem with the 2x4 setup occurs because it is difficult to design a manifold that provides equal cylinder-to-cylinder mixture distribution when the primary carburetion is not even at the center of the

Another factory performance setup that was once popular was the dual four-barrel manifold. These were generally reserved for race cars on Nascar ovals or dragstrips. This expensive Z-28 Camero option with Holley carbs and a cross-ram manifold was for Trans-Am road racing.

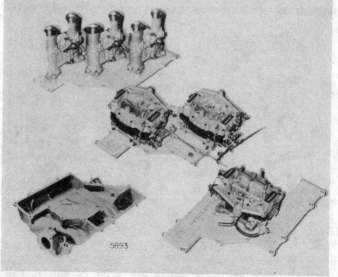

With the removable top that is a feature of most cross-rams, you can have a variety of tops fitted with different carburetion, even Webers or a single four-barrel.

manifold. Obviously, for most operation, the cylinders at the front of the engine aren't going to be fed as well as those that are near the rear carburetor. Also, a problem with all multiple carburetion systems is that to *fully* take advantage of the fuel-air delivery capacity of these systems at high rpm, the engine must necessarily be modified to an extent that low-speed efficiency is reduced. For example, to mount two four-barrels on a 327 Chevy street engine, and fully utilize all the potential available in the induction, the engine should have a minimum of 10:1 compression, lots of timing advance and a hot solid-lifter cam and related valvetrain. You can't just bolt two big carbs onto a stock engine and expect the same power increase that a high-speed race engine would appreciate.

"Ram" Manifolds

Aside from standard-type manifolds for the 2x4 combination, there are also the more exotic "ram" manifolds. One of these, the cross-ram, has been used on some limited OEM applications as well as on the racing circuits. This is a type of single-plane design in which each four-barrel feeds all four cylinders on one bank through long runners that cross under the plenum (for a ram-tuning effect).

A well-known example would be the cross-ram with dual Holley four-barrels that was once an option on the Z/28 Camaro. Actually, this very expensive option paralleled the design of

The so-called tunnel-ram manifold was developed specifically for very high-rpm drag engines. The extra length of each runner provides maximum "ram tuning" intake boost into each cylinder but this effect occurs only within a narrow rpm range.

the most popular aftermarket racing cross-rams of that period and wasn't really intended by Chevrolet to be used on the street. It was listed as an option to make the free-breathing setup legal to run on the production-based cars Chevrolet was running in Trans-Am sedan racing.

Going back into performance history even further, we can remember the long cross-rams used by Chrysler Corporation to keep their big wedges on top in both drag racing and Nascar stock car racing. The combination of the long, swoopy ram manifolds and the equally impressive free-flowing cast-iron headers earned the 426

Max-Wedge engine the nickname "The Orange Monster."

A later type of ram manifold that is extremely popular in drag racing today is the "tunnel-ram" design. This induction is characterized by two four-barrels (sometimes a single four-barrel) on top of a huge plenum chamber, which in turn sits on long, almost-individual runners that connect to the ports, like a high-rise manifold mutated into a giant from a 1950's atomic science-fiction movie.

The specialty manufacturers are constantly coming out with "new, improved" variations of the basic tunnel-ram concept, but they can't

For maximum acceleration performance the carbs used on large-plenum manifolds, such as the typical tunnel-ram or cross-ram, require a tremendous amount of accelerator pump discharge. These Holley "center-squirter" carbs do just that but they are designed for racing and they use fuel at an astonishing rate.

The "eyewash" appeal of a pair of big four-barrels may encourage you to apply race-car carburetion to a street machine, but in most cases you'll find it unsatisfactory, as excessive fuel consumption and hard starting are common.

keep up with the tricky racers, who spend countless hours polishing and contour-massaging the interior passages of their manifolds in the search for an extra horsepower or two. Although such manifolds can be considered the highest advances of the manifold-maker's art for drag racing use, they have little advantage for street engines.

Street racers and "street freaks" often install tunnel-ram manifolds on street machines because they make the carburetors stick out through the hood for a real race-car appearance, but they aren't entirely practical for street use. Given two equally-modified mild street engines, one with a tunnel-ram and the other with a good single-plane four-barrel manifold, we'd bet on the single-four car every time for all but top-end performance.

Some other drawbacks to ram manifolds for street use include linkage problems and the lack of manifold heat. Without the exhaust cross-over passage (from the center of one head to the other) underneath the carburetor base, you can forget about "getting into it" on a cool evening after the drive-in movie is over (without a long warm-up). Manifold heat is a design factor of all street manifolds to help reduce warm-up time and emissions. Linkage problems are another matter, especially when you consider the sideways placement of the carburetors required on many ram manifolds.

Tri-Power

"Tri-power," even today the words still sound like magic, hearkening back to those descendants of the Olds J-2 heritage, the early GTO's and "Total

This has to bring tears to the eye of any true performance fan. The legendary Mopar "triple-deuce" setup, complete with aluminum high-rise manifold and three of Holleys finest two-barrels, was a popular performance option in the 60's. A well sorted tri-power induction will give respectable economy, since it cruises only on the center two-barrel carb, and still give astonishing performance when all six throttles reach full open.

Edelbrock still sells the Mopar big- and smallblock tri-power manifolds and replacement carbs are available from Holley. This is, however, an expensive setup and though used tri-power inductions are available on the used market, many have been damaged beyond repair by inept amateur tuneup artists.

If you're determined to use some kind of multiple carburetion, one of the most successful designs for street use has been the "tri-power." Detroit has offered a variety of such intakes for early muscle cars, such as this 435-hp Corvette system. You may find a system like this for your engine in your dealer's parts book.

Performance" Fords. Compared to the 2x4 manifolds, the three two-barrel induction sacrifices some total cfm capacity for a more streetable runner design. The three carburetors are linked with a progressive linkage that allows the engine to run most of the time on the center two-barrel, just like a stock engine, and cut in the two end carburetors when maximum performance is desired. The beauty of the tri-power setup over the 2x4 is that when the 3x2 is operating in the single-two barrel mode, the center, or "primary," carburetor is in a central location on the manifold, and can therefore deliver a more equal charge to all the cylinders.

Also, for a street engine the total cfm capacity of a 3x2 is of a more usable nature than that of the 2x4. For example, if your stock two-barrel carburetor is of 300-cfm capacity, adding two more for a 3x2 gives a total of 900 cfm, which is plenty healthy. However, when you start with even small 600-cfm four-barrel carbs, a 2x4

setup is going to total at least 1200 cfm—maybe a little too healthy! And your stock throttle linkage is more likely to hook right up to the center carb on a 3x2, likewise for your choke linkage and heat-riser tubing.

There are still some specialty catalogs that list 3x2 setups for popular engines, but such inductions are pretty rare on the streets these days. The last usage of the design by Detroit was on the Mopar 340's and 440's with the "Six-Pack" option, and the fabled "435-hp" Corvette 427 Rats. The former units represented a unique bow from Detroit to the hot rodder, since those Mopar Six-Packs came out of their respective showrooms with a factory-installed aluminum Edelbrock manifold!

Since those days, most wise street enthusiasts have decided it was better to have carburetor problems with only one carburetor rather than three, and have stayed with the single-four-barrel design for simplicity and ease of maintenance.

Most carb makers supply gaskets and hardware to mount their product correctly. This is an example of Holley installation wares.

Manifold adapters are available to mount various carbs on different manifolds.

The used parts shelf at your local speed shop can help you save a few precious dollars. This is a fine way to obtain a rare manifold/carb combination but be prepared to check that the manifold has not been imporperly machined and be ready to completely rebuild any used carburetor. If you're a novice to hot rodding this is a good way to get in over your head, fast!

Manifold Selection Hints

1) Multiple carburetion systems require some degree of "finesse" and mechanical skill to install and maintain—don't get in over your head.

2) Buying a new manifold is often your best bet. Used manifolds may be damaged (cracked, etc.) or may have been machined to match milled heads. *Always* check used manifolds on your engine for bolt/hole alignment before you lay out "the green."

3) Make sure that the manifold that you intend to use will accept the carburetor you have chosen. Spread-bore carbs (Rochester Quadrajet, Carter Thermo-Quad, etc.) use a different family of manifolds than the standard Holley four barrel.

4) Some manifold manufacturers offer "installation kits" that supply all (or most) the hardware needed for the bolt on. If you don't have ready access to a "bolt-bin," they are a worthwhile investment.

5) Run through the installation in your mind first. If you have all you need on hand, the job will go much easier—avoid frustration, be prepared.

6) Remember, if the cylinder head "deck" surfaces have been milled, the intake manifold mating surfaces should have been milled also to insure bolt/hole, port/runner alignment.

7) Clean all surfaces of the manifold before final assembly. Residual sand particles extant in the casting can find their way into engine oil (from the valley area) and into the cylinders (from the ports).

8) Follow recommended bolt-torque techniques. You can damage aluminum manifolds and allow air/water leaks by improper tightening. Bring all bolts up to final torque values in several steps.

9) If the engine will be operated in daily street driving, do not block the heat-riser passages, they help cold-engine fuel atomizing and improve driveability.

10) If your engine has the stock exhaust manifolds, check the heat-riser valves. A valve stuck closed will cause troublesome "percolation" and vapor lock.

A performance intake manifold and carburetor are basic to the needs of a high-performance engine, whether for street or strip. Follow through here as Ron Headlee (Ron's Exxon in Fullerton, Calif.) installs a Holley Street Dominator on his 327 Chevy and tops it with a Carter 4-barrel.

Before taking any bolts out of the stock manifold, you must drain the engine coolant. Drain from the radiator and remove the upper hose.

Naturally, the carburetor must be removed if you're going to use it on the new manifold. The cast-iron, stock manifold is heavy enough to remove without the additional carburetor weight.

Disconnect the distributor wiring, mark the distributor rotor orientation with reference to the firewall, note the distributor housing orientation with reference to the manifold, and remove the distributor. If you do not turn the crankshaft while the distributor is out these two references will allow you to get the ignition reinstalled in approximately the correct timing to restart the engine.

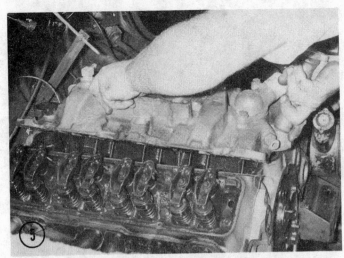

After pulling the throttle linkage and hoses out of the way, you can take off the manifold when you're sure *all* of the bolts are out. You may have to pry with a screwdriver against the heads or block to break the manifold gasket seal.

With the manifold off, your first duty is to clean all the gasket surfaces on the heads and block with solvent and a scraper. Use rags in the ports and oil valley to catch the scrapings. Don't gouge the metal or you'll have leaks.

With the surfaces cleaned of old gasket and sealer, new gasket sealer (in this case Permatex was used) is liberally coated around the ports and on the ends of the block.

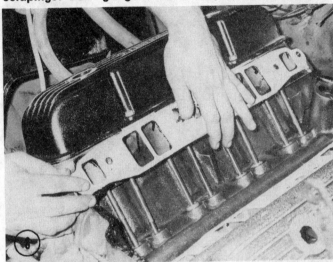

The gaskets should be carefully set in place before the manifold is installed. Then coat the gasket mating surfaces with sealer. You may find that factory (in this case Chevrolet) gaskets fit and seal better than cheaper replacements

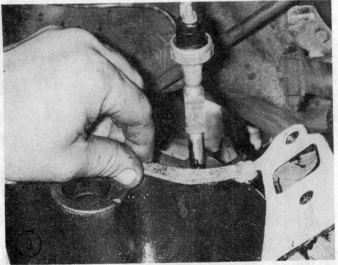

It's important to get the rear block gasket glued down firmly or it can slip out during the manifold installation and cause oil leaks. Note here that the stock oil pressure sending unit has been spaced upward to clear the manifold.

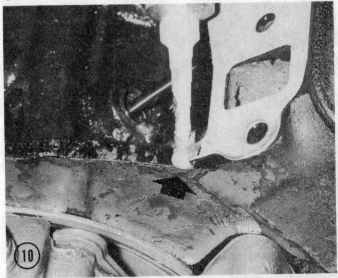

The seal at the corner between the heads and the end gaskets is very important. To avoid oil leaks here, Ron is using 3M silicone sealant at the four corners to improve the seal.

This is the fun part, seeing that new manifold go into place! Take care to set it straight down, so as not to dislodge any of the gaskets.

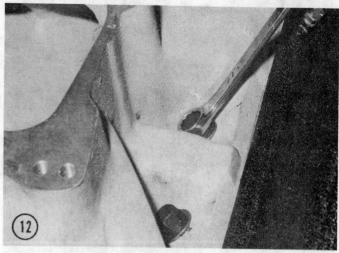

Depending on the manifold design you may have to use small header bolts to have room for your wrench, though a socket and flex will work on most bolts. Don't tighten any of the bolts until all have been started.

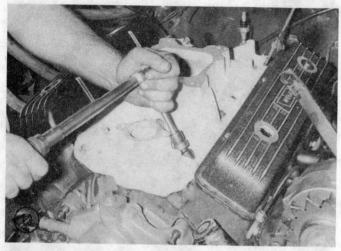

Washers should be used under the manifold bolts, so as not to chew up the soft aluminum. Follow the tightening sequence shown in the shop manual, torque the bolts to an even 15 ft-lb all around, then go back again in sequence to 25 ft-lb.

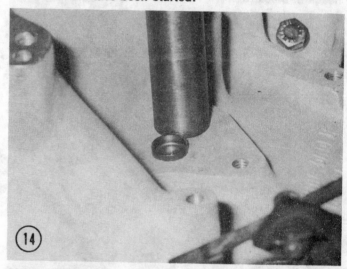

Most modern performance manifolds have a provision for EGR hookup, a smog device your older car may or may not have. If not needed plug the holes with a pair of small freeze plugs (arrow) driven in with a hammer and drift.

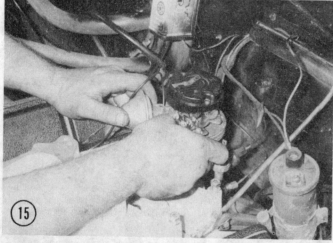

Realigning the rotor to the mark you made previously, reinstall the distributor, and realign the distributor housing with the corresponding reference. Run your hand over the back of the manifold-to-block surface one more time to check that the rear gasket stayed in place.

Now you can bolt down the coil and hook it to the distributor lead and the hot wire from the ignition switch.

48

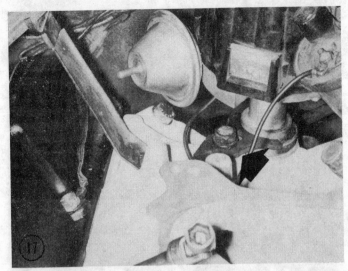

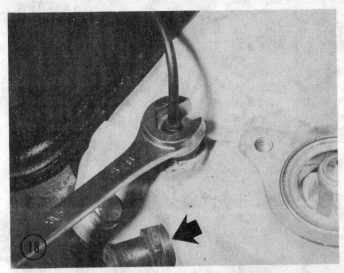

Put the distributor cap and wires back on, but don't fasten the distributor retaining bolt tight (arrow) because the timing will have to be set after the engine is restarted.

At this point, the water temperature gauge sender is coated with sealer and installed, as is the fitting for the heater hose (arrow) and thermostat.

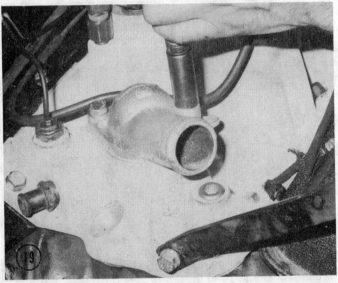

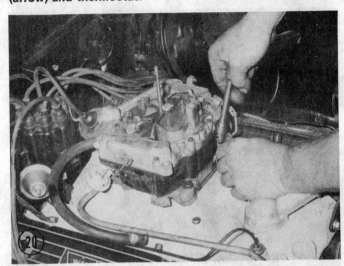

Coat the cleaned water neck and gasket with sealer and install.

Everything takes shape as the carburetor goes back on. Check the carburetor base for flatness and make certain the carb base gasket is in good shape to prevent any vacuum leaks.

Save all the vacuum and smog fittings off your stock manifold for installation on the new one. Some of the fittings may require brass adapters (available at auto parts stores) to fit the new manifold.

In your haste to drive off with the new manifold don't forget to hook up your heater hoses. This may be the opportune time to replace split or cracked hoses.

CLIFFORD RESEARCH has been the leader in performance equipment for inline engines for many years. In intake manifolds, their lineup includes high-flow types for two and four-barrel carburetors, as well as exotic multiple-Weber setups for popular Ford, Chevrolet and Mopar engines.

EDELBROCK almost "wrote the book" on modern performance street and race manifolds. They also offer marine equipment, flathead Ford equipment, tunnel and cross-ram setups, and they have developed an electronic fuel injection unit for the Chevy smallblock.

HOLLEY has only been in the intake manifold market for a few years, but their 75 years of experience in carburetor design gives them an edge. Holley offers the Street Dominator and Strip Dominator series along with manifold installation kits and carburetion from small two-barrels to huge fours.

IECO is an unfamiliar name to some, but good news for owners of Pintos, Vegas and Corvairs, for which IECO manufactures everything from suspensions to induction systems.

MOON EQUIPMENT COMPANY is well known for their line of aluminum fuel tanks and other products for race cars, street rods and performance boats. Among the goodies are exotic manifolds for mounting a quartet of Italian Weber carbs or Autolite inline carbs on Ford or Chevrolet engines.

SPEARCO PERFORMANCE PRODUCTS has concentrated its efforts in supplying the needs of popular American and imported compact cars, such as the Pinto, Vega and Capri with their line of products including everything in inductions from four-barrel manifolds to Weber setups to turbocharger kits.

OFFENHAUSER has been around since the beginning. Not only do they still make a line of manifolds for the venerable Ford flathead, they also have a full line of innovative equipment for today's engines.

TEAM G is the name of a new line of racing and street manifolds that have the stamp of approval from none other than Bill "Grumpy" Jenkins himself. These manifolds feature the latest in induction designs for low-rpm response on mildy-modified engines, and have a flange to accept Holley or spread-bore carbs.

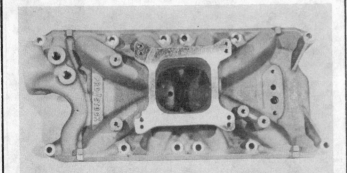

PRO/STOCK may be a new name but they're going after the other companies with a line of street manifolds designed for the most popular smallblock engines. Pro/Stock manifolds are designed to accept either stock or performance carburetion.

WEIAND'S complete line of intake manifolds covers the gamut of usage from street to drags to circle track. Weiand also manufactures a complete line of carb adapters and manifolds for the Vega and Pinto four-cylinder engines.

CARBURETORS & FUEL SYSTEMS

As you may have gathered from the preceeding chapter on intake manifolds, multiple carburetion isn't nearly as popular today as it once was. The revolution in street machine intake systems is the result of sophistication in the modern high-performance four-barrel carburetor. Even before fuel economy and emissions were important concerns of the hot rodder, the bulk of intake manifold research and development had been concentrated on producing better manifolds for single four-barrel applications. The development of a wide range of performance four-barrel carburetor sizes by specialty carburetor companies has pretty much relegated the twin-four setup to the dragstrip, and the 3x2 to the 60's musclecar restorer and nostalgia fans.

The four-barrel carburetor is so attractive for street use because it works just like the best multiple-carburetor setup with a well-designed progressive linkage. In the case of the single-four, the primary and secondary portions work almost independently—like two separate carburetors. When the engine is under normal load and throttle application, it runs only on the primary throats of the four-barrel carb. The secondary throats open only on demand or with application of full throttle. This ability to suit both the "slow" and the "go" engine modes, like a multiple-carburetion setup with progressive linkage but without the hassle of more than one carburetor, has made the four-barrel carburetor the king of street performance.

When we discussed intake manifold design, we mentioned that one of the advantages of a 3x2 setup compared to a dual-four setup is that the engine is fed in the "primary" mode with a carburetor (the middle one) that is centered on the manifold. This promotes more even mixture distribution between cylinders, which is also one of the prime advantages of the single-four setup. With *all* of the carburetor throats, both primary and secondary, located at the center of the intake manifold, the single-four-barrel carburetor provides even better cylinder-to-cylinder distribution in all rpm ranges than any multiple-carburetion scheme going (with the possible exception of the most exotic one-venturi-for-every-port type). It has been the single four-barrel induction that has allowed the specialty intake manifold companies to concentrate

The latest high-velocity intake manifolds for four-barrel carbs usually provide all the performance a street machine needs, retaining good fuel economy along with excellent low- and mid-range response.

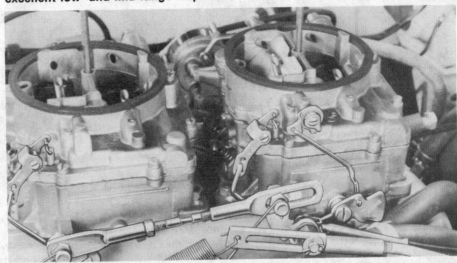

When Detroit was embroiled in the horsepower wars with their factory musclecars, the hottest options were the dual four-barrel setups like this for the 426 Hemi. Streetability was retained by using progressive linkage, shown here with the slotted secondary link.

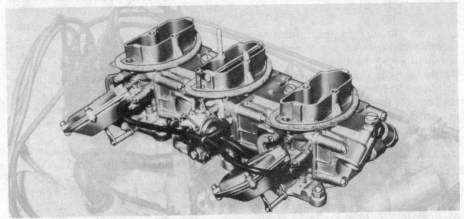

The Holley triple-deuce setup was offered on several Chrysler and Chevrolet high-performance engines. They proved nearly the ultimate in eye appeal and work fine but they should be left to the more advanced student of performance carb tuning.

53

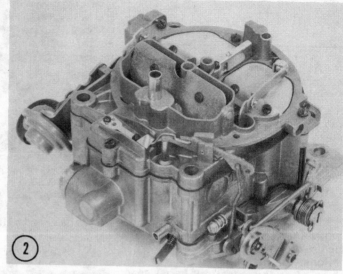

Factory original four-barrel carbs provide respectable performance but are designed to feed engines with a fairly modest rpm limit. If the engine is modified to gain maximum performance at 4500-plus rpm consider a high-performance replacement. **The examples shown here can be suitably tuned for modest performance. They are: 1) Holley model 4360 four-barrel; 2) the Rochester Quadra Jet; 3) the Ford Autolite four-barrel; and 4) Carter 9000-series AFB.**

their efforts in a search for the optimum street induction with good mileage.

The CFM Game

The carburetor manufacturers meanwhile haven't been exactly idle, either (if you'll excuse the pun). The single four-barrel carburetor has been extensively developed and programmed to suit every purpose from street performance to all-out racing to RV economy. Who would have thought back in the Fifties that today there would be more performance in a single carburetor than we had back then in three or four of the popular two-barrels?

Today we have available a wide variety of carburetor sizes within the basic four-barrel design. Two factors are important in determining the most desirable carburetor size for your engine—the displacement and the maximum intended engine speed. This only makes sense. The tighter you turn an engine, the more air-fuel the carb has to supply, but given the same engine speed, a larger engine can usually use a larger carburetor.

Carburetors today are rated according to their maximum airflow capacity as measured in cubic feet per minute (cfm) of air. You can get four-barrel carbs with as little as 450-cfm capacity, and others with as much as 1150 cfm, and choosing the wrong carburetor size for a street engine is probably the most common mistake in hot rodding.

There are no hard-and-fast rules in any aspect of engine modification but to give you a simple guide to carburetion planning we'll share a "secret formula" with you. Multiply your engine displacement (in cubic inches) by the maximum rpm to which you plan to run it (be practical about the rpm limit you pick, it's getting more and more difficult to utilize a high-winding engine today). Divide this number by the constant 3456 and see what you come up with. For instance, with a 350 cubic inch Chevy in your van and probable maximum engine speed of 5000 rpm (in street use), you come up with 1,750,000. Dividing this by our constant of 3456 gives us an airflow requirement of about 504 cfm. So this van should be carbureted just about right with a 500-cfm carb.

This may seem a little small to some of you, especially when there are so many larger carbs available that will bolt right on just as easily, but given a modern intake manifold that maintains good mixture velocity and has good distribution, a small "efficiency" carburetor should give you the crispest throttle response, good gas mileage and better performance.

Four-Barrel Designs

Just how much carburetion you can use on the street is also affected by the carburetor design. In performance four-barrel carburetors there are two types of primary and secondary venturi arrangements. Until recently the most common design has been the "standard-flange" type, in which both the primary and secondary throttle bores are the same size or nearly so. However, there is now a trend in both performance and OEM Detroit carburetors toward the so-called "spread-bore" design, in which the secondary throttle bores are considerably larger than the primaries. The spread-bore design takes full advantage of the "progressive" nature of the four-barrel carburetor. If has a small primary venturi size for best engine economy, low emissions and low-rpm throttle response and it has two large bores at the rear to handle the engine air demands at higher rpm. There should be little question why the specialty intake manifold companies have devoted a lot of research to this type of carburetion.

The subject of manifolds brings up another point about four-barrel carbs that should be mentioned, usually you need a different manifold for each type of venturi arrangement. A spread-bore carb will not fit on a standard-flange manifold or vice-versa. It's possible to change from one carb to the other on the same manifold, but only with the help of a carb adapter and an adapter will raise your carburetor at least ½ inch. Check your air-cleaner-stud-to-hood clearance before you consider this.

Actually, the specialty companies came up with their spread-bore carburetors to have a performance carb that would directly replace the Rochester Quadrajet that has been original equipment on GM cars using four-barrel carburetion. Then, because these carburetors became so successful in the hot rod market and because invariably there are many enthusiasts who would like to retain their *stock* carburetor but switch to a performance manifold, manifolds designed for the spread-bore type carbs became a natural by-product.

Four-barrel carburetors differ in ways other than just the size of the venturis. A major difference is the operation of the secondary barrels, some are operated mechanically and others are controlled by vacuum. Virtually all OEM and specialty street designs are of the latter type, vacuum.

When many enthusiasts and even some experienced mechanics talk about vacuum-secondary carburetors, they have the mistaken impression that the rear throttles are working off straight *manifold vacuum*. Since we know that intake manifold vacuum nearly disappears when we drop the hammer, this would hardly seem like a good way to trigger our "high performance" half of the carb. The vacuum signal for the secondaries is obtained from a sensing orifice in the primary venturis of the carburetor, above the throttle plates. The vacuum signal is created by airflow through the venturi and it increases as engine rpm goes up and more air-fuel is flowing through the primaries. Simply, when enough air-

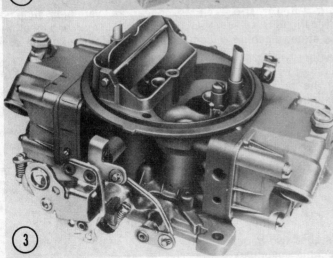

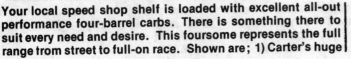

Your local speed shop shelf is loaded with excellent all-out performance four-barrel carbs. There is something there to suit every need and desire. This foursome represents the full range from street to full-on race. Shown are; 1) Carter's huge Thermo Quad, an excellent street/strip performer; 2) Holley model 4165 "spread bore" double-pumper; 3) the legendary Holley double-pumper; and 4) the gigantic Holley 4500 Dominator race-only carburetor.

Bottom view of the Quadra Jet shows the so-called spread-bore design with small primary throttles and large secondaries. This provides good low-end throttle response and good high-rpm, wide-open-throttle flow.

The V-6 engine is now considered the performance engine of the future and more equipment is available all the time, such as this package from Holley with their aluminum manifold, valve covers and #4360 four-barrel. Its 450-cfm rating is just right for the new V-6's.

flow is sensed at the primaries, the vacuum signal is strong enough to overcome the spring holding back the diaphram that operates the secondaries. This diaphragm activates a linkage connected to the secondary throttles, which then open to supply the extra fuel and air needed for high-rpm or heavy-load situations.

The mechanical method of secondary operation (no vacuum diaphram) we mentioned first is generally found only on racing specialty carburetors. This type of secondary control usually takes the form of a rod-link from the primary throttle arm that fits into a slot on the activating lever of the secondary throttles. The slot provides some delay, allowing the primaries to open a certain distance before the secondary butterflies start to open. This delay prevents the secondaries from opening "too soon" during low-speed high-load situations, preventing a severely lean condition. Most modern mechanical-secondary carbs are also equipped with additional

accelerator pump(s) on the secondary side to help overcome the lean metering created when all the throttles are suddenly opened simultaneously. The most famous example of a mechanical-secondary operation is the Holley "double-pumper" series of carbs, so-named because of the double set of accelerator pumps.

The vacuum-operation style has been the OEM favorite for many years, and with good reason, because it gives excellent low-speed performance without sacrificing high-speed power. It is undoubtedly the most practical selection for the average performance or hot rod engine. Despite the abundance of manual-operation kits available from speed equipment companies to convert a vacuum carb to manual, they are often unsatisfying. The gear-drives and sheet-metal-screw-in-the-secondary-slot "tricks" are OK for certain types of racing (where the carburetors contend only with supplying full-throttle needs), but such modifications leave a lot to be desired on a street machine

that must contend with low-speed travel, hills and other aspects of traffic. Most of the manual-secondary modifications actually make the average-geared street machine *slower* because they cause bogging, backfiring and stalling when the throttle is opened.

Carburetor Jetting

There are a number of worthwhile carburetor modifications we can recommend that will prove useful for more than simply assuaging your "if it came out of the box, it won't work" fears. In fact, unless the carburetor you select is designed by the manufacturer as specifically set up for your exact engine/car combination, improvements can no doubt be made in air-fuel ratio metering. With all the variables possible in a specially-built street machine (compared to a fixed OEM application), variables such as transmission type, rear end gearing, cam profile, manifold, exhaust sys-

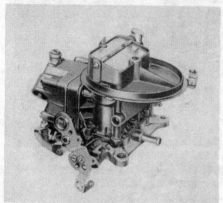

For smaller engines (or smaller egos) there are many good two-barrel performance carbs. Holley model 2300 has put out over 500 hp.

The Holley 5200 is a staged two-barrel (progressive primary and secondary operation) built under license from Weber of Italy. Found on Pintos, Vegas and small Mopars, this carb is very popular for performance minicars.

It is even possible to adapt a four-barrel to a small four-banger. The Holley R-6299 is often chosen for this conversion.

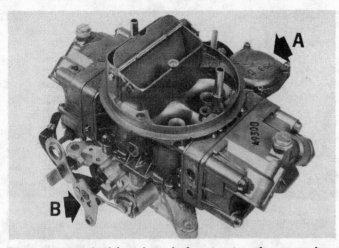

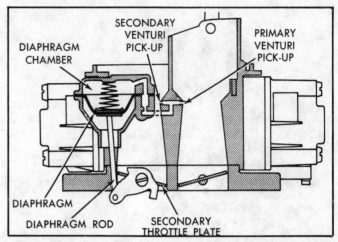

The most practical four-barrels for street performance have vacuum secondaries like the famous Holley 3310. At right you can see the vacuum diaphragm (A). Stay away from cheap modification kits that attach to the secondary link (B), or you may have *worse* low-rpm performance than before.

Holley vacuum secondary is not controlled by direct manifold vacuum. Schematic shows that air *velocity* past primary and secondary ports controls vacuum in the diaphragm chamber, opening or closing the secondary blades.

tem, compression ratio and even driving habits, it would be a near miracle if the carburetor you picked worked *exactly* right for your engine without a little "tailoring."

The primary consideration for any street carburetion system should be the air-fuel ratio measured at the tailpipe. An exhaust gas analyzer can be invaluable for this type of tuning, whether you take the car to a pro shop for testing or use one of the relatively inexpensive home air-fuel meters now on the market.

The air-fuel ratio of your engine is largely determined by the size of your main jets, and before you begin your carburetion modifications, it's not a bad idea to record your engine air-fuel

ratio with the OEM equipment still in place, as a baseline against which to compare your new carb. There is a so-called "ideal mixture" of 14.9:1 (known as the stoichiometric mixture), which means that for every clump of gasoline that is completely burned 14.9 times that much air (by mass) is also consumed. But, in reality, gasoline combustion in an engine is not complete and residual by-products of combustion cause the actual air requirement to be lowered somewhat. For maximum performance the wide-open-throttle air-fuel ratio is generally considered to be about 12:1.

If a modification to the engine has caused the air-fuel mixture to be changed dramatically, the fuel meter-

ing inside the carb will have to be altered. In most cases this necessitates that the carb metering jets be changed. Usually a trial-and-error method is required, changing the jets and rechecking the tailpipe readings, until the best performance is obtained. This is among the most basic of carburetor tuning techniques and is generally a simple operation, once the carburetor assembly or tuneup manual is used to determine where the main jets are located and how they are removed and replaced (four-barrel carbs will have both primary and secondary metering jets, the primary jets control most of the metering and the secondary jets only control the additional fuel "dumped in" at wide-open throttle).

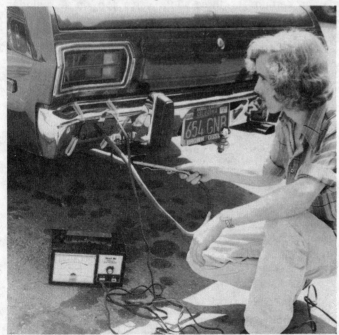

There are now exhaust gas analyzers on the market that are relatively inexpensive and have a great many uses in fine-tuning for the best air-fuel ratio for performance.

With a long set of leads portable analyzers like this Hawk can be used at the engine compartment for static tuning of the engine, as well as carried on the dash for on-the-road checks. It's almost like having your own chassis dyno!

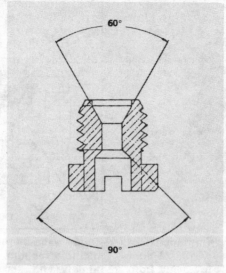

HOLLEY MAIN JET CHART			
Jet No.	Drill Size	Jet No.	Drill Size
40	.040	71	.076
41	.041	72	.079
42	.042	73	.079
43	.043	74	.081
44	.044	75	.082
45	.045	76	.084
47	.047	77	.086
48	.048	78	.089
49	.048	79	.091
50	.049	80	.093
51	.050	81	.093
52	.052	82	.093
53	.052	83	.094
54	.053	84	.099
55	.054	85	.100
56	.055	86	.101
57	.056	87	.103
58	.057	88	.104
59	.058	89	.104
60	.060	90	.104
61	.060	91	.105
62	.061	92	.105
63	.062	93	.105
64	.064	94	.108
65	.065	95	.118
66	.066	96	.118
67	.068	97	.125
68	.069	98	.125
69	.070	99	.125
70	.073	100	.128

Your parts store or speed shop probably carries a full line of these Holley Trick Kits. They not only have all the parts necessary for a rebuild, but also performance parts and a set of instructions on carb modifications.

Jets are usually numbered according to the size of the metering orifice (normally measured to the nearest one-thousandth of an inch). But sometimes other numbering criteria are used—the fuel flow rate (rather than orifice diameter) or just arbitrary "part numbers." Since one numbering system cannot be directly compared to another, try to stay with one system, and ask the manufacturer if you have any doubt about the numbering system on the jets you are buying. Jets are available at speed shops and many performance auto parts stores.

Most dyno tuners and carburetor experts recommend changing jets only one or two sizes at a time. If you find that your engine is running lean and the number on your stock jet is 60, then switch to a number 61 or 62 (don't just jump to a 65 to see how it runs). Drive

Carb manufacturers claim that the entry and exit angles of the jets are such that drilling a jet may ruin the flow pattern. They would prefer you to buy new jet sizes for tuning.

your car for a while with the new jets (obviously they should be changed in sets on a four-barrel carburetor—primary pairs and/or secondary pairs) and then go back and recheck the air-fuel after all the regular carburetor adjustments like float level, fast idle, choke adjustment, etc., have been checked. This will tell you if you're going in the right direction.

If you don't have access to an air-fuel meter, to a certain extent, you can tell the relative ratio by "reading" the spark plugs and tailpipe color. Black, sooty deposits on the spark plugs after some hard running (not idling in traffic) indicate the carburetion is rich, (but can also mean excessive oil burning) while white spots or an overall light-colored-appearance generally indicate a lean condition. The same is true for your

The above chart provides a cross-reference for jet numbers to orifice diameter. However, flow rate is determined by flow testing.

tailpipe. In both plugs and tailpipes, a dry, light brown or grey appearance indicates close to optimum air-fuel ratio.

In the past, many hot rodders would change carburetor jetting by simply drilling out the stock jets with a pin-vise and a tiny set of drills. Most carburetor manufacturers today do not recommend this time-honored practice. This can adversely affect the flow characteristics of the jet, because most jets do not have a simple hole through the middle. The metering orifice may be tapered or flared at one or both ends (something like a three-angle valve job on a cylinder head) and drilling will remove this flare and change the fuel flow or leave some very tiny burrs inside the orifice that may actually *reduce* fuel flow.

There is enough difference in the

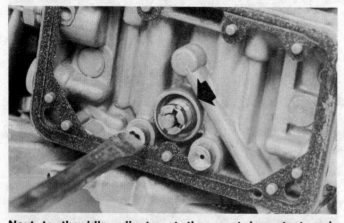

Next to the idle adjustment the most important carb adjustment is made by changing jet sizes. On Holleys this is easily done by removing the float bowl and screwing in the new jets with a wide-tip screwdriver or a jet wrench. Arrow indicates location of the power valve, which can also be changed to tailor mid-range economy.

Holley offers a complete line of replacement and performance parts for their four-barrels, including new secondary diaphragms and springs at left, and secondary metering plates. Replaceable metering *plates* are used in some Holley carbs, instead of individual jets, to meter fuel flow.

manufacturing of replacement jets that Holley offers two kinds of jets, standard and "close limit." The close limit jets are said to be more precise in their fuel metering, and are sold mainly "for OEM applications to obtain tighter carburetor emission flow limits." They manufacture these special jets to extra-close tolerances which Holley says reduces by 60% the "jet flow variations" that can occur with standard jets. While this is not strictly a problem for the average street rodder looking for a few horsepower, it does show that we're dealing with more than a simple hole in a piece of metal.

Other Metering Types

In some carburetors you may not find simple removable jets. In the case of many four-barrel carburetors, specifically some Holleys, the secondary barrels don't have jets but a "metering plate," which is a thin removable piece with drilled restrictions in it. Again, the restriction orifice is not a simple drilled hole, but a combination of several holes, and drilling is not the recommended way to change the

metered flow. You have to buy another metering plate with the right-size holes in it. And since each plate has metered holes for both main and idle fuel flow, this can be a real "kettle of fish" if you aren't careful in your selection. Holley lists a wide assortment of these in their catalog to suit just about any application.

Just to throw another curve at the uninitiated, there are also carburetors in which you can change more than just the jets to change the air-fuel ratio. Carter carburetors such as the AFB and Thermo-Quad, as well as most OEM General Motors Rochester Quadrajet carburetors, utilize main jets in conjunction with tapered metering rods.

The metering rod hangs vertically and fits into the hole in the jet. As engine and venturi vacuum change with the amount of throttle opening, the tapered metering rods pull out of the jet to allow more fuel to pass through. This creates what amounts to a variable-orifice jet. In some cases, the rods are "stepped" in size, in addition to their general taper. The larger thicknesses toward the top of

the rod restrict the jet more and are called "economy steps." Conversely, the smaller portions near the tip of the rods are the "power" steps.

These carburetors really pose no more problem to fine-tune to fit your situation than carburetors with removable jets. Special metering rods and the jets to match them are just as available as regular jets. Carter markets them in skin-packed "strip kits" with a full range of various tapers and two-step or three-step models that allow fine tuning to every situation.

Just as with regular jets, hot rodders traditionally have taken their own approaches to modifying the fuel flow of Carter and Quadrajet carbs. They sometimes drill the jets and modify the metering rods by grinding off portions of the tapered or stepped areas. Obviously this takes a rather light touch because the rods are quite small and we doubt seriously if the average hot rodder is capable of sufficient "eyeball engineering with micrometer eyes" to modify his metering rods and still have them exhibit desired fuel flow characteristics. In all cases the average rodder would be wise

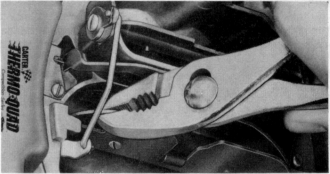

On Holleys and most other vacuum secondary four-barrels, the only way to adjust operation of the secondary is by changing the tension of the vacuum diaphragm spring. Holley codes their springs for different tensions: White for the lightest, Yellow for light, then Purple, plain for medium, Brown for medium-heavy, and Black for the heaviest. The heavier springs make the secondaries open later.

This adjustment screw on the Carter Thermo-Quad controls operation of the secondary air valve (next to it is a lock-screw). Adjusting the screw controls timing of the vacuum air valve (secondary flow) tip in. The corner of the air valve is notched so pliers can be used to adjust the wide open position of the valve.

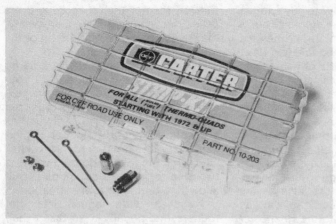

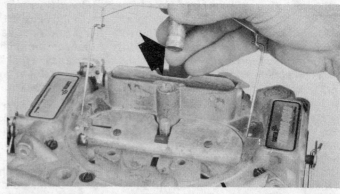

Most of the performance carburetor manufacturers have special tuning kits available like this selection of metering rods, jets and other small parts for Carter four-barrels.

Thermo Quads and other Carters use metering rods controlled by the step-up piston (arrow) and spring. Optional rods can be used to feed more fuel, and special springs can be used to tailor the step-up piston/rod action for any desired performance profile.

to buy new jets and/or rods rather than modifying, no matter what kind of carburetor he is using.

In addition to juggling the jets and metering rods, Carter carbs offer an additional tuning route. The tension of the metering rod springs can also be changed. Carter markets a set of springs, each having a different tension, or you can use a less reliable technique called the "cut-and-try." Either stretching the spring to increase the tension or cutting off a little at a time to weaken it is not recommended as a permanent fix.

The "Power" Circuit

If you've got the air-fuel ratio worked out to give throttle response, good spark plug life and clean emissions, then your fine-tuning is almost finished. The power circuit of a carburetor, which dumps in the extra fuel needed when you suddenly deck the pedal, may not affect the part-throttle air-fuel ratio reading, but it can have a definite effect on driveability and performance. If, when accelerating with your new carburetion system,

you experience a "bog" or a "surge" condition, then you may have to modify or adjust your power system.

Having the basic jetting either too rich or too lean can cause these problems, too, which is why you should get into the ballpark on jetting first. A "bog" can indicate richness. This is caused by either rich jetting, too much or too little fuel being passed in the accelerator-pump system or just having too big a carburetor. Assuming that you have selected the correct carburetor size for your engine and have the main jetting close, you can proceed

On some carbs accelerator pump shot is controlled by the link-and-arm arrangement. To increase the amount of the accelerator pump shot the link is moved to a hole that is closer to the arm pivot. This increases the amount of travel per pump stroke.

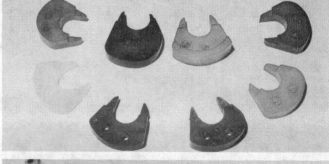

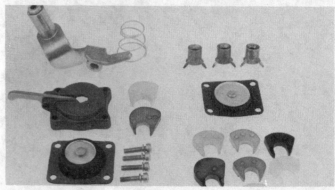

Among the popular performance modifications for Holley carbs is the addition of the "Reo" accelerator pump (left) that supplies a bigger squirt of fuel. Because it is thicker than the stock pump, you may have to use a ¼-inch spacer under the carburetor for clearance. Also available in Holley parts kits are a variety of profiled plastic cams for the accelerator pump lever, making it possible to tailor pump duration/volume action to your engine/throttle requirements.

One of the most important carb tuneup checks is setting the float level. The Holley float level can be set with the external adjusting screw, while the engine is running.

Even though the Holley float level can be adjusted externally, for maximum accuracy the bowl should be removed and the float level set dry. When the bowl is inverted the clearance between the top of the float and the inside of the bowl should be set to Holley recommended "dry float setting" specs.

to "tune up" your accelerator-pump system.

If the engine stumbles or backfires when you rapidly depress the accelerator pedal, but runs smoothly when the pedal is pushed slowly, your accelerator pump may be squirting the incorrect amount of fuel into the venturi. Most accelerator pumps are controlled by a linkage rod from the throttle arm, and where this rod fits into the actuating arm of the accelerator pump there should be several holes. Stock carburetors usually come out of the box with the linkage rod in the center or furthest-out hole, but, with a bogging condition, you may want to move the rod to increase the accelerator pump "squirt." Moving the rod further in on the accelerator-pump arm will increase the squirt by increasing the pump-arm travel and moving the link to the hole furthest from the pump plunger *will reduce* the squirt.

An over-rich accelerator pump

squirt will often not be detected by "seat-of-the-pants" tuning. However, excess fuel injected into the engine every time the throttle is opened will, over a period of time, cause black colored plugs and pipes, promote fouling and difficult starting. A very over-rich pump squirt will cause black smoke during acceleration and reduced throttle response.

There are hundreds of different carburetor modifications that you may find in enthusiast publications. We won't go into all of them here. Most are suited only for racing applications and would be of questionable benefit on the street, where economy and emissions, as well as performance, must always be considered. The most important thing that we wish to emphasize in this chapter is the selection of the proper carburetion and manifolding for your engine, and dialing them in for the best possible throttle response. To do this we

suggest making a few adjustments and jet changes, not a complete hot-rod "rebop" that only runs great "foot to the wood."

Carbs Need Clean Air Too

Obviously, or maybe not so obviously to the neophyte, there's a lot more to carburetion than just a manifold and carburetor. How the carburetor is fed fuel and *air* can have a lot to do with overall performance.

On the question of air supply, it should go without saying that an engine needs a clean source of air. Whatever goes through your carburetor along with the air is going to wind up inside your combustion chambers. This is obviously no place for dirt or dust, which can wear out an engine in short order. A few long drives down a dirt road without an air cleaner can be enough to seriously affect your engine's oil consumption

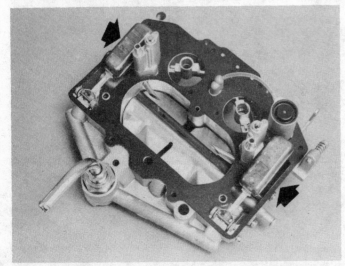

On some carbs the float level cannot be adjusted externally. For example, on the Thermo Quad the top section of the carb must be removed to uncover the floats and bowls.

Float setting specs for the Thermo Quad call for a certain clearance between the top of the float and gasket surface of the top section. This setting is adjusted by removing the float and bending the tang which rides against the inlet needle.

61

rate, permanently.

Assuming then that we must have an air cleaner, what kind? The hot rodder has even more choice here than in his carburetion! The stock air cleaner can usually be fitted to the performance carburetor, unless the use of a high-rise manifold creates clearance problems. However, the modifications you're making to your stock engine can create a need for more-than-stock filtration and airflow. This need is generally fulfilled by specialty filters, which are available in a wide range of sizes and styles, to suit every need from a subtle street machine to a killer off-road basher.

By having the filter element exposed around the complete circumference of the cleaner, these filters offer less restriction than a stock cleaner that has only one small opening for the air. They look good as well. When shopping, read the package carefully to make sure that there is a readily available filter element that fits it; you don't want to get stuck in East Podunk looking for an element that is only made by the air cleaner manufacturer in Hollywood.

Near the end of the factory musclecar era in the late Sixties so-called "cold-air packages" were hot items for manufacturers to advertise as options. Basically, Detroit had learned from drag racers that cool "non-underhood" air made more horsepower—racers used scoops and ducting to pick up cold air from the overhood air stream or from under the front bumper and grille area.

While the day of the factory supercar is gone forever, the specialty manufacturers have come through again with bolt-on cold-air packages that can be adapted to just about any vehicle. Remember that for every ten degrees you can lower the intake charge temperature, you can gain 1% in engine power. Several of the specialty "ram air" systems incorporate an air cleaner and are of low-enough profile to be used even with most high-rise manifolds.

Fuel Pumps

How the fuel gets to your carburetor is equally important for performance purposes. A stock engine is perfectly happy with a stock fuel pump, line, etc., but you and I are asking for something more than stock in every department. Once again, the least-restrictive path is the best. Stock fuel pumps are adequate (with 3-5 psi pressure) to supply the stock carburetor in normal driving, but often fall short at higher rpm when forced to feed

Using a performance manifold on some cars with limited hood clearance like Corvettes and Trans-Ams may require you to use a low-profile air cleaner such as this high-flow unit from Moroso. Any high-performance street engine should be fitted with a high-flow air cleaner at all times!

Ram-air is an effective trick for more performance on the street. Ready-made units are available from some sources, or you could duct cold grille air to your stock air cleaner with clothes dryer hose. Similar cold-air packages were used on some factory muscle cars and can often be adapted to late model engines.

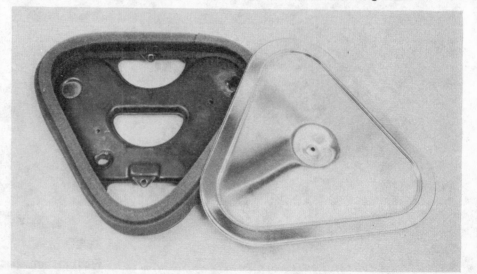

Though there are many excellent specialty high-performance air cleaners some of the original factory hi-po air cleaners work just fine. At wide open throttle a hi-po carb needs lots of air so look for a filter with as much area as practicable. A large diameter, tall element is desirable.

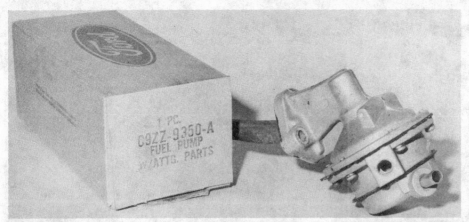

The local dealer's parts shelf may have the part you need. For example, smallblock Fords can gain from using the Boss 302 mechanical fuel pump (built by Carter for Ford). However, many of these "special" parts are no longer stocked by most dealers and, in most cases, the local speed shop can provide a comparable replacement, sometimes at a cheaper cost!

The Carter Competition Series mechanical fuel pump is preferred by many Nascar engine builders (electric pumps are not legal in Nascar competition). This pump has a reputation for delivering a high volume of fuel at a constant 8 psi pressure.

a thirstier-than-stock carburetor. Specialty manufacturers like Holley, Carter and Stewart-Warner all offer high-performance fuel pumps for both racing and street usage.

The simplest by far to install are the "performance mechanical" pumps. These bolt on to your engine in place of the stock pump, and provide considerably greater fuel delivery rate (gallons per hour) and at a higher, more steady pressure such as 4½-8 psi. For most street engines, this should be more than adequate for fuel supply, although there are "racing" versions of these pumps that put out even more.

You may be interested in utilizing another type of fuel pump, the electric. Auxiliary electric fuel pumps have been around as long as hot rodding it seems, and they are still common today. There are various kinds of high-volume and low-volume electric pumps on the market. Some are suitable as direct replacements for your stock mechanical pump, others work well as a supplement to the stock pump. It's a fact that any pump, whether mechanical or electric, is better for *pushing* fuel than for pulling it, yet every stock engine-mounted pump operates by drawing fuel from the fuel tank all the way up to the engine.

One of the main advantages of an auxiliary electric fuel pump is that it can take the load off your mechanical unit. By mounting an electric pump at the rear of the car, as close to the fuel tank as possible, the engine mechanical pump has a much easier task of pushing the fuel up to your carburetor. Another advantage of the electric pump is that it should, if

Holley sells a complete line of fuel system accessories to complement their carburetors. They can provide everything from the fuel tank forward and feature mechanical and electrical performance pumps, even chrome-plated mechanical pumps!

Too much fuel pressure can overpower the "needle-and-seat" valve that meters fuel into the float bowl and create flooding, but too little pressure will starve the engine at higher engine speeds. You must use some kind of pressure regulator if you are using a high-pressure pump. To the right of this Holley 97-gallon-per-hour electric pump is their adjustable fuel pressure regulator.

This is an all-out racing fuel system but it shows some excellent features for a high-performance approach. Neat steel-braid fuel line of large diameter feeds fuel into a cool can. Cooling the fuel increases its density, increasing the relative amount of fuel carried into the engine. A Y-fitting splits the fuel line to feed two four-barrel carbs. Dual pressure regulators are used to insure sufficient *volume* as well as sufficient *pressure* to the carbs (one pressure regulator may restrict the total *volume* of fuel fed to the carb(s), especially a problem when two carbs are used on a very high-horsepower engine).

mounted near the fuel tank, virtually eliminate the occurrence of vapor-lock.

There are a number of high-volume electric fuel pumps on the market today that are capable of serving as the only source of engine fuel delivery. With these pumps the frictional horse-power loss of the mechanical pump can be eliminated. Aluminum cover plates to replace the mechanical pump in these applications are available in most speed shops.

One of the advantages of an electric pump system is that on a rare occasion when you run out of gas, you don't have to wear your battery down

trying to prime the fuel pump after you put in the gas from your spare can. (You simply turn on the electric pump and wait for it to slow down, telling you the "pipeline" is full once again and the engine is ready to restart.)

There are two ways to wire up an electric pump, either through the ignition switch, or with a separate toggle switch. If you wire through the ignition switch, don't leave the ignition on for long periods without the engine running as carburetor flooding is possible. The advantage of the separate switch is that the electric pump

can act as an anti-theft device. By leaving the power to the pump in the "off" position when you leave your vehicle, anyone who subsequently tries to start your car without turning on the pump will only be able to drive a half-block or so before the engine quits. You do have to get into the habit yourself of turning on the switch before starting your car, and turning it off when parking, but that 50¢ toggle switch can be a lifesaver if someone does try to steal your machine and, after considering the time and money you have invested in your car, that's pretty important!

In case you're wondering, here's what the inside of an electric fuel pump (Carter) looks like. Most units run reliably for many years.

Something often forgotten in the rush to build a performance induction is good fuel filtration. This Holley inline fuel filter has a replaceable element and filters well without restricting fuel flow to the carb.

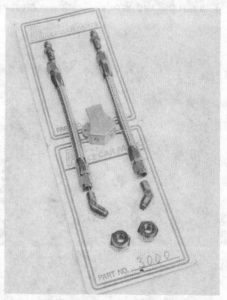

Your speed shop probably has a variety of fuel lines to suit your installation, from rubber hose to braided steel to Holley dual-line kits with chromed steel tubing.

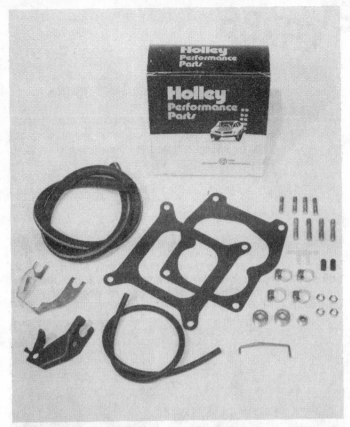

To go along with their manifolds, Holley markets these installation kits with everything you need to bolt a new carb into the manifold. They have all the miscellaneous parts needed to perform a "perfessional" installation.

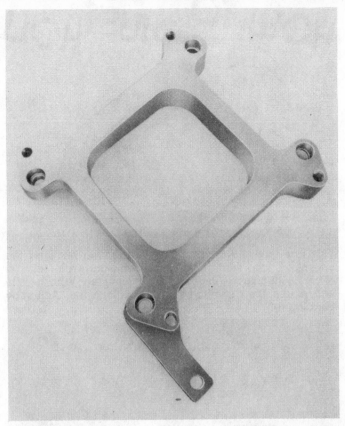

A plethora of carburetor adapters are available in speed shops. This B&B adapter mounts a Holley carburetor sideways so that the butterflies will open in line with the manifold runners.

Carburetion Installation Hints

1) Some carburetors are designed for racing use only, as with the double-pumper series, the Dominator, etc. Don't get talked into a "good deal" on a used race carb that you intend to use on the street, stay with the recommended types.

2) Spread-bore carburetors use their own family of manifolds that have a plenum to match the large secondary throttle bores. Make sure the carburetor you select will attach directly to the manifold—try to avoid adapters as they can cause vacuum leaks, make linkage and choke connections difficult and may cause hood/air cleaner interference.

3) Never rely on the throttle return spring that is built into the carburetor. Always reconnect the stock return spring. Nothing is more scary than your throttle staying stuck "to the floor."

4) Use accepted methods for routing and connecting fuel lines. More than a few engine compartment fires have been the result of leaky fuel lines.

5) In-line fuel filters will prevent dirt, rust and whatever else is pumped into your tank that you didn't want, from getting into the small fuel and air passages in the carb metering system. These foreign particles can cause idling problems and poor performance.

6) If you are using a thick easily-compressed carburetor base gasket (like most anti-percolation designs), *do not* over tighten these bolts because you will surely distort the secondary throttle bores, perhaps enough to prevent them from opening. Thin gaskets help prevent base distortion.

7) If your car uses a throttle cable instead of mechanical linkage, adjust the cable so that just as your foot reaches the floor, the carburetor is fully open. If your foot is not on the floor when the carb is wide open, additional pressure on the pedal will eventually break the cable.

8) Never use silicone rubber sealant on surfaces that come in contact with gasoline, it will dissolve the rubber into gooey chunks that do a great job of clogging up your carburetor.

9) Many new carburetor designs use electric chokes (no need to use bimetal manifold heated elements or hot water, etc.). These are easy to hook up, reliable, and should be used whenever possible in a carburetor swap.

10) STP's gas additive is very effective in keeping your carburetor's "insides" clean. Also, many racers have said that you can pick up a hundredth or two by adding a can to a full tank.

HOW TO ADJUST HOLLEY CARBS

This is a typical 600-cfm Holley four-barrel, showing the emissions type vent valve which connects (from tube at arrow) to the charcoal vapor recovery cannister. With throttle at curb idle, there should be .015-inch clearance. Adjust by bending rod.

Loosening three screws on the choke body allows you to adjust the choke. Use the reference marks indicated here when leaning or richening the choke to obtain the best cold-start idle.

To adjust the secondary throttle stop on Holleys, back this secondary stop screw out until the secondaries are fully closed. Then turn the screw in until it just touches the stop on the lever, then one-fourth turn more. Ordinarily this adjustment is not necessary unless the secondary throttle plates have been completely removed.

The accelerator pump linkage is adjusted by holding this nut with a 3/8-inch wrench and unscrewing the screw until all play is removed. Too tight or too loose will affect the pump stroke. Plastic screw adjusts the idle mixture.

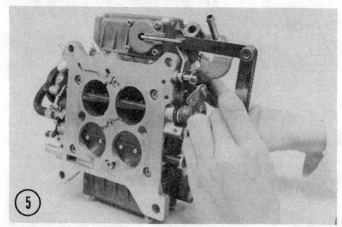

The accelerator pump lever should always be capable of .015- to .020-inch additional travel beyond the screw when the throttle is wide open.

The small screwdriver here points out the Holley fuel level sight hole (normally covered by a screw). If you elect to set the float level with the engine running, float level can be varied by loosening the lockscrew (arrow) and using a wrench on the nut to raise or lower the needle assembly. Adjust until the fuel just comes up to the level of the sight plug hole.

HOW TO ADJUST CARTER CARBS

On a typical Carter four-barrel such as this 9000 Series of 625-cfm capacity, the idle speed screw is easily reached, located next to the throttle arm. In this case, no speed solenoid adjustment is needed.

Carters usually have two idle mixture screws located at the front. Using a vacuum gauge or a tachometer, slowly adjust the screws to achieve the highest vacuum or rpm readings at idle. If this raises your idle speed beyond specs, back off the idle *speed* screw. Adjust both mix screws to the same number of turns.

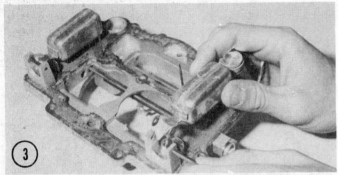

When the carburetor top is removed the floats can be adjusted. Removing these pins frees the floats and bending of the float tangs will correct float levels. Don't bend in place or you could damage needle and seats. Carter tuning specs give float clearance between top of the float and *bottom* of the carb top, when the assembly is turned upside down as shown here.

Under the float pins are the needle and seat assemblies, which should be replaced during carb rebuild. They have a wide-based slot for removal with a special tool or very wide-tip screwdriver. Too small a screwdriver can chew up the brass assembly.

With the carb cover inverted, the floats should be nearly parallel to the top with 9/32-inch between the float and the top gasket. This float (foreground) needs adjusting.

This is the adjustment for the choke countershaft lever on the 9000. Loosen this screw, hold the choke butterfly closed and then retighten.

On most other carburetors, a jet change is simple. Carters and Rochesters use pairs of metering rods as well as jets. A Carter Strip-Kit, which contains a variety of rich and lean jets and rods, is invaluable in tuning.

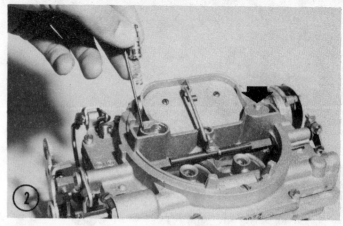

Removing a screw (arrow) releases the metering rod and step-up piston covers. This is done before removing the carburetor bowl cover.

The float bowl cover has to be removed to get the primary jets. There is a variety of sizes in the Strip-Kit. Enlarge or reduce the jet orifice size in one-step increments until you have the best air-fuel ratio for your engine equipment.

Here the screwdriver indicates the location of the primary jets and the arrows show the secondary jets, which are normally hidden by the float bowl baffles (which have been removed in the above photo).

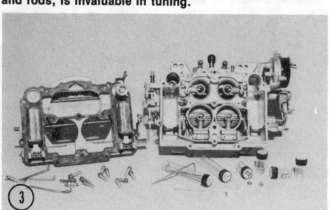

As with most other carb jets, the Carter jets have thin slots on each side of the center hole. Either use a Carter jet-wrench to remove them or a screwdriver blade that exactly fits. Too small a screwdriver may chew up the soft brass of the jet, complicating removal and installation.

Different step-up pistons are part of the Strip-Kit and can be additional help in tuning, as can the different step-up piston springs (arrow), making the Carter one of the easiest four-barrels to tailor to your needs.

HOW TO ADJUST ROCHESTER CARBS

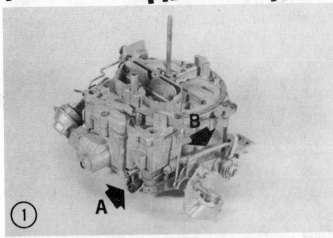

① The Rochester 4MV, otherwise known as the Quadra-Jet, is the standard four-barrel on all GM cars. Arrow (A) indicates the idle speed-setting screw, while arrow (B) shows the accelerating pump arm with two linkage holes.

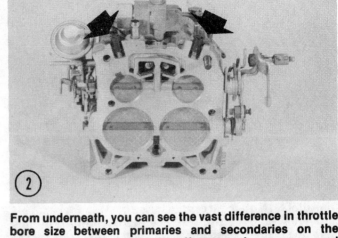

② From underneath, you can see the vast difference in throttle bore size between primaries and secondaries on the Quadra-Jet, the reason it offers good economy and performance. The arrows here indicate the idle mixture screws.

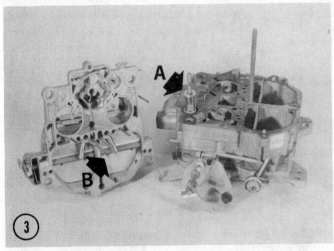

③ With the cover removed, you can examine the accelerator pump (A) and the three-step secondary metering rods (B), which can also be removed without taking off the bowl cover.

④ Here the gasket is removed so you can better see the float chamber and the primary metering rods (arrow). The accelerating pump and spring are in the foreground here.

⑤ The float bowl fuel baffle (arrow) must be removed to adjust the float level. The float tang must be held (gently) down against the needle and seat while the float level measurement is taken at the other end (ruler). Do not bend the float tang while float is in place, or you could damage the needle and seat assembly.

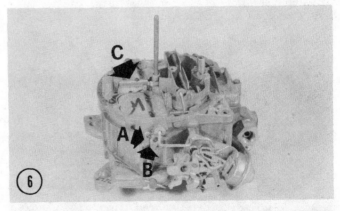

⑥ The operation of the secondary air valve is adjusted with this screw (A), but the Allen lockscrew (B) must be loosened before you can adjust it. The opening of the secondary air valve actually controls lifting of the secondary metering rods through this arm (C). Removing this arm allows you to change secondary metering rods without removing the carb bowl cover.

HOW TO ADJUST AUTOLITE CARBS

The Autolite/Motorcraft carburetor is a basic and dependable carburetor in both two and four-barrel forms. On this pre-smog model, speed idle is adjusted at (A). Note (B) the number of adjustment holes for the accelerator pump rod. Maximum pump shot can be achieved by using the top hole here and inside hole at pump arm end (C).

Secondary operation of the Autolite four-barrel is via a linkage rod (A) hooked to the secondary diaphragm (B) that opens when vacuum is high enough in the primary venturis.

By loosening three screws on the choke housing, you can rotate the housing to richen or lean the choke operation. Move it only a notch at a time, with relation to reference mark at (A). If your engine idles rough when hot, you need to replace the hot idle compensator (B). It is not adjustable.

With the air horn cover removed, everything in the Autolite carb is accessible. Popping off two spring clips with a screwdriver releases the floats for removal. When working with the cover off, don't lose the two metal baffles (arrows) at each end of the fuel bowl pressure equalizer.

Removing the secondary float here reveals the needle-and-seat assembly (A) and the removable jets (B). Do not adjust the float while in place, or you'll damage the needle-seat.

The idle dashpot controls how fast the carb returns to idle, and helps prevent hot-weather stalling. If it doesn't properly dampen throttle return it must be replaced.

HOW TO INSTALL BRAIDED FUEL LINES

Stainless-steel braided hoses are as durable as they are good looking. If they have any drawback, it is that they are expensive and their inside diameter is always considerably smaller than the outside diameter, compared to any non-covered type hose.

Plumbing fuel lines to the carb is always a problem. The super-slick setup is braided hose. Easy to remove and replace without leakage, even this complicated tri-power fuel line is a snap with braided hose.

For the expensive aircraft look without the bother of adapting special AN fittings everywhere, you can use "Econo-Seal" hose ends from Earl's. These anodized-aluminum fittings can be used with either standard hoses or stainless, and contain a stainless screw-type clamp inside, allowing them to be fitted on radiator hoses, etc.

Dave Russell's Race Car Parts has a complete line of AN (Army-Navy) hoses and fittings for just about every need. They also have chromed steel fittings.

Since AN fittings have their own special threads, you may need adapters to fit stainless-braided hoses to your brakes or engine parts. There are adapters to go from standard threads and pipe threads to the AN threads.

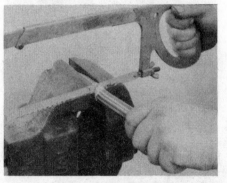

You can buy hoses ready-made, or buy the fittings and bulk line and cut to exacty fit your requirements. Wrap the hose with silver duct tape and hold in a vise to neatly cut the length you need with a fine hacksaw.

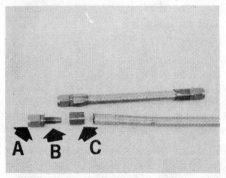

Here's a complete Race Car Parts hose with one ready for assembly. The fitting is actually three pieces, the swiveling end (A), threaded male nipple (B), and female-threaded nut (C). Assembled, they make a tight, high-pressure seal on the hose.

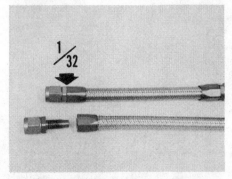

If you've made a clean cut in the hose, you can remove the tape and push the female nut over the hose until it bottoms out inside. Then thread the male nipple into the nut. When fully-tightened, the nut will have 1/32-inch clearance from the nipple.

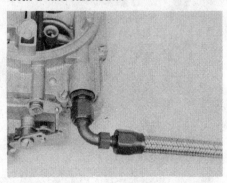

Braided lines look especially trick in your fuel system and brake lines. Here a Race Car Parts big-bore carb fitting is installed in a Carter to accept angled high-flow hose end. No more chewing up rubber hoses with standard screw-type hose clamps!

HOW TO INSTALL AN ELECTRIC FUEL PUMP

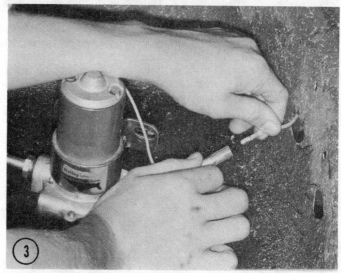

Installation of a specialty electric fuel pump is a simple job, but pump replacement is most important. If possible, mount the pump near the fuel tank and *below* it, as pumps are designed to push fuel not to pull. Depression in the trunk of this Camaro was the easiest place. Drill holes for mounting the pump and routing the fuel lines.

The two holes for the fuel lines should be enlarged with tin snips to keep the metal from chafing the hoses. Also use heavy tape or grommets on the hoses for extra protection.

Run a "hot" wire from the "Ign" side of your ignition switch to the pump, which is at the rear of the car. Use crimp-on quick-disconnect terminals for easy pump removal.

The hot wire is wired through a Hobbs pressure switch mounted on the engine from a "T" at the oil pressure gauge sending unit. The switch serves as a safety device by cutting off electricity to the fuel pump in the event of an engine failure (drop in oil pressure opens switch). You also need an override hookup with a toggle on the dash that allows you to power the fuel pump when starting (when oil pressure would be too low).

Here's the Holley fuel pump and lines in the Camaro trunk. A ground wire connects the pump motor to a clean ground on the sheetmetal (top). Use a secret toggle switch in the hot wire, and you have a simple way to prevent car theft, too.

You could make your own cool-can, but ready-made ones like this Moroso unit have heavy insulation inside and out for best efficiency in cooling your fuel.

The Moroso can features a drain petcock at the bottom and two stainless steel clamps with mounting brackets.

You'll probably have to remove one front wheel to have access to the fenderwell to drill can mounting holes.

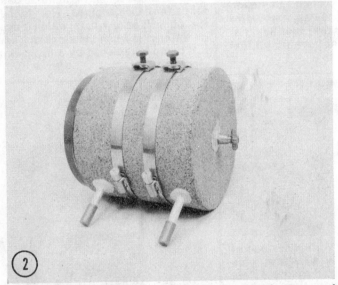

It's not easy with today's crowded engine compartments, but try to find a good location for the can that is away from the radiator and exhaust heat.

The bottom hose from the can is hooked to your fuel pump, and the top hose to the carburetor. Here you can see the internal insulation. You only need to add ice when running, but keep the can filled with water or anti-freeze.

73

MOROSO SALES is the serious racer's delight. They specialize in hard-to-find performance items and most of their products can be used as effectively on a street machine as they can on a Pro Stocker. They have air cleaners, carb tuneup tools and fuel system components to match your heart's desires.

B&B PERFORMANCE offers everything the racer or street machiner needs in the way of accessories for the high performance fuel system, including carb adapters, spacers, carburetor holders for bench work, fuel line Y's, and fuel line taps for hooking up fuel pressure gauges easily.

CAL CUSTOM manufactures a whole range of dress-up and functional parts for performance engines. Here is their fuel pump blockoff plate, which is used on the engine when the stock mechanical pump is replaced by a heavy-duty electric pump.

CARTER CARBURETOR COMPANY makes a lot more than their famous four-barrel carburetors. They also make performance electric and mechanical fuel pumps, and a full line of parts packages for tuning Carter carbs.

EARL'S SUPPLY COMPANY is one of the leading names in aircraft surplus and in supplying braided stainless steel hoses and anodized fittings. They're safer, last longer and look good in the engine compartment. Earl's also offers aircraft quality fuel filters that utilize bronze filter elements.

EDELBROCK EQUIPMENT CO., while best known for their intake manifolds also markets carburetor tuning kits, carburetor adapters, fuel line kits, special linkage and many other fuel system accessories for performance.

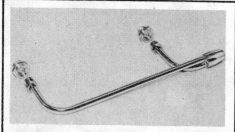

EELCO MANUFACTURING is well-known for their line of chromed accessories such as this dual-line kit for dual-inlet Holley four-barrel carbs.

HOLLEY CARBURETOR COMPANY is the most famous name in competition fuel system components. Not only do they manufacture their many carburetors, but offer a complete "system" that includes performance intake manifolds, gasket packages, trick kits for carb modifications, fuel lines and both electric and mechanical fuel pumps.

HOOKER HEADERS might seem like an unlikely name in this chapter, but in addition to their fine line of performance exhaust system components such as headers and mufflers, Hooker also markets a line of high-performance air filters, which are washable foam.

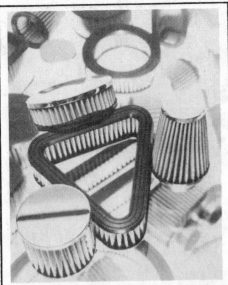

K&N FILTERS has basically only one product line, air filters, but they cover this field extensively, with special models for street, race, off-road racing, motorcycles, VW's, and their catalog of special filter sizes and shapes suits the needs of hot rodders well.

RIDGEWAY RACING ASSOCIATES is a group of ex-racers who decided to manufacture products they would have liked to use when they were racing. One such item is this set of studs and large, knurled knobs for holding the float bowls on Holleys. They make jet changes fast and easy.

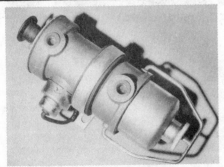

STEWART-WARNER is one of the oldest names in performance electric fuel pumps. Their Model 240 (shown) is a rugged performer that features a removeable filter element, and the rubber boot at top covers a screw that adjusts fuel pressure.

MOON EQUIPMENT COMPANY offers a variety of fuel system components, from their spun-aluminum fuel tanks to Weber carburetors, even aluminum outside fuel filler caps like this.

RITE AUTOTRONICS CORP. is better known to most car enthusiasts as RAC, the name under which they market a variety of products from gauges to test equipment. Among their products that apply to your fuel system are their inexpensive chromed air cleaners and portable exhaust gas analyzer.

TRANS-DAPT has one of the biggest selections of fuel system accessories such as carburetor adapters, linkages and special air cleaners. This is one of their insulated carburetor heat shields, a thickly-gasketed spacer to keep Holley carbs running cool.

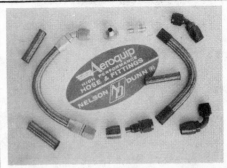

NELSON-DUNN one of the west coasts largest supplier of the famous Aeroquip brand braided hose, they have a wide variety of special adapters and fittings for plumbing racing and high-performance engines.

OFFENHAUSER EQUIPMENT CO. has a variety of fuel system components that include carb adaptors, such as these for spacing the Quadra-Jet and other spread-bore carbs, and their "economy" adaptor which mounts a two barrel to a four-barrel manifold.

ROCKET RACING PRODUCTS makes a wide variety of performance products from chassis components to engine goodies. Their fuel system pieces range from simple dress-up items to this performance mechanical fuel pump with a capacity of 80-GPH.

IGNITION SYSTEMS

Of all the specialty products designed to replace or supplement stock engine systems, the ignition system is paradoxically the easiest to understand and yet the least understood. Even though we are living in an electronic age, surrounded by electricity and many marvelous electricity-using devices, there are still many of us who view anything electrical in the same category as nuclear physics, alchemy, magic and why our favorite sports team doesn't win more often. Since the development of the computer, the transistor, and the microprocessing chip, the electronic age has become an ongoing miracle of miniaturization and packaging. (The current plethora of TV video games and pocket electronic calculators are but two examples of how electronics is affecting our lives more and more every day.) It was inevitable that numerous companies would jump on the technological bandwagon and try to sell us anything "electronic." From toothbrushes to shoe polishers to medical thermometers, musical instruments and fireplaces, there is no end to the list, as long as the advertising can use catch phrases like "transistorized," "solid state," "fully electronic," or "programmable."

Thus, it was equally predictable to find that the automotive factory and specialty promotions people would utilize the confusion about such matters to sell every type of electronic doodad conceivable. It so happens that the new electronic age has brought with it some great advancements for automotive electrical systems, as well as many pieces of hyped junk aimed at those whose knowledge of automotive electrical matters is "thin." Before we get into a discussion of the various types of electronic goodies for your car, specifically the variety of ignition systems, let's go back a ways and determine the basic rules that govern the operation of your stock ignition system.

Until a few years ago, all production cars had basically the same type of breaker-point-controlled ignition system, consisting of a coil, distributor, secondary wires and spark plugs. This system was developed by James F. Kettering in the 1920's, and since that time it has been the standard ignition on nearly every spark-ignited auto engine in the world.

Looking at the design of an internal combustion engine, we know that the mixture of air and fuel for each

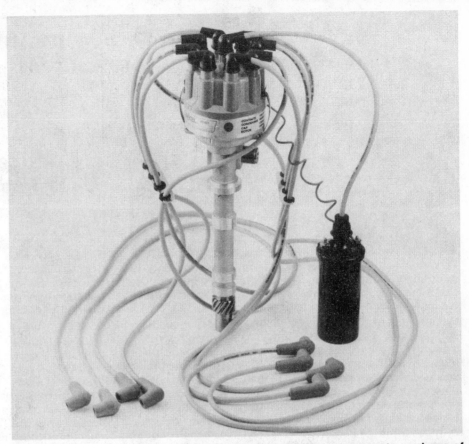

The ignition system is one of the most important engine components, and one of the least suited to high-performance usage. Stock systems can be modified for reasonably consistent high-rpm operation but for absolute reliability at very high power levels a specially-designed ignition should be used. Suitable systems (an Accel dual-point distributor is shown here) are available from several manufacturers.

Not all systems are suited for street operation. Though this Hays "crank-triggered" system works great on a pure racing engine, it should be avoided on a street engine. It has no provisions for normal variable timing advance.

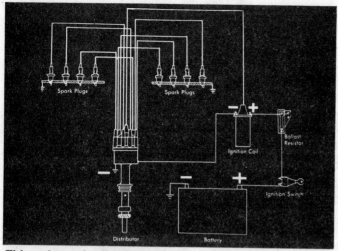

This schematic diagram shows the major components of an ordinary ignition system. The distributor and the coil are the primary components and are often replaced or modified for high-performance applications.

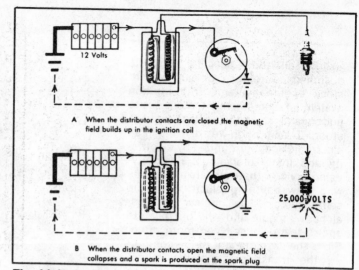

A When the distributor contacts are closed the magnetic field builds up in the ignition coil

B When the distributor contacts open the magnetic field collapses and a spark is produced at the spark plug

The high energy to create the spark at the plug gap is generated by the coil. The breaker points inside the distributor control the primary circuit.

cylinder must be ignited, and for the multiple cylinders to work together smoothly, these firings must be accurately timed to occur in a specific sequence and at precisely the right time within the four-stroke cycle. The firing of the separate cylinder mixtures is accomplished by spark plugs, each with a built-in gap, to be bridged by electrical energy supplied by the "secondary" system through the secondary ignition wires.

A distributor connected mechanically to the engine crankshaft fires each of these plugs in the proper order. The plug wires are connected to the distributor cap. Under this cap, a rotor takes voltage from a central terminal and distributes it to the terminals where each of the spark plug wires are connected. Inside the distri-

butor housing, below the rotor, a contact switch (usually called the distributor "points") opens and closes. This switch is activated by a follower block that rides on the contour of a cam mounted on the distributor shaft. And since the distributor shaft is often driven by a gear connection with the camshaft and turns at camshaft speed (one-half engine speed), the distributor shaft rotates once for every two revolutions of the crankshaft—two revolutions will allow all cylinders to complete the full four cycles.

Firing the spark plugs when they are under considerable pressure inside the cylinders takes a lot of voltage or energy. So the coil is used as a transformer, boosting the 12 battery volts to 12,000 or more volts. The points close and open once for each

cylinder firing, allowing the coil to build up the required high voltage, and then "dumping" it through the distributor cap, rotor and plug wire as the cylinder is ready to be fired. The battery voltage "side" of the system is called the primary circuit, and the "after-coil" high-voltage system is called the secondary.

All of the above sounds fine in theory, and the "conventional" ignition system has done a creditable job of keeping our cars running for many years. Where this design exhibits some shortcomings, however, is when it is adapted for high-rpm performance. Special components have been developed to replace every part of the conventional system, permitting engines to reach full power potential at high speeds.

A single-point distributor can provide excellent performance to 6000 rpm, however, it must be carefully maintained. Note how the rubbing block on the pivot arm of the breaker point rides up on the distributor cam lobes, breaking the primary circuit and triggering the secondary voltage in the coil.

Some improvements in your ignition performance can be made by substituting performance breaker points in place of the stockers. Stiffer breaker arm spring tension allows the engine to rev higher before bounce and misfire occur. But don't go too heavy on tension. These Sorensen "cross-cut" points are designed to ventilate the contacts for cooler operation, reducing the rate of burning and pitting.

One of the cheapest and easiest routes to better ignition performance is to replace the stock coil with a special high-voltage coil. These coils have a greater ratio between the primary and secondary windings. This creates a greater "step-up" of the voltage in the secondary circuit, resulting in higher spark energy. Hi-po coils are available from several manufacturers. Here are: the MSD Blaster, the Mallory transformer, and the Accel Super Coil.

Let's start with one of the most common terms—voltage. Electricity at its simplest can be compared to a watering system. Instead of molecules of water, electrons are what run through the system, and conductive wires play the part of the hoses. Voltage is simply the electrical *pressure* pushing these electrons along. The more voltage you have, the easier the electrons are able to "squirt" across a resistive gap.

During operation of the engine the secondary voltage finds a resistive atmosphere when it gets to the spark plug; jumping the gap in high cylinder pressure is like trying to water the lawn against a heavy headwind! Therefore, a minimum amount of voltage is necessary to fire the plugs in a running engine, say 15,000 volts under stock conditions. When you have a high-performance engine with higher compression, you need even more voltage.

High-performance coils are available from a number of companies to increase secondary voltage. But beware, these "hot" coils develop the additional potential by placing more demand on the primary side of the system. More primary current is needed to produce more secondary volt-age—you never get something for nothing. The points (or electronic control boxes discussed later) must be able to reliably carry this increase in energy flow, which is no small amount for the "killer" racing coils. Further, the cap, rotor and plug wires can only handle a certain amount of voltage, maybe 32,000 volts in top form. While it's a good idea to have a coil that will produce a few thousand extra volts to make up for voltage lost due to resistance in these components (especially the wires and spark plugs), a 60,000 volt system may never build to full potential before the spark jumps

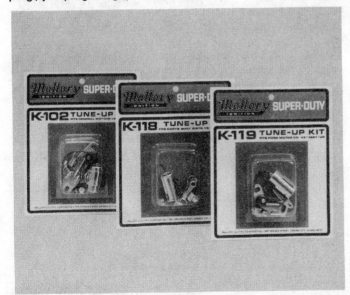

The standard point-type ignition is simple, reliable and inexpensive but it must be carefully maintained. Fortunately, several manufacturers provide a wide array of special performance or "super-duty" replacement parts. They are available at most speed shops and insure top ignition quality. The illustrated Mallory packages are excellent "kit-type" tune-up aids that supply all needed components.

Many performance ignition manufacturers offer special hi-po tuneup kits like this one from Mallory, which includes heavy-duty coil, cap, rotor, point set and condenser.

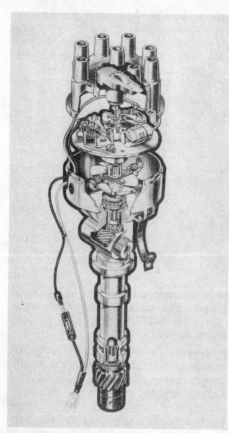
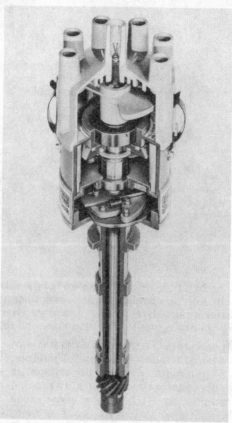
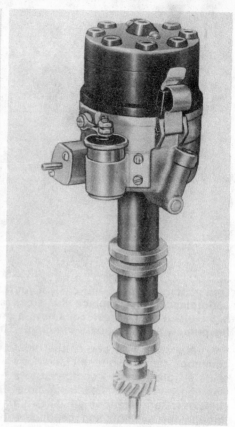

Specially designed performance distributors are plentiful. They often permit you to vary the advance rate by making simple internal adjustments. Many also have provisions for dual points, permitting longer coil "saturation" times at high rpm. The samples shown here include (left to right): the Accel, the Cragar, and the Mallory dual-point models.

the plug gap. But these high-voltage coils will build to firing potential faster, and that leads us on to the problems with time.

A major problem of igniting the high-performance engine is the *time available* for the coil to build sufficient secondary voltage for ignition (rise time). The higher the crank speed, the less time is available and thus secondary voltage can drop off. One of the time-honored hot rodding tricks for creating more time for voltage accumulation is the installation of dual points.

Basically, two sets of points are used, wired in parallel and staggered in their opening and closing times. The spark isn't fired until both sets of points open (the last set to open is called the "break" set of points). But since the earlier closing set (the "make" set) of points is already beginning to build up voltage the overall period (engine degrees) available for coil saturation is extended. While this won't give you any more horsepower under normal circumstances, it will allow your engine to run better at higher engine speeds, where it can take advantage of the other modifications you may have made.

A dual-point conversion is simple to perform. Accel and other companies have kits to do this and they have been tremendously popular for years. Most of the factories have also made such systems at one time for their high-performance models. For instance, Autolite/Motorcraft has a conversion kit that fits most Ford distributors. It comes with simple instructions and sells for less than $15. GM offers a similar kit, and Mopar distributions can also be converted with the factory P-parts.

While we're still talking about point-type ignitions, we can now mention another problem that crops up when you have a leaden right foot—point bounce. The movable contact arm of a set of points is kept closed (touching the stationary contact) by a thin, metal leaf spring. When the high spots on lobes of the distributor cam push against the rubbing block attached to the movable contact arm, the points open. A certain minimum

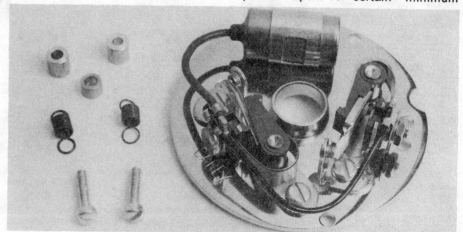

One of the oldest hot rod ignition tricks is converting a standard distributor to accept two sets of points. When two point assemblies are used, one set "makes" the circuit and the other "breaks" it. The break set operates slightly later than the make set. This permits the primary circuit to be applied to the coil for a slightly longer period of time, even at very high engine (and distributor) speeds. The result is higher and more consistant secondary voltage. The conversion kit shown here fits into any Delco/GM distributor and is available from Sig Erson Cams.

amount of tension is necessary to make the rubbing block closely follow the distributor cam, and the faster the engine is turning, the more spring tension is necessary. If you've been to the drag strip and heard the exhaust note of a pure stock car "break up" as it went through the lights, it may have been because the points were bouncing off the distributor cam.

To combat this problem, some point sets are made with extra spring tension. Unfortunately, the heavier spring tension brings with it a few drawbacks, the most common of which is accelerated rubbing-block wear (meaning that the points won't last as long as stock). You should have your distributor tested on a machine (found in most tuneup shops and well-equipped service stations) to see at what rpm (the machine spins the distributor while it shows you exactly how it would fire on your engine) the stock points or the high-performance points will bounce.

There are some specialty point sets that will go to 10,000 rpm before bouncing, but the heavy spring tension will do more than wear out the rubbing block in a hurry. Such heavy pressure can also ruin the distributor by placing such a heavy side-load on the cam that the distributor shaft bushings wear out quickly, leaving you with erratic spark timing and accelerated distributor cap wear. But if you select the proper units made by Accel, Mallory or other well-known manufacturers, you will have the best compromise between spring pressure and high-rpm potential.

Beyond Points

In a continuing effort to combat the limitations a conventional ignition system imposes on high-speed engine performance, Detroit engineers and the performance manufacturers have devised a number of components to supplement or replace the standard parts. Three of the basic types include transistor and/or capacitive-discharge (CD) units, breakerless ignitions, and multiple-spark ignitions. The CD and/or transistor ignition conversion is one of the easiest, so let's discuss it first. The major component added to your system when you install a transistor control unit is a set of electronic goodies contained in what many refer to as the mysterious "black box." Inside this electronic module there is such electronic esoterica as a transformer, capacitor, oscillator and power-switching transistor. In the case of a CD unit these parts boost battery voltage and then store it in a capaci-

tor, for release to the coil when the points say so (some CD units can also be used with breakerless, non-point-type distributors—more about this later). However, in the case of non-CD transistor ignition control boxes, this added voltage boost is not provided; the box just reduces the "load" on the points for added contact life.

There are two important differences here between the transistor/CD and the conventional setup. If stock points are used with the electronic conversion, they are only used as a low-amperage switching device; the actual switching is done by the transistor circuitry in the control box. While in a conventional ignition

the points may have to handle three to ten amps of current, with a CD they handle less than *one-tenth* amp. The real load (the voltage applied to the coil) is handled by the transistors. Thus, point wear, caused by high current arcing, is substantially reduced with the addition of a CD.

The conventional ignition system only works with about 12 volts when the engine is starting. This full 12 volts is fed to the ignition coil to insure the highest secondary level (actually less than 12 volts is applied since the starter motor draws a large current and lowers battery voltage). After the engine has started, however, the ignition ballast resistor cuts down this voltage to

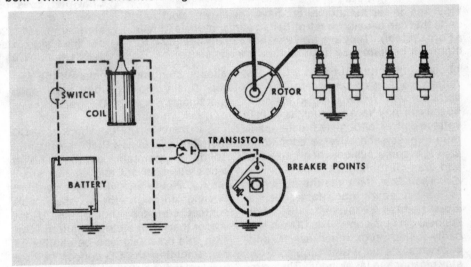

A transistorized ignition operates in much the same manner as a standard ignition except that the primary circuit is not routed directly through the distributor points. The circuit is switched by transistors in the control module, but the switching is still controlled by a separate very low voltage circuit across the distributor breaker points. This greatly increases breaker-point life expectancy.

The setup shown here was used by Pro-Stock star Bill Jenkins before he converted to a breakerless system. It consists of a #1110985 Corvette distributor (modified) with Mallory points (two sets) and a Prestolite 201-252 transistor package. Any similar well-designed breaker system would work fine on a street machine.

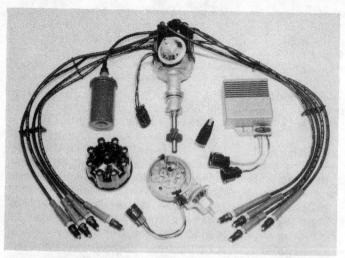

Most major car manufacturers have their own electronic units that can usually be retrofitted to earlier models (this is a Ford system). They are, however, not usually designed for high-rpm performance use and they are expensive.

Chevrolet does offer a performance unit in their parts book. A magnetic pulse-type system, the one shown (with distributor #1111263) is designed for racing, featuring a bearings supported centershaft and no vacuum advance mechanism. This is strictly "high llama" racing stuff.

about eight volts. But with a CD, *the battery voltage is jumped to 300-400 volts before it is delivered to the coil*, so the coil may have as much as 40,000 volts to deliver, enough to fire the spark plugs under such adverse conditions as high compression, rich mixtures and even oil fouling.

The CD system has the ability to deliver the spark much faster than a stock points-type system; it's a hot spark and a quick one. The CD can fire badly-fouled plugs much easier, and even when the plugs aren't fouled, they stay cleaner and last longer. The extra voltage also makes starting easier in cold weather. As an example, the air-cooled Porsche engine has traditionally had a tendency to foul spark plugs during long periods of low-speed operation. Mechanics quickly learned the answer to this problem was the installation of a CD ignition. To

silence customer complaints the factory finally took the hint and began installing Bosch CD ignitions as original equipment.

If there is any drawback to a CD installation, it is only that there are still points to maintain, as the rubbing block will wear out and change spark timing. However, with less current flowing through them, the point contact surfaces should last a lot longer than with a stock ignition. But even this drawback can be eliminated by combining the CD concept with a breakerless ignition triggering device, which brings us to...

Breakerless Ignitions

There are several alternate means that have been developed by electronic ignition manufacturers to trigger the coil. One is the breakerless "magnetic" type developed by Prestolite and

Delco-Remy. The second most popular type (used by many performance manufacturers) is the "photocell" type. In the former design, the points are replaced by a small magnetic coil or "pole piece," and the point cam is replaced by a "reluctor." The reluctor turns like the point cam but instead of having lobes it has one precisely-machined triangular shaped core piece for every cylinder. As each core passes by the pole piece, it generates a small electric pulse without actually touching the magnet on the pole piece (they are separated by a close air gap of about .006-inch). The electric signal is routed to a control box (similar in appearance to a CD box) and transistorized circuitry switches the coil primary current.

With no rubbing-contact action, there is virtually nothing to wear out, so timing stays precise for the life of

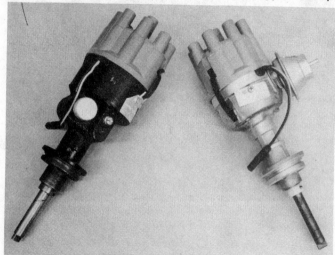

Chrysler offers two hi-po breakerless distributors. The race-only model (left) is cast iron and has no vacuum-advance mechanism. The street model (right) is aluminum, has vacuum advance and is cheaper.

The Chrysler breakerless distributors have magnetic pulse switching activators but the race distributor (right) has a different magnetic reluctor than the street model. Separate power modules are also available or the systems can be bought in complete kits.

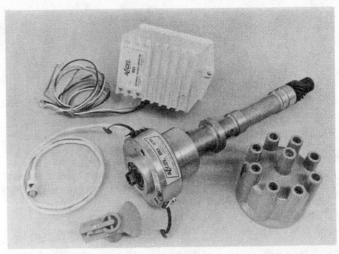

Very popular today are the many electronic ignitions that eliminate the points altogether. This Hays conversion kit can easily be installed in a stock distributor. Note the magnetic reluctor (arrow) slips over the stock breaker-point cam.

The Accel BEI system is a distant relative of the first breakerless ignitions ever used on Indy-type Offys. It uses an LED triggering device and is noted for reliability (when properly installed).

the car, which is exactly what we want to keep our cars running cleaner, longer. Even at high speeds, the timing control is quite accurate, because there are no points to bounce, and the switching speed of the transistorized circuitry is much faster than that of the stock points and cam lobe.

In the late 1960's, Detroit experimented with various kinds of transistorized ignitions on some of the factory muscle cars, notably the '64-'67 Ford 427, some '67-'69 Olds and Pontiacs, and the Chevy fans could get the Delco-Remy Magnetic-Pulse system on the big-block (L-88 and 435-hp) Corvette in '67 and later on the '70 and '71 LT-1

smallblocks. These were limited options on special models, and it remained for Chrysler Corporation to make the first full commitment to breakerless ignition. They offered it in 1972 as an option on some models, then took the big plunge in '73 by offering it as standard equipment across the board. (Their system is a magnetic-pulse type based on the Prestolite design.) Subsequently, in 1975 all of the other manufacturers switched to similar electronic ignitions (due to stringent government emissions requirements, and the threat that future legislation would require new cars to maintain new-car emissions levels for 50,000 miles without a

tuneup).

The second type of breakerless ignition is the photocell-controlled design. This system is found in many of the best specialty units, like the Accel BEI (Breakerless Electronic Ignition), Mallory Unilite, Borg-Warner's Power Brute, and the Allison Opto XR-700. All of these ignitions have some design differences, but basically they all replace the stock points with a special light-control rotor and a light-emitting diode, or LED as they are called today in electronic-ese. Some of these ignitions have a special distributor with a built-in LED system, and some use add-on conversions for LED use in stock distributors.

The Mallory Unilite is an electronic distributor designed for direct replacement, pre-assembled. This unusual unit uses a light-emitting diode instead of a magnetic pickup, and the electronics are all *inside* the distributor body. There is no separate amplifier box to install.

The Delco breakerless triggering device is typical of most magnetic pulse systems. The eight pointed spikes on the pole piece (left) coincide with the eight points on the magnetic core (the pole piece attaches to the distributor shaft). During one rotation the spikes align eight separate times, each time sending a small magnetic signal to the transistor box that switches the primary coil current.

A unique twist to transistorized ignition is provided by the Autotronic Controls MSD box. Special switching circuits load the primary side of the coil several times during every firing cycle, giving several secondary sparks at the plug.

The stock Delco/GM breakerless HEI system is definitely *not* designed for high performance use but the Autotronic conversion kit adds a multiple-spark box and a high-output coil to the stock HEI coil, making it into a suitable performance ignition.

The add-on kits are usually cheaper and incredibly easy to install. These kits generally have the LED and an optical sensor located on the same plate, which screws down to the distributor advance plate just like a set of points. The stock distributor cam is left in place but is no longer used with the light-trigger kits. The LED and sensor are aligned so the LED shines on the sensor separated by a small gap. A special trigger or "shutter" wheel installs over the stock rotor in such a way that the outer edge fits between the LED and the sensor. As the trigger-wheel turns with distributor rotation, precise slits in this wheel correspond to firings of plugs. When a slit aligns with the LED, it allows the light from the LED to hit the sensor, which in turn signals the control box to switch the primary circuit of the coil. What could be simpler? Like the magnetic-pulse units, the LED-controlled ignitions eliminate point

bounce and dwell variations, and in the case of LED/CD units they increase secondary current output, and offer faster rise time.

A third type of ignition available now is the multiple-spark discharge. The electronic wizards at Autotronic Controls came up with this idea, but we're sure it won't remain as the only such system for very long. The basic difference between the Autotronic MSD (Multiple-Spark-Discharge) and any other ignition is that instead of firing just one fat spark for each cylinder, it fires one fat spark and then a series of smaller sparks through 20 degrees of crankshaft rotation.

The signal to fire comes from either breaker points or any of the breakerless pickup units and is sent to an "input amplifier." This signal is then shuttled to a "duration control computer" which determines the length of time the MSD should spark. Two additional computers con-

trol the actual firing, releasing 450 volts stored in the capacitor (like a CD) to the coil. The coil builds very high secondary voltage and continues to spark as long as the duration computer tells it to.

The MSD offers a very high spark energy and the beauty of it is that it can be triggered by any kind of ignition. You can use it with stock points, factory breakerless or nearly any of the specialty conversions. Multiple spark discharge systems, however, have yet to be proven to produce more power than a well designed conventional CD or transistorized unit. A system that provides a "hot" reliable spark at a reasonable price is always the "best" choice.

The Total Ignition System

Obviously, there's more than just what goes inside the distributor to building optimum ignition for your high-performance street engine. If you

Autotronic Controls, the company that originated the multiple-spark discharge ignition, also has this unit (right) for Chryslers with factory electronic ignition. Their control module plugs right into the stock harness.

Remember when installing any of the breakerless conversion kits that the electronic "black box" is sensitive to heat and vibration, and must be located away from exhaust manifolds and other hot parts.

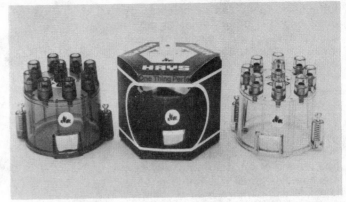

Before modifying your ignition, make sure all of your stock parts are in perfect order, including your cap and rotor. If in doubt, replace them with performance counterparts.

Once considered strictly for looks, clear see-thru plastic distributor caps like these from Hays are built to high standards to handle the extra voltage of hot ignitions. Also, when trouble-shooting you can tell at a glance if the points are working.

expect the distributor to do its best work, upgrading should also take place in the cap, rotor, coil, wires and plugs.

Spark plugs and wires play an important role in keeping your engine performing well. There isn't much advice we can give you about upgrading your spark plugs, the special types of racing plugs available are unsuitable for street engines. We can suggest that by tuning for the best air-fuel ratio and checking or "reading" the spark plug conditions as you make other modifications, you carefully determine the best plug heat range for your use. We might suggest if you're experiencing short plug life due to high compression that you investigate using commercial or truck plugs, such as those made by Autolite. They have heavier electrodes and are designed to withstand sustained high loads.

Plug wires have come a long way since the days when you only had two choices, either stock wires or the

"Packard 440" wires (steel-core type every hot rod used to run). Today we're concerned with the sound coming from our high-powered FM radios and expensive speakers, so the solid-core wires that used to create radio static are seldom seen anymore on anything but race cars.

Luckily, the wire companies have come up with greatly improved suppression wires (meaning they suppress radio interference) that are perfectly good for high-performance use. Instead of a wire core, they feature a core filled with a flexible and elastic textile impregnated with carbon conductor. These wires can stand a great deal more flexing and pulling than the old resistance-type wires, and are offered today with colorful and tough silicone outer jackets that resist heat, oil, smog and other contaminants. When attached with good terminals and protected by silicone boots, these wires should last for several years on your street

machine, even with the heat of tubing headers. Just remember that any resistance wire can be ruined by excessive handling and stretching, so never pull on the silicone cable itself to remove a wire from a plug, pull it off by the boot only.

How do you tell when a set of wires is ready for replacement? By using an ohmmeter you can check the resistance of each plug wire and the coil wire. The lower the resistance, the better the wire's condition, but remember that resistance will be greater in the longer plug cables. Most wires will show a resistance of about 20,000 ohms, but if you're in doubt about your readings on a particular wire, just check a brand new wire of the same length for comparison. An infinity reading on the meter means there is a break somewhere in the wire. This can happen especially with a hot ignition system if the plug wire terminals aren't crimped on perfectly. Leaking wires or

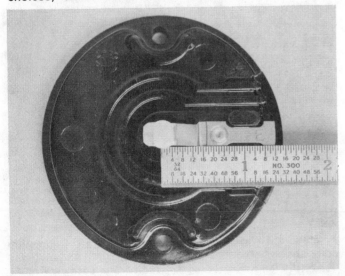

Here's a super low-dollar tip. Many smog-type distributors have short rotor blades (note this Delco smog rotor blade is stamped with an "E"). Early rotors have longer blades and provide more accurate spark distribution.

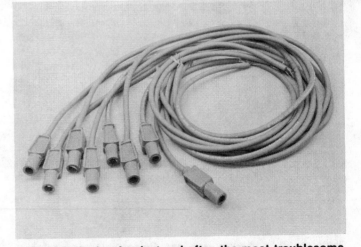

Undoubtedly the simplest and often the most troublesome link in the ignition chain is the spark plug wire set. Stock radio-suppression wires are fairly fragile and will often allow secondary voltage to crossfire or leak to ground. They must be replaced by hi-po wires with solid wire core and silicone jacket material.

terminals usually can be detected by observing the idling engine at night. Blue sparks around the wires or plugs mean there's voltage that's being wasted.

The Advance Game

Ignition advance is an important part of the ignition game. For maximum economy and performance the functioning of the distributor advance mechanism must be understood, checked and perhaps altered slightly.

Ignition timing, as we have mentioned, is controlled by the distributor assembly. Ignition advance, however, is a critical factor that is adjusted and tailored to the engine's requirements in three ways: by setting of initial advance to the specified mark on the damper (with a timing light); through the centifugal advance mechanism that increases ignition timing as engine speed increases; and with the vacuum advance diaphram that provides advance to suit the idle and cruise requirements and improve overall efficiency. Each of these systems must be working properly (meeting all engine requirements throughout the rpm range) or some areas of engine performance will suffer.

Since all of these factors interrelate and vary with engine speed and/or intake manifold vacuum, it is very difficult to adjust and evaluate the result of each one individually on a running engine. Enter the "Sun" machine. This is not a high-wattage hair dryer, but a special instrument (most often manufactured by Sun Corporation) that is designed to simulate various engine speeds so that

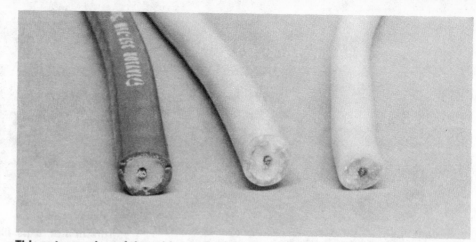

This cutaway view of three hi-po wires shows the basic construction used by most manufacturers. The core is usually made of several strands of wire (often copper plated for increased conductivity). A special silicone material surrounds the wire to add insulation but this material is designed to give greater flexibility. The outer sheathing is also silicone but is of a higher density for greater heat resistance and durability.

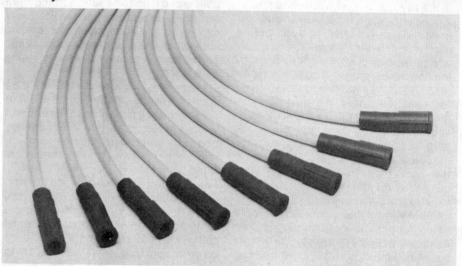

The newest wire from Accel is a full 9mm in diameter, with 67% more insulation than stock factory wires. Crossfiring, a problem with very high energy ignitions, is considerably less likely with the added insulation.

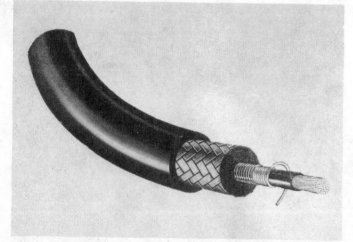

Metal conductor wires are less susceptible to accidental core breakage, unlike carbon-core wires which are easily damaged. This cutaway of a Sorensen Mono-Mag wire shows how they use a monel steel wire in addition to the standard insulation giving metallic-core performance without radio static.

A close-up view of two wires gives an interesting comparison between a carbon-core wire (left) and a unique solid-silicone insulated wire. This carbon-core wire has a silicone jacket for increased heat resistance but the core is still susceptible to breakage. The solid-silicone wire is unique and available only from Speed Industries. It is a very rugged wire.

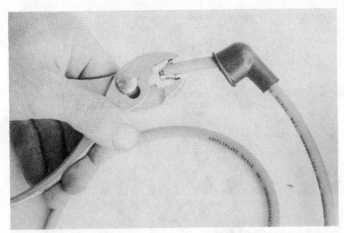

The only trick to installing new plug wires is to make certain that the distributor terminals are properly fastened in place. After the wire is cut to the proper length, the insulation is stripped back for a short distance and the core is folded back along the insulation so it will make full contact with the terminal. The terminal can be crimped with pliers as shown here but a special crimping tool does a much better job.

Many wire kits permit you to make up the cables to custom lengths, but it's important to make truly secure crimpings on the cable terminals. These two dies (available from Accel) can be used along with an ordinary hammer to make the job easier and more certain.

A variety of terminals and boots are available, including straight, angled, distributor cap ends and plug ends. In the center here are Rajah screw-together spark plug terminals (instead of the more common crimp type) that are favored by some engine builders.

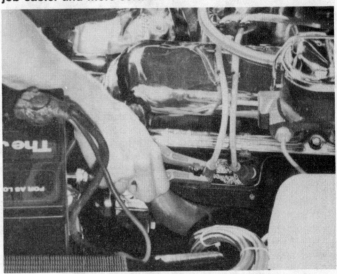

Silicone-jacketed cables are good for resisting engine compartment heat, especially on header-equipped cars, but they must be handled with care as they stretch easily. Insulated plug-cable pliers are helpful to take them off the plugs, and grab them only by the boot, not the wire.

all facets of distributor operation can be evaluated and adjusted. A large number of well-equipped speed and repair shops have Sun machines and the small investment required to have your distributor "recurved" is often very worthwhile.

"Total advance" is a term that means the total ignition advance when the initial and centrifugal are "full in." This does not include vacuum advance. To measure "total," a timing light and a degreed balancer are required, although it can be done without a fully-degreed balancer by the addition of an appropriate timing tape or marks at 20, 25, 30 and 35 degrees before top dead center. While observing with the timing light, the engine is

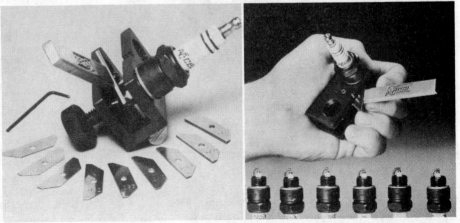

If you're a stickler for precision, this new Accel spark plug gapper is just the thing for your tool box. Tightening the adjuster knob with a spark plug in place makes a precise gap with both electrode surfaces parallel.

If you're reworking your stock distributor to change the advance curve, this should be done *only* on a distributor testing machine, which you should be able to find in most large service garages. The machine is also useful for checking the rpm at which point "bounce" will occur.

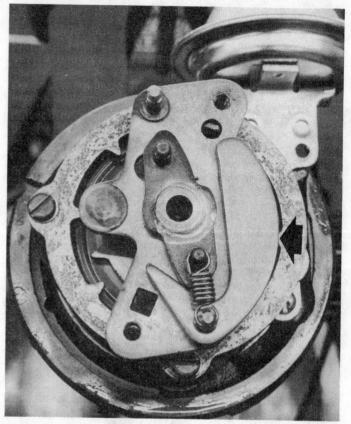

A distributor normally has two centrifugal advance weight springs (arrow indicates one). The spring tension works with the advance weight shape and size to control the rate of advance. Kits are available in speed shops to vary spring tension or weight size, providing a "faster" curve for better low-end performance.

brought up in rpm (with the vacuum advance hose disconnected) until no further increase in advance is seen on the balancer. This maximum advance is called total advance. Total and the rpm at which it occurs are the most important variables in ignition tuning.

If you talk to drag racers, you may know they try to run as much total ignition advance as the engine will withstand, but street enthusiasts, un-fortunately, have to contend with poor quality gasoline and long periods of low-speed operation. Having more initial timing advance and modifying the advance curve in the distributor to come in "earlier" can have a dramatic effect on street performance. But the amount of "total advance" will, in the end, be determined by the limit at which your favorite high-test causes the engine to detonate.

The modern, stock engine has only about 4 degrees (BTDC) of initial (on the crankshaft) advance due to smog restrictions. This accounts, in part, for their sluggish performance. These smog engines also have a lazy advance that doesn't reach full-on until 4000 rpm or more, and some smog devices don't allow advance to take place until the car is in high gear, or is about ready to overheat.

Here's another trick for point-type distributors. The shape of the lobes on the distributor cam will affect the opening and closing rate of the points and the engine speed at which the points "float." Some manufacturers offer specially ground distributor cams which will allow the engine to go to higher speeds before misfire occurs.

The vacuum advance mechanism is not needed on a distributor that operates *only* at very high speeds (racing), but if you drive the car around on the streets at part throttle, vacuum advance will greatly increase economy. Usually, several vacuum control units are available from the manufacturer to control the total amount of vacuum advance and at what manifold vacuum level the mechanism will bring in the advance.

On our performance street engine, we'll need a little more advance to take advantage of our other modifications and to restore fuel economy. Assuming we won't be running as lean a mixture as stock, and that we will hopefully have more even mixture distribution, we'll want to set something on the order of 8-10 degrees of initial advance at the crank. By checking the distributor with a sun machine and substituting and/or adjusting advance weight springs, we can tailor our advance curve to begin advancing at about 1000 rpm (engine rpm) and to develop a total ignition advance of 28-32 degrees, measured on the crank, by 3200-3600 rpm.

These specifications are general, and a number of factors could modify them. For instance, cars with air conditioning may need slightly more advance on the crank and slightly less in the distributor, and cars with low gear ratios like 3.55 to 4.11 or large displacement engines—i.e. the 440 Chrysler can also use more initial advance. At the same time that you're working on the advance curve, take your advance weights off, clean them thoroughly and lightly lubricate them with distributor cam grease to insure smooth operation. A little rust or dirt here can cause that sluggish feeling to come back. With everything you've invested in your pride and joy, this would be a shame especially when you're on your way to becoming King of the Street!

Ignition Installation Hints

1) Electronic ignition conversion kits offer advantages but are not essential. A dual (or even single) point distributor that is in good shape and is equipped with high-performance points and condenser will provide a "hot" ignition.

2) A high energy coil develops more spark energy by drawing more primary current (more load on the 12-volt system). This higher draw will reduce breaker-point life (non-electronic systems) and place additional strains on electronic "black boxes." Stay with a stock-output coil for street use.

3) *All* electronic control boxes are more susceptible to heat and vibration failure than are stock breaker point/coil systems. Electronics have come a long way in sophistication and reliability in the last few years, but a toasted transistor in the "boonies" is always a possibility. Potential failure can be minimized by mounting the electronics in the coolest location, for a few degrees cooler operation can double or triple the life expectancy.

4) The real advantage in using an electronic "switch" to carry the coil-current load is reduced point wear and system maintenance. When the points are replaced with a magnetic pickup, spark plugs are the only item requiring periodic replacement, with the exception of ignition timing, which must be checked every time plugs are replaced (variations occur from timing chain stretch, distributor bushing wear, etc.).

5) Most specialty ignitions require at least some rewiring be done under the hood. If reliability and optimum performance are what you're looking for (if not, why are you installing electronic igni-

tion?), rewiring should be done neatly and with proper terminals, wire ends, splices, crimping pliers, etc. Nothing looks or works better than "sano."

6) Vacuum advance, which should be maintained for optimum gas mileage, can often be hooked up to two vacuum ports on the manifold/carburetor (for timed or non-timed vacuum). The *timed* port is always at the carb, has no vacuum at idle (and therefore no advance), but as the throttle is opened, vacuum builds to a peak at about one-quarter to one-third full throttle. If your engine has a tendency to ping at part throttle you may be better off connecting the vacuum advance to a non-timed (direct) vacuum port. These are most often found on the base of the carburetor or directly in the intake manifold (possibly next to the vacuum line for the power brakes). When the vacuum advance is connected to a non-timed source, the engine will have full (or nearly full) vacuum advance at idle. Full advance will also come in at any part throttle cruise, but as soon as the throttle is advanced to any acceleration "mode," the vacuum advance will drop out and ignition advance will be controlled only by the centrifugal advance mechanism. It will often be necessary to "experiment" with each of these to determine the best setup.

7) A common mistake that a lot a street performance enthusiasts make is installing too-cold spark plugs. An engine that must run wide-open throttle during most of its life, like a drag or Nascar motor, will need very cold plugs (meaning that the insulator is kept cooler—relatively—by a more directed heat-dissipation path to the plug body). A street engine, however, must have

much warmer plugs to insure sufficient temperature to burn off carbon deposits and permit reliable combustion. A good rule of thumb is to run the manufacturer's recommended heat range or, depending on engine conditions, *one* step hotter or colder. And remember, warmer plugs will have to be inspected and, perhaps, replaced more often.

8) In bracket cars or other off-road applications where it is desirable to eliminate the vacuum advance unit or its function, pinning or welding the advance plate solid with the plate mount is often done. But one potential problem, again very often overlooked, is the rotor-to-cap "timing" or position during the spark jump. Moving the advance plate will change the position of the rotor in relation to the distributor cap when the plug is to fire, and if the rotor is between two cap contacts, it may fire two plugs simultaneously.

9) Mechanical advance (built-in centrifugal mechanism) will also, to no small degree, determine how well the engine will run. A quick advance will usually improve low-speed torque, however, it can also promote ping. A slow advance curve will often allow the use of poorer quality gas to the detriment of performance. Tuning your advance curve (properly) will require using a distributor machine that "runs the distributor up" for advance vs rpm checking.

10) Finally, all spark plug wires should be routed away from exhaust manifold/header pipes, and should be kept separate in wire looms or supports. Spark plug ends should have boots—not exposed clips—and spark plug wires should be trimmed to the minimum necessary length.

Although most breakerless ignition conversions can be made with the distributor in the engine, removal makes for an easier job. Remove the distributor cap and mark with chalk on the engine or firewall where the rotor is pointing (indexing the centershaft position with reference to the cam). Also mark an index on the distributor housing and on the manifold. Realigning these two references when the distributor is reinstalled will insure approximately correct ignition timing when the engine is restarted.

Remove the vacuum line from the vacuum advance unit (arrow) and take the lead wire off the coil. With the help of a distributor wrench to remove the distributor hold-down bolt (hard to reach on Chevys and other cars with rear-mounted distributors), you can remove the distributor.

With the distributor mounted in a bench-vise or distributor machine, you can start to remove the stock parts. Here the rotor screws are removed.

The instruction sheet says to cut the primary lead wire, but you can pull the grommet from the distributor housing and remove the lead without damage, leaving something for your spare parts box. Then put the grommet back in place (without wire).

You can now remove the stock set of breaker points and the condenser. You won't ever need them again with a pointless electronic ignition like this Accel conversion kit.

Since you have the distributor this far apart, you should take the time to clean and lube the advance weights with a dab of distributor cam lubricant. The conversion starts when you install the sensor plate and leads, using the existing holes in the breaker plate. Use the clip provided to hold the sensor leads.

The Accel kit furnishes a gauge (arrow) for positioning the sensor an exact distance from the breaker cam. Tighten the hold-down screw when the sensor is spaced correctly.

The trigger-wheel is retained by the two screws that mount the rotor; two longer ones are supplied.

Four sheetmetal screws are provided for mounting the power module to the fenderwell or firewall. Mount it somewhere away from engine heat that may destroy the transistor circuits.

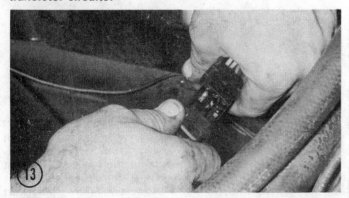

There's a bundle of five wires in the Accel harness. You hook the harness plug to the five-wire plug on the electronic power module.

Now the eight-bladed trigger wheel can be slipped over the advance weights. Take care not to nick the wheel during installation; there's a cut-out at one end of the wheel that allows you to slip it over the weights (arrow).

Since you won't be adjusting any points anymore, you can remove the "window" from the cap by bending the tab inside. Toss the stock metal window (right) in parts bin. The cap is then installed with the new sensor leads coming through the window hole, and the plastic Accel window is installed over the grommet.

Taking into account the amount that the rotor will turn as the drive gear engages helical gear on the camshaft, reinstall the distributor so that the rotor is pointing at the mark on the firewall. Realign the index marks on the distributor housing and manifold and tighten the hold-down bolt.

The two leads with connectors (shown here) are attached to the leads from the distributor sensor. Of the other three wires, the brown is attached to the negative terminal of the coil, the red to the positive coil terminal, and the black wire to a good ground. You're all done now except for starting the engine and checking/resetting the initial timing. Re-attach the vacuum hose to the distributor (plug the hose to prevent a vacuum leak when you start the engine and set the timing).

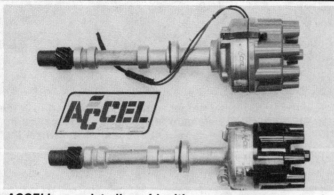

ACCEL's complete line of ignition components covers the field from spark plugs to wires to performance coils to complete electronic and conventional breaker-point high-rpm distributors. Their breakerless BEI system is used by many professional racers.

Autotronic Controls Corp. has a unique ignition system they call multiple-spark-discharge. The MSD unit fires many times for each firing of a cylinder instead of just once. A mini computer controls the capacitor discharge circuit during each firing "period," delivering a long, hot spark that is good up to 12,000 rpm. It can be used with points or breakerless distributors of nearly any type or make.

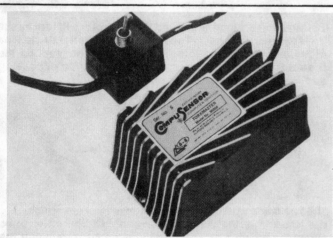

Clifford Research sells more than just their line of speed equipment for inline fours and sixes, they also market the Clifford-Jacobs CompuSensor electronic ignition. With a built-in "computer" to determine the engine spark needs, the CompuSensor is said to deliver only the voltage the engine needs, without failing at high rpm.

ALLISON XR·700

Allison Automotive Company offers this Opto-Electronic ignition conversion. Using a light-trigger instead of the more common magnetic-pulse system, the Allison conversion offers more spark energy for performance and improved spark plug life and better starting in cold weather.

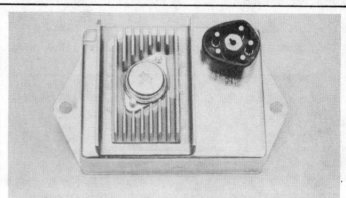

Chrysler Direct Connection has the electronic ignition system that started the OEM movements. Available to retrofit most Chrysler engines. These reliable breakerless distributors are available in street and racing versions.

Cragar may not be as well known for their ignition products as their famous custom wheels, but their dual-point distributor offers precision quality with ball bearings and features an adjustable advance curve.

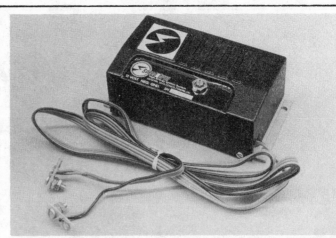

EELCO has several products in their line that would appeal to the ignition shopper, among them this inexpensive kit for altering the advance curve in Delco distributors, bringing full advance in by 2000-2500 rpm.

General Nucleonics manufactures the Speedatron CD ignition that has proven very successful under hard conditions such as turbocharged and LPG-fuel applications. Hookup is very simple (just keep the unit away from engine heat) and the unit puts out a tremendous amount of spark energy.

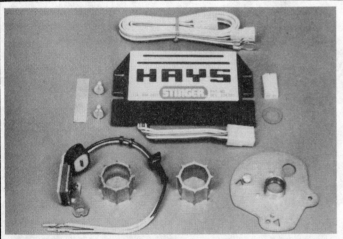

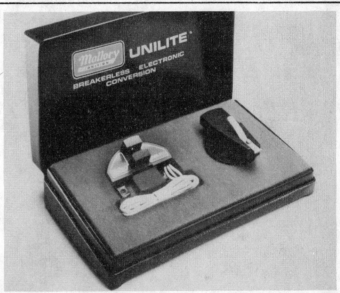

Hays Sales is one of the biggest names in special ignition parts. Their catalog is filled with such goodies as wire crimping tools, wire sets with silicone boots and jacketing, heavy-duty caps and coils, and their Stinger electronic ignition conversion kits, which bolt into stock distributors.

Mallory's newest product for your ignition needs is the Unilite kit for breakerless electronic ignition. A bolt-in conversion, the Unilite uses a light-triggered approach to replacing the ignition points.

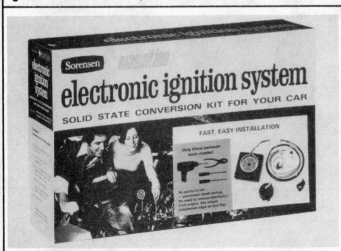

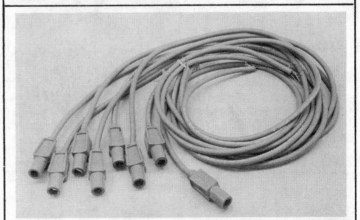

Sorensen not only manufactures and sells their well-known Mono-Mag wire sets, they also offer caps, coils, point sets and complete electronic ignition conversion kits.

Taylor's "Kool-Blue" ignition wire sets feature molded boots at the spark plug end for secure connections. These silicone-jacketed suppression wires are long enough for any application and come with crimp-on terminals for the distributor ends.

93

CAMSHAFTS & VALVETRAINS

The camshaft has often been described as the "heart" of an internal combustion engine. While an efficient street engine can be assembled with a perfectly stock valvetrain, the true performance engine requires something a bit more. The camshaft controls the operation of the valves. It will, therefore, affect the functioning of the other performance equipment you add to your engine. All of the standard hi-po items (such as increased carburetion, a better exhaust system, special ignition, etc.) serve to increase the breathing efficiency of the engine, but they are, in turn, limited by the engine valve action. After all, the valve operation determines how much is going to be taken into the cylinders and how much is going to be exhausted. If you look at the role of the valves in this way, it is easy to understand how important the camshaft and valvetrain are.

To be basic for a moment, the camshaft is driven from the crankshaft by gears or by a chain and gear combination. The lobes, which are sort of egg-shaped in profile, impart a reciprocating motion to the lifters. As the aptly-named lifters move up and down, they transfer this motion to the pushrods (also aptly-named). The pushrods push up against the ends of the rocker arms, whose opposite ends (like a seesaw) push down on the stems of the valves.

The valves are kept closed by

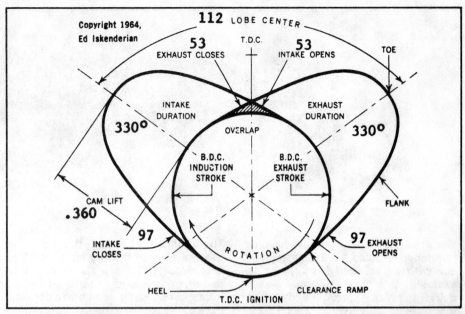

There is perhaps more confusion about the operation of the camshaft than any other system. This schematic diagram shows the basic nomenclature of the cam lobes, their relation to each other, and the physical location of the important "events" (valve opening and closing points). The exact figures shown are typical for a hi-po cam but the opening and closing points, the lobe center, the overlap, and the cam lobe lift will vary from one specific design to another.

heavy springs which are held to the stems by spring retainers and valve locks. When the valves are not being operated (opened) by the rocker arms, these springs hold the valves on the valve seats and keep the other valve gear—the rockers, pushrods and lifters—in constant contact (less design clearances). By following the geometry from the "spring-loaded" valve back through the rocker arm and pushrod, you can see how the valve springs keep the lifters in contact with

the camshaft, to follow the contour of the lobes.

The main point should be clear by now, the shape and size of the camshaft lobes will determine when each valve opens and closes (how long they stay open or closed), how high the valve lifts off the seat, and the *rate* at which they open and close. Obviously, if the lobes are taller, they will open the valves further. If the part of the lobe that opens and closes the valves is "fatter" (as viewed from the end of the cam), it will keep the valves open longer. The rate at which a lobe "gets fat," or further away from the center-line, *determines the rate at which the valves open and close*, the third factor in lobe profile.

Reams and reams of material have been written about camshaft design and valvetrain geometry, particularly as they relate to performance and racing engines, but we'll forego some of the more esoteric discussions. There's as much confusion about camshafts and related valvetrain equipment as any other phase of engine building, and this is an area where the often-taken-for-granted formula of "bigger must be better" just doesn't work for a street engine. You might believe, as you listen to some of the tall tales swapped in bench racing circles about "hot" cams, that you need lots of "duration," "lift," and "overlap" to make your car go fast. Put simply, *lift* is the measurement (in inches) of how high the valve is held off the seat, *duration* is the time (in degrees of

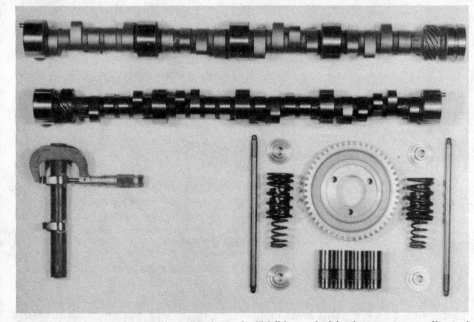

A complete cam and coordinated valvetrain "kit" is probably the most complicated of bolt-on parts to install (see following section for full details) but the results gained from all your other equipment can be either hurt or enhanced depending on the effect of the camshaft performance.

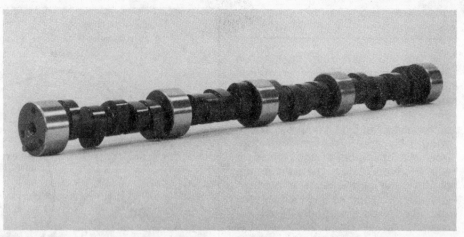

Many cam manufacturers have recently developed profiles for heavy modern cars with lazy rear end gears. A typical example, this Crower Torque-Master delivers low-rpm torque and performance (with excellent economy) up to about 5000 rpm in a street engine.

The camshaft is basically the "heart" of the engine. It is possible to greatly change the character of the engine merely by altering the cam design. However, like all mechanical devices, a camshaft is a combination of compromises. It is possible to gain good low-rpm torque and economy, or it is possible to get more high-rpm horsepower, or it is possible to obtain a strong mid-range power band (sacrificing a little at the rpm extremes). You can't have it all, so decide what you need, consult an expert if you can, and select the cam carefully.

crankshaft rotation) that the valve is held off the seat, and *overlap* is the period of time (in crank degrees) during which the intake and exhaust valve are simultaneously off their seats. All of these terms and a few more we'll get to later have a bearing on the power potential, rpm range and useful application suitability of a particular camshaft grind.

Duration

Probably the most important factor in camshaft selection is the duration. The air-fuel mixture we're trying to cram into the cylinders of a normally-aspirated (nonsupercharged) engine resists (because of inertia) being moved through the intake manifold, through the intake port and then past the open valve into the cylinders. The performance camshaft attempts to counter that sluggishness by keeping the valves open longer, i.e., opening the valves before the charge is actually needed, and keeping them open even after the piston has reached the bottom of the so-called intake stroke.

If our engine responded just the way a paper-theory examination would lead us to believe, the intake valve wouldn't have to open until TDC (top dead center) on the beginning of the intake stroke, and the valve could be closed again at the BDC (bottom dead center) beginning of the compression stroke. This would be fine for an engine that never had to run above 300-400 rpm, but the faster the engine runs, the sooner we have to initiate valve actions. In our paper example, the piston/rod/crank would travel through quite a few crankshaft degrees on the intake stroke before the column of intake air would begin flowing into the cylinder. Opening the intake right at TDC would not allow the maximum amount of air-fuel to flow into the cylinders. And, the faster the engine is

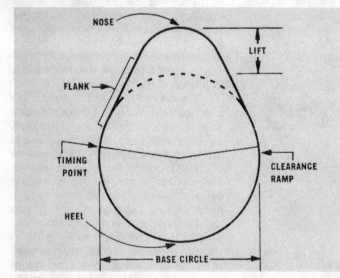

To speak the "cam language" you need to know the basic terminology. This diagram of a single cam lobe explains the basic terms. Most cams are "symmetric," meaning the intake and exhaust lobes are exactly the same. Some new racing cams have different lobe shapes for the exhaust and intake. And very recently some designers have used a different shape on the opening flank than that of the closing flank, but this is too exotic for most street engines.

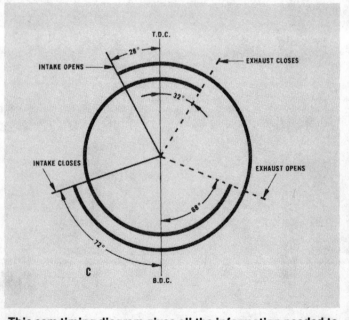

This cam timing diagram gives all the information needed to understand the basic performance characteristics of this specific grind. From the diagram we learn that this cam has duration of 280° on both intake and exhaust, and valve overlap of 60°. This is a mild street cam design.

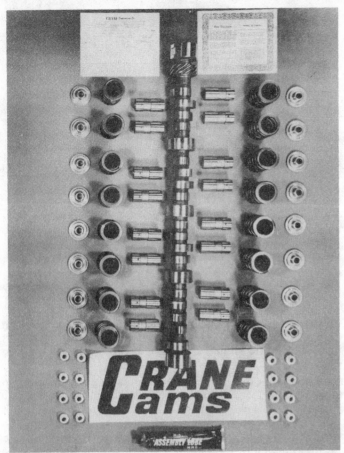

The best way to upgrade a basically stock engine is to install a cam and "kit." As shown, this usually includes a new cam, matching springs, and possibly lightweight retainers, new valve seals and lifters. The job is easy when you have all the right parts.

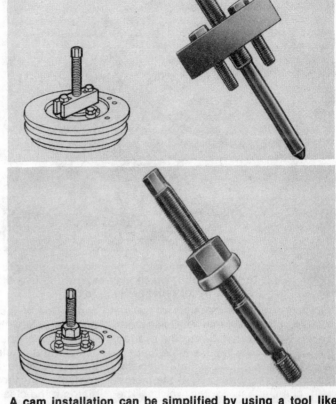

A cam installation can be simplified by using a tool like this dampener puller (top)/installer (bottom) that can be rented or purchased at most auto stores. These super-strong tools are made by the Owatonna Tool Company.

running, the less "real time" there is available for filling the cylinder. Therefore, as engine speed goes up, it is possible to give more "lead" to the intake charge (open the intake valve earlier before the piston arrives at TDC).

By the same token, when the piston is coming up to compress the inducted mixture, it takes some time before the pressure builds to the point where the intake charge might be pushed backward past the open intake valve. In fact, at higher engine speeds, where the intake charge builds considerable momentum as it moves into the cylinder, effective cylinder filling can still take place for 50-100 degrees of crankshaft rotation *after* BDC. Because of this, it is possible to keep the intake valve open until the piston has moved well past BDC.

All of this sounds fine, but this business of duration is very closely tied to the desired rpm range of the engine, so what works for one narrow rpm range probably won't work as effectively at a higher or lower engine speed. Obviously, unless we're running at the correct speed and throttle position (requiring a specific amount

of intake "lead"), the intake valves are either going to be opening too soon, in which case the residual exhaust charge may dilute the incoming intake mix, or opening too late, in which case the incoming charge will not have been given enough lead time for maximum cylinder filling. The closing times are likewise in a direct relationship to the engine rpm range. The exhaust valve timing is just as critical as the intake. Moving that collection of heat and spent gasses out of the cylinders also takes time and is affected by momentum, and this must also be anticipated by exhaust valve timing.

Because most enthusiasts (even a few racers) don't fully appreciate that duration must be keyed to the intended use and rpm range of the engine, many camshaft manufacturers play up duration numbers in their advertising. Unfortunately, all camshaft manufacturers don't use the same method of measuring camshaft duration. Total duration can be measured from the exact point when the valve moves off the seat, or it can be measured after the valve is lifted some arbitrary amount. Measuring from the beginning of valve movement gives the biggest numbers

for "advertised" duration, however, the mixture doesn't really begin to flow past the valve as soon as it opens (nonsupercharged). Most experts seem to agree that measuring the duration from a point after the valve is already in the lift phase and at a corresponding point in the closing cycle is more accurate and more realistic. Since actual valve lift can vary according to the engine and type of rocker arm used, the *general* measurement of .050-inch of camshaft lobe (lifter) lift is used, although this is not universally accepted in the industry. This results in a shorter duration figure, but one more indicative of the cam's effectiveness.

Lift

The other figure frequently bandied about is the amount of valve lift. Theoretically, the more the valve is lifted, the more charge that can enter or exit the cylinder and the more power the engine will produce. But, every engine has specific charge-flow requirements for different engine speeds, and lift works with the duration to determine total flow.

In any engine, you can only go so

Radical camshaft profiles mean that the valves are going to come closer to the pistons, which may require the use of special pistons with flycut relief areas (arrow).

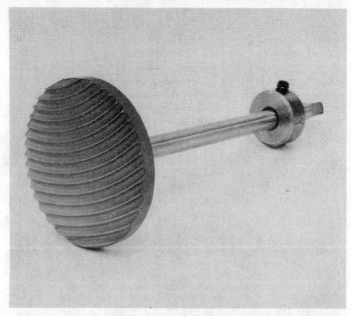

Iskenderian makes this piston-notching tool for relieving stock pistons to clear valves used with high-lift cams. Pistons should be rebalanced after such a cutting job.

far with valve lift because of valve-head-to-piston clearance. Since both valves will be open during the overlap period (even on a stock engine there is a certain amount of overlap—discussed in next section), at TDC the piston will come close to the valves. The stock pistons are designed to clear the valves, either by having flat tops (with mild cams) or some sort of depressions (with higher-performance grinds) so there will be no interference. When you install a performance cam with more lift, duration, or overlap, the valves will naturally come closer to the pistons. This could be disastrous if they are allowed to contact! Major cam manufacturers recommend minimum of .080-inch clearance between the pistons and intake valves and at least .100-inch clearance for the exhaust valves, since they will expand more (because they are not cooled by the incoming mixture, as are the intake valves).

Total lift must take into account the rocker arm ratio, because on most stock engines the rocker arm multiplies camshaft lift by a factor of about 1.5-1.6. Thus, a cam with .297-inch lift "at the lobe," working through a rocker arm of 1.6:1 ratio, gives a total of .475-inch lift "at the valve." Most of the cam manufacturers list the lift at the valve in their specifications (sounds more impressive).

The manufacturer should be able to make a recommendation about piston-to-valve if the cam is used with a standard piston, but to be perfectly safe when installing a high-lift cam, you should always check the clear-

ance. One of the easiest methods for doing this is with modeling clay.

Remove one cylinder head and place strips of clay over the areas on the piston where the valves could make contact. You need only do this for one piston if the clearance is ample (more than .080-inch intake, .100-inch exhaust), however, if minimum acceptable clearance is detected (or close to it) all pistons should be checked, as variations usually occur. Coat the valve heads for that cylinder with oil (so they won't stick to the clay during the test)

and install the head, cam and valvetrain just as you would in final assembly with the correct head gasket, bolt torque and valve lash. Now turn the engine over by hand. Go through two complete revolutions. Remove the head again. The valves will have squished down the clay on the piston and you have but to slice the clay through the middle with a razor blade and peel one half away. It's a simple matter at this point to measure with a machinist's rule the thinnest section of clay (where the valve depressed it) to

When the amount of lift imparted to the lifter by the cam lobe is transferred to the valves by the rockerarm, it will be increased by mechanical leverage built into the rockerarm. This is called the rockerarm ratio. Note here that the distance between the pushrod cup and the center of the rocker pivot slot is shorter than the distance between the valvetip pallet and pivot slot. The ratio between these diameters is the rockerarm ratio and is the amount by which the cam lobe lift will be multiplied to determine the lift at the valve.

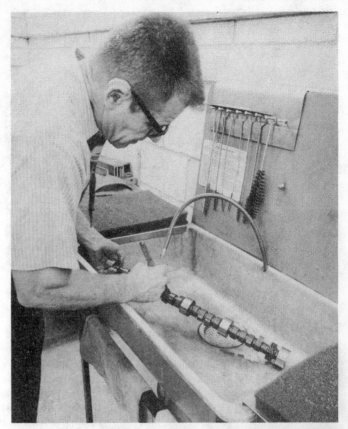

Cam design is important and no one knows all the answers. This cam cabinet is in one of the most famous race shops in the country. Sometimes it is completely filled with various camshafts that they are testing and evaluating, all in an effort to find those last few important race-winning horses.

Some engine builders change cams almost as often as you and I change our socks. Unless you have an unlimited budget and an equal amount of time, don't worry about finding the "ultimate" shaft for your street machine. It's better to be conservative and talk to as many experts as you can to get a concensus.

determine the actual clearance between the valves and piston. The figures given for minimum allowable clearance take into account valve float, timing chain stretch and connecting rod stretch, all of which require that the valves do more than "just clear" the pistons.

Overlap

Another important factor in cam design is overlap; the length of time both valves are open as the piston nears TDC on the changeover from the exhaust to the intake phase. This is determined by the *lobe displacement angle* of the cam design. This angle expresses, in camshaft degrees, how far apart the centerlines of the intake and exhaust lobes are for a particular cylinder. The wider the "spread," the larger the displacement angle, the less overlap there will be, and vice-versa.

Most camshafts have lobe center angles between 105-115 degrees (of camshaft rotation, which is half the number of crankshaft degrees). Racing engines use the lower figures, street engines the higher ones. The racing engine builder wants more overlap because it increases high-rpm

flow. Simultaneously keeping the intake and exhaust valves open longer also means the exhaust can have more scavenging effect on the intake charge, that is, as the exhaust gasses rush out they will tend to help overcome the

inertia of the intake charge and help "pull" the air-fuel into the cylinder. Further, the little bit of intake charge that is lost out the exhaust port cools the exhaust valve. On a street engine, however, this wastes fuel, creates high

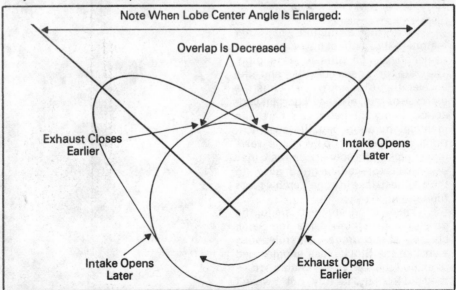

The phasing of the exhaust lobe to the intake will affect the overlap period. As the displacement angle is increased, the overlap will be reduced and the engine will have better low-rpm performance. As the displacement angle is reduced overlap increases and high-rpm performance is enhanced. Pro-Stock racing cams may have angles as small as 108°, while street cams generally have 112-118° angles.

Over the years solid lifters have gained a reputation for reliability but they require periodic clearance adjustment. The tools required are simple: a wrench (here posi-lock adjusters are shown and an Allen wrench is needed for the lock) and a feeler gauge.

The best way to set the valve clearance is with the engine running and up to operating temperature. However, engine oil will splash out of the rocker boxes unless you have some homemade splash guards like these.

emissions due to the unburned fuel in the exhaust system, and creates a very rough idle (because the increased overlap works effectively only at high rpm).

Most street cams have at least 110 degree lobe centers, and the many "ecology," "RV," and "mileage" cam grinds offered today have displacement angles of 112-115 degrees. In these cases, the reduced overlap period means fuel isn't drawn out with the exhaust. This reduces potential top speed of the engine somewhat, but usually provides a torque bonus at the lower end.

Rate

There are a number of other factors that can affect how a particular camshaft design runs in an engine. The rate or speed of lift, and the acceleration of the lifter, which is the increase of rate, are too important variables. Two camshafts can have the identical duration and lift specifications, and yet, by opening the valve more quickly (not sooner), one cam may be a much more radical grind, allowing the engine to take in considerably more fuel and air.

These factors are the basis for the development of the cams for Stock classes at the drags. The rulebooks said that the Stock class engines had to exhibit the same lift and duration as they did from the factory, but it wasn't long before the enterprising cam grinders and hot rodders found out they could increase the rate and acceleration of lift and still stay within the rules. Such designs are called "cheater" camshafts.

Although these rate and acceleration measurements are important to the cam designer, you won't find such specifications listed in anybody's cam catalog. Generally, you needn't concern yourself with these figures unless you are building an engine for one of those specialized drag or circle track classes where a "stock specs" cam is required.

Lifter Types

Besides the specifications on how a camshaft design dictates valve movement, there are other differences between cams. The basic material of the camshaft, for instance, may vary. The amount of valve spring pressure can have a direct bearing on how long a particular cam will live in a

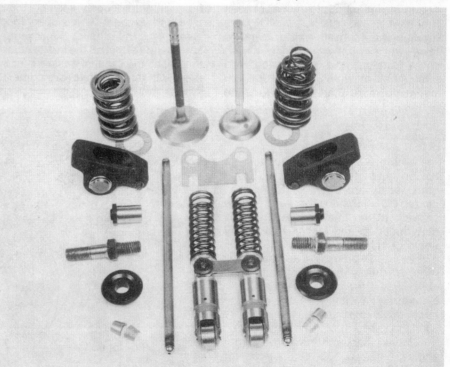

This exotica makes a pretty picture but it should be reserved for a high-dollar racing engine. Every one of these special components is designed to help accomplish one thing—increase the valve opening rate. Opening the valve as fast as possible helps the engine make bunches of power, but high-rate cams just cause everything to bend and break, so you have to beef up the entire valvetrain assembly.

Here are three basic lifter types: from left, a "mushroom" lifter, racing solid, and hydraulic lifter. The solid at left is designed with a larger (mushroom) diameter at the cam face than at the body, allowing such lifters to follow more radical cam profiles.

Inside the typical hydraulic lifter is a piston, springs and a valve button that operate under oil pressure to "sense" the operating clearance and compensate so there is no operating lash. This keeps the timing from varying regardless if the engine is cold or hot.

certain application, and the camshaft has to be machined from the right material in order to withstand the spring pressure forcing the lifters to follow the lobe profile. The "racier" the profile and the heavier the spring pressure, the tougher the cam material has to be.

Stock cams and almost all performance street cams are machined from cast iron. They may also be treated with one or more specialized metal-finishing or heat-treating processes to insure wear longevity. For racing engines the requirements are tougher, so most solid-lifter "hot" cams feature an overlay of special alloy steel over the tops of the cast-iron lobes. This hard surface is designed to withstand high valve-spring loads and high rpm, but requires lots of lubrication to survive. The lubrication flow generally is sufficient only at 3500 rpm or more, so such cams are decidedly not for

low-rpm or street use. A third type of camshaft material is the strongest yet, steel billet. The strongest racing valve springs not only put a heavy load on the cam/lifter contact surfaces, they also exert tremendous bending loads on the shaft itself. Although the cam is supported in the block by five bearings (typical V-8 engine), the pressure of the springs (several hundred pounds) is applied alternately along the length of the cam, rather than steadily, which could induce flex and breakage unless the shaft were completely rigid. Cam manufacturers machine their finest racing cams out of solid steel billets (very expensive) rather than castings, and use special alloy steels.

The type of camshaft material chosen is usually related to the type of usage involved, the amount of spring pressure such a grind would call for, and the *type of lifter*. The types you may see advertised or listed in a

manufacturer's catalog include solid, hydraulic, mushroom and roller lifters. We'll mention the latter two just in passing, as they are strictly racing-oriented.

The roller lifter has a steel roller to roll over instead of scuff over the cam surface, permitting super-high spring pressure to be used in a racing engine. Thus, higher engine speeds are attainable, and even more important, the roller lifter is able to closely follow the extremely radical profiles of racing cams, allowing faster valve acceleration than is possible with the standard solid- or hydraulic-lifter-equipped cam. Because of the very high spring pressures normally employed with roller cams they are usually ground on steel billets.

Because roller cams aren't allowed in certain racing classes, in recent years the "mushroom" lifter has been developed. The mechanical rela-

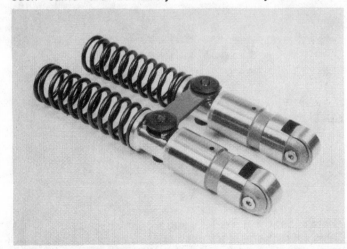

Roller cams and roller lifters are designed to open the valves very, very quickly. This is just fine, but in order to control the valve, tremendous spring pressure is also needed. This adds strain to the valvetrain and your wallet.

Mushroom lifters are helpful when roller lifters must be avoided but increased valve-lift rate is desired. They aren't as good as rollers, but they will accommodate faster valve-lift rate cams than regular lifters. However, you need a tool like this to relieve the underside of the lifter bore so the lip on the lifter won't hit the block a full lift.

tionship between the lobe surface that opens the valve and the diameter of the base of the lifter limits the acceleration rate of the lifter/valve. This is pretty advanced for most amateur mechanics but the simple fact is, if the diameter of the base of the lifter is made larger, it is possible to accelerate the valves away from the seats more quickly. This simply permits the valves to get out of the way of the incoming and outgoing gasses more quickly (hopefully resulting in more power). To gain this advantage cam designers have made standard lifters with a larger-than-stock section at the base and have designed special cam lobe shapes to match the special lifters. The engine must be specially-machined at the bottom of the lifter bores to use these lifters, and they aren't recommended for street engines, since their main purpose is to follow very radical grinds.

The solid lifter and the hydraulic lifter are the two main types that have been used with success on high-performance engines. However, today there are no production V-8 engines available with solid lifters.

The solid lifter is said to offer quicker and higher revving potential, and are used with many types of grinds, from mild street cams to wild racing profiles. They have two drawbacks, noise and need for occasional adjustment. Because they operate with a certain amount of "lash" (clearance required to allow for heat expansion) between the rocker arm tip and the valve stem, they are noisier and require periodic lash adjustment. There are those hot rodders, however, who love the "solid-lifter sound" because it really makes their street engine sound hot.

The development of high-bleed-rate hydraulic lifters has made "juice" lifters increasingly popular for street performance engines. They are quiet and don't require adjustments. A plunger, spring and disc "valve" work with oil pressure to "sense" the operating clearance and automatically make up the difference as the valvetrain expands. Hydraulic lifter "pump-up" refers to a condition that occurs when the disc valve allows the lifter to fill with oil, because the lifter has trouble following the cam profile during high-rpm operation. When this happens the plunger of the lifter valve moves up, raising the pushrod seat higher in the lifter, temporarily holding the valves off the seats. This kills power instantly, and keeps it dead until the plunger slowly bleeds back to its normal position. Special anti-pump-up lifters are available today that combat this problem by adding a special bleed hole for high-rpm oil pressure that allows rapid "recovery" after valve float. The modern hydraulic cam is definitely the most practical type for any street engine.

The Camshaft "Kit"

A camshaft should never be installed without the proper lifters. Hydraulic cams should not be used with solid lifters, and vice-versa. Also, never use *used* lifters with a new cam, or mix lifter and cam brands (some are ground on different tapers), and they must be of compatible-wearing materials since both wear-in at the same time.

In addition to a set of new lifters, there are a few other parts you should consider buying at the same time as your camshaft. Most camshaft manufacturers offer camshaft "kits" to go along with each cam. These kits generally include everything needed to upgrade the valvetrain to accommodate the level of performance provided by the new cam. This includes components such as special pushrods, valve springs, spring retainers, retainer locks, valve spring shims, valve stem seals, and even a tube of special break-in lubricant.

The reason for the special springs should be self-evident by now, extra spring pressure keeps the lifters in contact with the cam at high rpm, even though the lobe profile may be more radical. Good valve springs are really the key to high rpm performance. Weak springs allow the valves to occasionally bounce off the seats, a condition called "valve float," which instantly kills power and may even cause the valves to hit the pistons.

Everything in the valvetrain is interrelated, so the use of higher spring pressure requires heavier-duty components throughout the system. Almost invariably when performance valve springs are installed, special retainers are installed at the same time. These retainers are sized for the springs they come with; they should be stronger than stock to take the extra spring pressure, and the one characteristic most performance retainers share is light weight. Shedding weight in valvetrain components, even if it's only a gram here and there, is important in high-rpm race engines, but for the street, your main consideration in the long run should be durability.

Spring retainers are generally made from one of three basic materials: aluminum, hardened steel and exotic titanium alloy. What the designer is looking for is high strength combined with light weight. Many

This Bill Jenkins Pro-Stock valvetrain has more tricks than a Hong Kong hooker. Large-diameter springs, special rockerarms, offset pushrods, roller lifters, rocker stud tie-bar, titanium spring retainers and specially modified pushrod guideplates all add up to bundles of money, bushels of headaches and a lot of power. Unless you race for big money, you don't need any of this stuff!

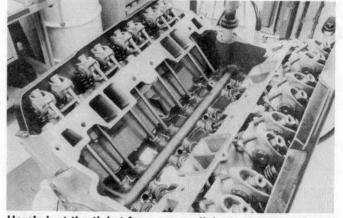

Here's just the ticket for a super-slick street setup. Stock-type solid lifters, stock pushrods, stock guideplates, stock springs, steel retainers, and stock-ratio roller rockerarms add up to inexpensive and reliable power up to 7500 rpm. These are all super-duty factory parts (except for the roller rockers) and they do the job on any engine in the 1.25-1.50 horsepower/inch range.

Aluminum spring retainers look neat in anodized colors, but chrome-moly steel retainers like these are much stronger, and the slight additional weight isn't important on a street machine engine (which usually runs under 7500 rpm).

Stock valve locks (or "keepers") should not be reused when you update your valvetrain with performance springs and retainers. These little pieces of steel are all that stand between long engine life and a dropped valve, so use only the best. Most cam kits come with hardened keepers.

specialty performance retainers are machined of aluminum and this material has proven fairly suitable for many purposes. Although it isn't very strong compared to stock steel retainers, it does have lightness going for it. With the special demands of racing, though, titanium has come into more and more use. It's much more durable than aluminum and still much lighter than steel, but it's also nasty in the expense department. Leave it to the racer who has high-buck sponsors to pay for such esoterica. Heat-treated steel retainers are best for street engines. Steel retainers are sometimes heavier but always stronger than aluminum, and since aluminum is softer than steel it can be chewed up by sharp edges on stiff valve springs. However, if you insist on lightweight aluminum, make sure they're heat-treated and hard-anodized to prevent wear.

Next in line for discussion is the lowly pushrod. Pushrods are seldom seen and not very glamorous, but they have an important job to do. They must accurately transfer lifter motion to the valve, even under heavy resistance from the spring. Generally speaking, there is nothing wrong with your stock pushrods as long as they are straight and compatible with your new lifters and rocker gear. They almost never "wear out." But when you add the extra pressure of racing performance valve springs, heavier-duty parts are recommended. Pushrods included in cam kits by most cam manufacturers are considerably stronger and more rigid than stockers, being made most often of seamless 4130 chrome-moly tubing, either in 5/16-inch or 3/8-inch diameters. Other materials, such as aluminum and even titanium, have been tried in the past, but only chrome-moly steel, with hardened steel inserts at each end to take the extra wear factor incurred by the spring pressures, is the way to go.

As with spring retainers, it's important that pushrods be light in weight, but the most important consideration again is durability. What you look for in a performance pushrod is a high stiffness-to-mass ratio. And, above all, straightness must always be checked when installing any pushrods, particularly if they have been run at high speeds with high spring pressure. Rolling the pushrods across a piece of flat glass will quickly tell you if they are bent.

Valve Springs

Perhaps the most important components of any cam kit are the valve springs. When a valve momentarily hesitates to return to the seat as quickly as it should because of weak valve springs, you're in the market for at least one new valve or piston!

There are almost as many specialty valve springs as there are camshaft profiles, some for various kinds of racing and some for street use. Only

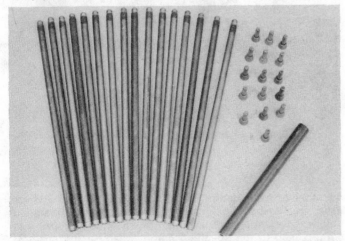

This set of custom high-strength chrome-moly pushrods is available from Chrysler. The lifter ends are already installed and the pushrod ends are to the right with the tool used to drive them into the tubes after the tubes are cut to the desired length.

When you get up there with valve spring pressure, you need stronger pushrods, and in particular you need hardened steel tips on them.

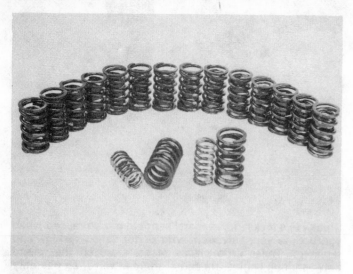

New valve springs should always be installed with a new cam and kit. Stock, weak or low-tension springs can cause valve float even at moderate rpm.

Shown here are two Isky cutters. At top is the cutter to widen the spring seats to take bigger springs, and bottom is the tool to machine the upper end of the valve guides (as on the two left guides, arrows) for high-performance stem seals.

by buying your springs as part of a kit from the same manufacturer as your cam can you be assured of getting exactly what you need and no more.

Too much valve spring pressure is just like too much cam duration or too much carburetion, unsuitable for street use. Very heavy spring pressures are necessary for racing engines to follow radical grinds at 9,000 rpm, but the higher the spring pressure, the more load on the parts (particularly the valves and rocker gear) and the greater the frictional drag at lower speeds.

Performance valve springs are made of a variety of special steels, with various advertised names such as Vasco-Jet 1000, Iskyloy, "battleship steel," Oteva alloy, etc., and in many configurations. For a number of high-performance applications, the required pressure is hard to build into just one spring, so valve springs usually are springs-within-springs. Stock springs often have an outer coil with a damper (flat-wound material that helps eliminate harmonics), while racing springs may consist of up to *three* coils. Since springs have an rpm range where their natural resonant frequency causes

them to "surge," the two and three-piece springs are wound to different harmonic frequencies and are often assembled with an interference fit to dampen vibrations.

The foremost concern is that the springs physically fit on your stock heads. The hi-po springs may be bigger in diameter and require machining of the spring seats on the heads (with a tool sold or rented by the cam company). This is not a difficult job to do and can often be done with a high-torque, slow-speed hand drill. With some engines you run the risk of

A valve spring puts out a certain pressure only at a specific height. Performance springs should be installed at the correct height to gain the same tension on all valves. A valve, retainer and keepers are assembled inside each guide and the space for the spring measured. If the space is bigger than needed, you have to shim the spring, if it's too small, you have to machine the seat.

A tester like this is helpful for checking that the new springs have the correct tension at the recommended installed height. The upper arm is pulled down until the spring is compressed to the specified height (read on the scale at right), and the spring pressure is read below (on scale obscured here by the hand). Springs that don't meet specs can be shimmed to reduce the installed height (increasing tension). However, if this may possibly lead to coil bind at full valve lift the spring must be discarded and replaced.

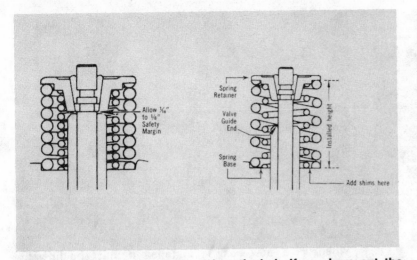

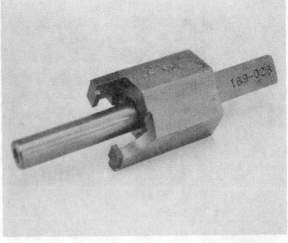

When installing valve springs, and particularly if you have cut the spring seats, you need to check the clearance between the retainer and the top of the guide. If there is less than 1/8-inch clearance at full lift of your cam, then you need to machine off some of the guide.

Most of the unique tools developed by Iskenderian for valvetrain work are available from the manufacturer on a rental basis, such as this one for cutting stems for oil seals.

cutting into the water-jacket part of the head, a problem particularly common on smallblock Chevrolet and Mopar heads, which are thin in this area. For street use, you should be able to find a spring that fits with minimum machining, or even some that are wound with smaller-diameter coils at the bottom (Chevy application only) to fit into stock seats, although some engines may require spring seat remachining.

It's also important that all the valve springs exert about the same pressure. This is sometimes difficult as factory tolerances and variations after a valve job can change the relationship of the valve in the head slightly, consequently there may be more or less distance between each of the valve stem/spring retainers and the spring seats. Since the amount cut from each valve face and seat varies, the spring "installed heights" will likewise vary. This means

that potential spring pressures (because they depend partly on the installed height of the spring) will be different. To correct this, shims are often used beneath the spring to bring them all to the height specified by the manufacturer. This is time-consuming but an important "custom" step in valvetrain prep.

After the valve and seat grinding has been done, install each valve, and without a spring in place install the retainers and locks. Pull the valve all the way up into its seat and use an inside micrometer or machinist's steel rule to measure the height between the spring seat and the bottom of the retainer (at the point where the spring will ride). If this measures, say 1.765 inches on a particular valve and the cam manufacturer recommends an installed height of 1.750-inch for the spring you want to use, then you need

.015-inch of spring seat shims to correct the variation. An assortment of spring shims is usually included with most cam kits.

Once all of your springs are properly shimmed and installed, there are a few other checks to make before you blast off. "Coil bind" is a phenomenon that can occur with high-lift cams. The coils of the valve spring may be brought close enough together at max lift that they all actually touch. You must make certain this doesn't happen. With everything installed, turn the engine over by hand until the valve is as far open as the cam will take it, and try a .010-inch feeler gauge between each of the spring coils (it should slip in at least two or three, usually at the top). Normally, if you buy a kit that includes springs with the cam and you install the springs to the manufacturer's specs spring bind will not be

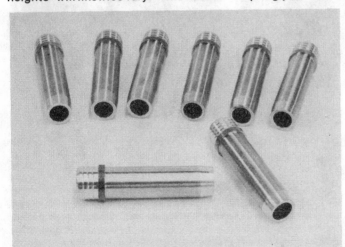

In some cases, when your valve guides are just worn too much, oil will get past even good valve stem seals. The only solution is to put new valve guides in the heads. These are bronze guide inserts which last a long time even with tight tolerances.

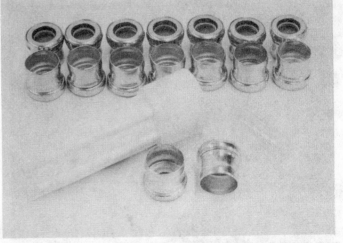

Valve stem oil seals keep oil from being sucked down the valve guides. Raymond high-performance seals are used by many professional engine builders. Usually the upper valve guide needs to be machined to fit these seals and they come with the proper installation tool.

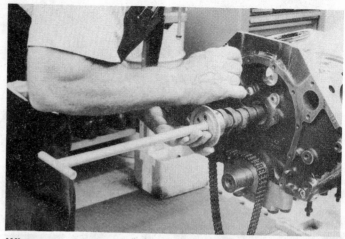

To make performance valve springs stronger than stock, a second spring is often added that fits inside the main spring. Additionally, a damper or flat coil may be added to reduce harmonic vibrations of the springs.

Whenever a new cam is installed it must be liberally lubricated with high-quality break-in lube. The easiest way to apply the lube is coat the lobes as the cam is slipped into the block. Slide it in carefully to prevent damage to the cam bearings.

a problem (unless the cam maker is totally out to lunch).

Another possible spot for mechanical interference to occur is between the spring retainer and the top of the valve guide. You should have a minimum of 1/16-inch of clearance here at full lift, otherwise you'll have to machine some material off the guide at the top.

There are myriad details to a "blueprinted" installation of a cam-shaft and related kit. We've only outlined for you the important considerations for a street engine. The illustrations that accompany and follow should answer any other questions you may have as a newcomer to performance valvetrain components. We should reinforce our hope that you'll "play it cool" when it comes to selection of components. Spend a few dollars to get the catalogs of the bigger companies, as they have a wealth of good information on all valvetrain parts. Note their recommendations for a particular grind's use, and make sure that the equipment on your engine is compatible. For instance, the manufacturer may recommend that a particular camshaft is best used with a stick shift and low rear end gears, or that another works best with high-compression pistons and extra carburetion and headers. If you have an automatic transmission with a vacuum shift

It's not absolutely necessary to "degree" the cam when you install it, but it's a damn good idea. You'll need a degree wheel, a dial indicator and a piston stop (to help find top dead center). Specific degreeing procedures are available on request from most cam manufacturers.

As long as you have the timing cover off to install your new cam, it would be a good time to check the condition of your timing chain and gears. If the chain is slack at all, it would be cheap insurance against future problems to install a new high-performance double-roller chain.

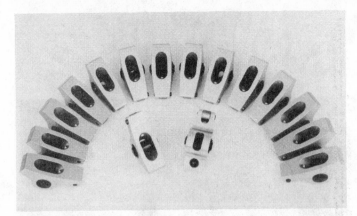

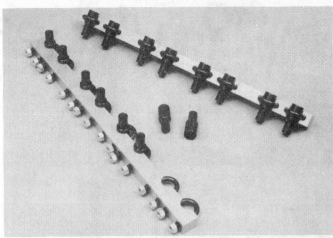

Stock rockerarms will suffice for most reasonable high-performance street engines. However, if you have some extra jingle to spend on your pride and joy, roller bearing-mounted rockerarms provide some benefits. They require less lubrication (meaning you can modify the oil system to keep more oil down in the crank assembly where it is most needed).

Recently rocker stud tie-bars or "girdles" have become popular on performance/racing engines. Supposedly they increase valve timing accuracy by reducing rockerarm stud flex. They are effective but are only required if you have a high-rate cam and some "extra" money.

modulator, then your choices are somewhat limited, because cams with a lot of overlap reduce your intake manifold vacuum and may change your shift characteristics. For street use, cams of around 230-degree duration (measured at .050-inch lobe lift) and .400-to .470-inch lift (at the spring) are a good starting point. If you have a special vehicle with special equipment or you contemplate unusual usage, such as low-speed off-road driving, then take the time to fill out one of the questionnaires found in many performance cam catalogs. Answer all the questions about your vehicle and engine (be realistic) and the manufacturer can recommend the right cam to make you happy, not sorry, that you modified your engine.

Valvetrain Installation Hints

1) The selection of a performance camshaft should not be a guessing game. Always let the cam grinder know the application, even if you are sure that you know the proper grind. His business is selling cams; the right cams for the purpose.

2) We feel that checking piston-to-valve clearance is an essential part of *every* camshaft installation. If you don't check, you are asking for serious trouble—bent valves, poor compression, and, in severe cases, broken valves that will require near complete engine disassembly at no small expense. If you are just not prepared to check this critical clearance, don't install a performance camshaft.

3) If the cam doesn't turn freely when it is placed in the block, do not proceed with assembly until the problem is corrected. Look for a nick or burr on a cam journal, an oversize journal, a bent camshaft, or if you have just installed new cam bearings, the problem is more than likely a crooked or distorted bearing that seated improperly in the block bore.

4) Always use Loctite on camshaft sprocket bolts—it never pays to take chances here.

5) When installing hydraulic lifters, it is always a good idea to "prime" the lifters with oil before you drop them in the bores. This can prevent bent push rods, difficult starting, and internal damage to the lifters.

6) Both lifter and cam contact surfaces should be coated with a prelube before the engine is fired up. There are many acceptable lubricants that can be used; most are black in color because they contain a "moly" compound suspended in a thick oil or grease. Many successful engine assemblers use STP instead of moly, but whatever type you choose, make sure that all contact surfaces are well coated.

7) If offset cam bushings or keys are used, the sprocket alignment marks will no longer align perfectly—as a result make sure that you do not install the chain with the sprocket advanced or retarded by one tooth. Also, piston-to-cam timing is moved. Make all clearance checks after cam timing has been finalized.

8) Inspect the helical drive gear that will mate with the camshaft.

There should be shiny spots that indicate the contact points with the previous cam's gear, but it should show no signs of galling or deep wear. If excessive wear is noted, replace the gear.

9) If you have installed new rocker arms or rocker shafts, they should be well lubricated before the engine is started. The best method of prelubing the rockertrain is using a pre-oiling tool to build full engine oil pressure *before* the engine is started (the crankshaft may have to be rotated—up to almost two full turns—to align the cam oil holes and the bearing supply holes before oil will flow into the rocker shafts or, in the case of pushrod lubricated rocker arms [Chevy], oil should be poured over the rockers and pivot balls before the valve covers are installed).

10) When a camshaft with higher-than-stock lift has been installed, make sure that sufficient clearance exists between the bottom of the retainers and the top of the valve guides to prevent metal-to-metal contact, plus allow additional clearance for umbrella seals, if used. With insufficient clearance, umbrella seals can be "chewed up" in short order.

HOW TO INSTALL A CAMSHAFT

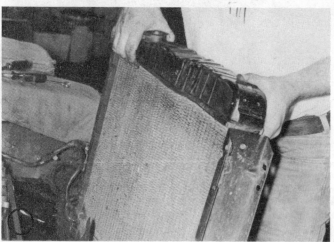

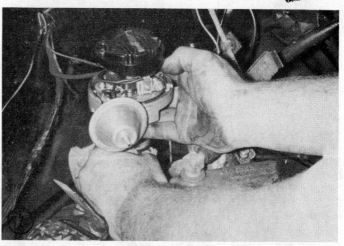

As with most engine disassembly procedures, you start by draining the cooling system. In the case of a cam change, you also need to remove the radiator for working room.

Mark the firewall with chalk to indicate where the rotor is pointing and mark the distributor housing/manifold reference. Remove the distributor.

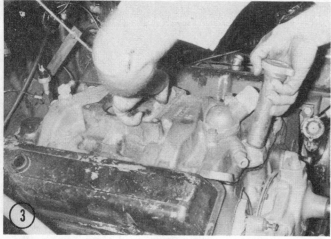

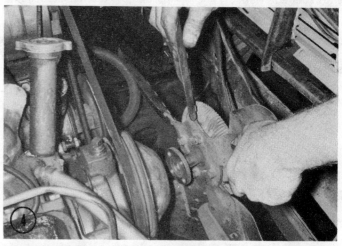

After removing and tagging all the lines, hoses and linkages attached to it, you can remove the carb and manifold to gain access to the lifters.

With the radiator out, you should have plenty of room to remove the fan bolts. Here's a good tip—loosen the belts *after* the fan bolts are broken loose.

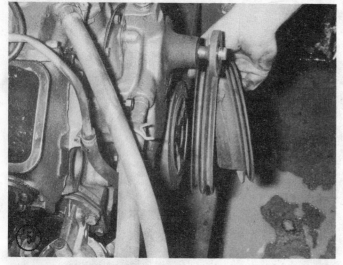

With the belts off, you can take the belt pulleys off the crankshaft vibration dampener.

A special puller will usually be required to remove the vibration damper (you can rent the puller at most rental suppliers). Leave the crank center bolt in place for the puller to push against.

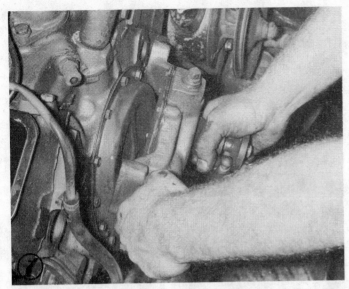

Remove the heater and radiator hoses and remove the water pump.

Normally you'll have to loosen all the oil pan bolts and lower the front of the pan slightly to clear the lower lip of the cover timing as you remove it.

Take off the valve covers and loosen the rockerarm adjusting nuts until the rockers can be tilted to the side, releasing the pushrods.

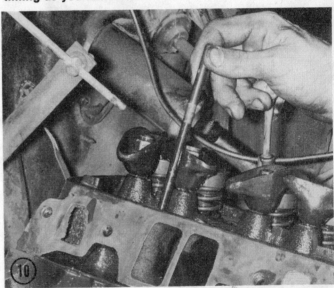

No need to remove the rockers completely, just enough to remove the stock pushrods.

When covered with oil the lifters may be hard to remove from the bores. You may have to use pliers but be careful not to scratch the lifters or the lifter bores.

After removing the timing chain and gears (see the section on replacement of these parts), screw a long bolt into the front of the cam to use as a handle, and slowly remove the cam. Be careful not to nick or scratch the cam bearings as the cam lobes move forward.

109

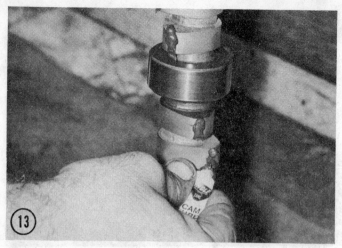

Most cam kits include special moly-based lube to assist camshaft break-in. We're using that supplied with the Engle street cam being installed by Ron Headlee of Fullerton, Calif. Use the lube liberally on all the lobes and camshaft bearing journals.

Again, be especially careful not to nick the cam bearings as you slip in the heavily lubed cam. Go *straight* in with the camshaft—slowly.

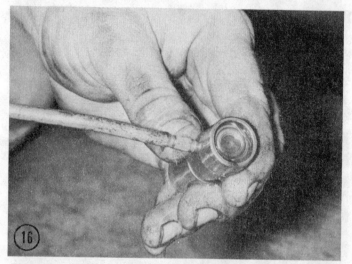

By the same token, the new lifters can use a little extra break-in lubricant. Use this on the bottom, sparingly.

Prior to installation, hydraulic lifters such as these should be primed with engine oil by squirting oil into the pressure hole or by soaking the entire lifter in a can of oil for several minutes.

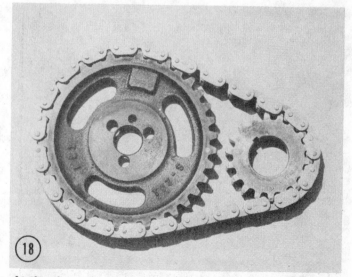

Wipe the lifter bores clean with a rag and install the new lifters. If you are reusing old lifters (a no-no with a new cam) each should be installed in the same bore out of which it came.

At the time of a camshaft change, you may want to also replace your stock timing chain and gears with high-performance ones like this Isky roller chain and steel gears.

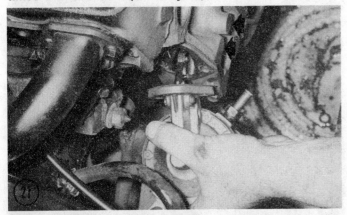

The cam and crank gears must align (arrows) when the chain is installed to make certain the cam is properly timed with the crank (or nearly so).

At this point the fuel pump can be reinstalled. The pump pushrod (not seen here) needs to be held up on the block while the pump is bolted on. This can be accomplished either by coating the pushrod with heavy grease to make it stick or (on later engines) using a stop bolt in one of these holes (arrows) to hold it until the pump is in place. Don't forget to remove the bolt and block off these holes after the job is done or else oil will blow out of the holes during restart.

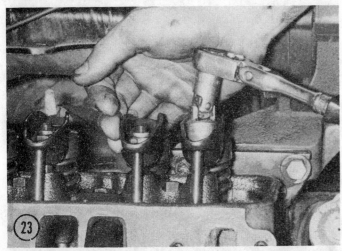

The new (or old) pushrods should be installed and the rockers tightened. Adjust the valve clearance according to the cam manufacturer's tech tag. You should also adjust the valves again after the engine has run at a fast idle for 30 minutes to "break in" the cam.

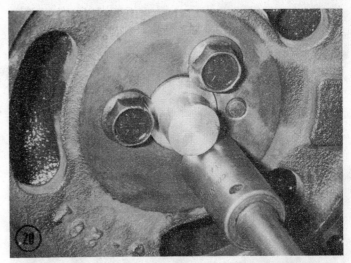

There are many solutions to prevent cam "walk" (the cam moves fore-and-aft in the block as the engine accelerates and decelerates), one of the simplest is this aluminum cam "button" from Iskenderian.

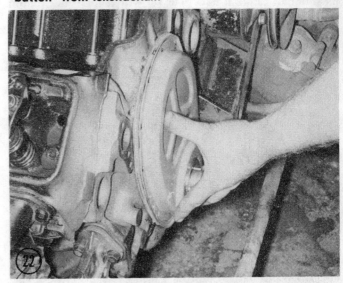

Coated with gasket sealer and a new gasket, the timing cover can be reinstalled and the oil pan can be bolted into place.

Reinstall the water pump, intake manifold, valve covers and the various hoses and belts. Put the radiator back in place and you're almost done!

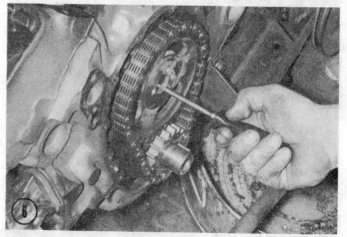

Iskenderian offers a new gear set with super-duty timing chain for all smallblock Chevys. The stock cam gear has nylon teeth and the crank gear is made of powdered iron, while the Isky cam gear is heat-treated steel and the crank gear is cast-iron.

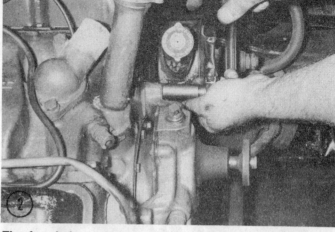

The fan, belts, pulleys, and the water pump must all be removed to get at the timing chain cover. Drain the water from the engine first, though.

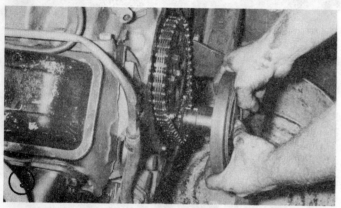

You'll need to rent or borrow a gear puller to remove the crankshaft vibration dampener, then the cover can be removed after you loosen the oil pan bolts and drop the pan down about ½ inch. Here the dampener is used to line up the index marks on the timing gears before removing the chain.

Remove the three bolts holding the cam gear to the camshaft snout and use a pair of prybars or screwdrivers to slip the cam gear off the index dowel, then remove the chain.

Although you can use heat to remove the crank gear, a gear puller is the cleanest and easiest way. Replace the woodruff keys (arrows) if they appear to be bent or worn. The new gear can be heated and installed with a brass or wooden drift and light hammer blows.

With the bottom gear in place on the crankshaft the new chain and cam gear are installed. A screwdriver shank is used through one of the cam gear bolt-holes to align it with the cam index dowel pin.

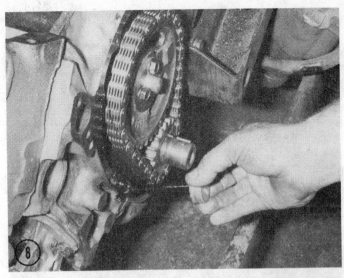

Before bolting up the cam gear, be sure the timing marks on the two gears line up exactly, as did the stock gears before removal. Place a ruler or straightedge between the cam centerline and crank centerline to be certain the marks are in line.

The cam gear bolts should be run in snug with Loctite on the threads and 35-45 ft-lb torque. Clean the block surface, coat with sealer, and install a new cam cover gasket.

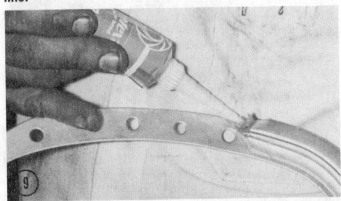

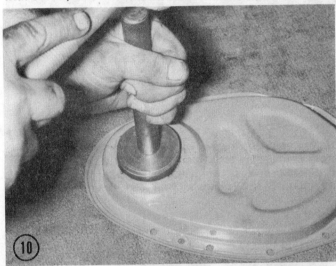

In our case, a Mr. Gasket quick-change cam cover was installed to avoid the future hassle of lowering the oil pan to change the cam or chain. The Mr. Gasket cover has an intermediate plate with a seal-lip for the oil pan. (The cover can be removed to gain access to the chain and cam without disturbing the forward pan seal, which is held in place by the intermediate plate.) A new seal is installed on the lip with gasket sealer and the ends sealed with a shot of Permatex silicone sealant.

If you're reusing the stock cam cover, be sure to replace the dampener seal. After the opening is swabbed with Permatex, a suitable driver is used to press in the new seal, with the seal lip facing rearward.

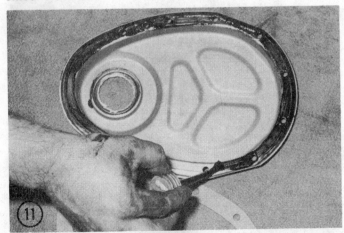

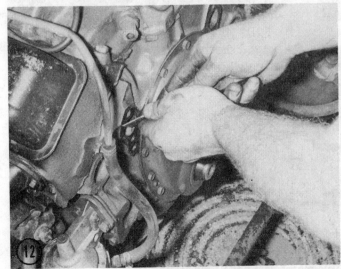

The Mr. Gasket intermediate plate is gasket/glued to the block and the oil pan is retightened. Another gasket is placed on the outside of the plate and the access cover installed. Coat the gasket flange of the cover with sealer, and use white grease on the inner flange of the dampener seal.

You can now reinstall the cover, vibration dampener, water pump and pulleys. Be sure to clean the block and install new water pump gaskets.

HOW TO INSTALL VALVE SPRINGS

Unless you need a valve job or are doing some other head work at the same time, there's no need to remove the head to install new performance valve springs and spring retainers. Start by removing your valve covers to expose the rockers.

On this big-block Ford, rocker arms are shaft-mounted, so loosening four bolts allows you to remove all the rockerarms from the head.

This might be a good time to take all the pushrods out for inspection. Just remember to keep them in order unless you're installing new ones at the same time as the new springs.

With the rockers and pushrods out of the way, you have a clear shot at the springs. Insert a special air pressure adapter (available at auto parts stores) in the spark plug hole and apply air pressure.

The pressure from the compressor will hold the valve up on the seat while you take off the springs, using a valve spring compressor like this one or the lever type, both available in parts stores.

While the spring compressor has the spring compressed, use a punch or screwdriver to tap the retainer so that the spring keepers come out.

The compressed spring and retainer come out easily now, but the valve stays up due to air pressure inside the chamber.

Still working on the first cylinder, use the same compressor on the new spring and retainer (here an Isky aluminum retainer and single spring) to compress them for installation. When they are down far enough over the valve stem, reinsert the keepers and then release the compressor tool. Now tackle the next valve for that cylinder. When both are done, move the air adapter to the next cylinder and repeat the procedure.

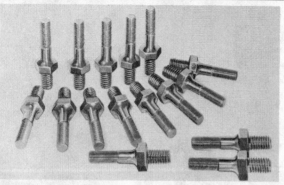

B & B Performance Products makes and sells a variety of performance engine and chassis parts, among them these high-strength steel screw-in rockerarm studs for Chevy engines.

Cam Dynamics is one of the relative newcomers to the business, however, they have been around long enough to gain a tremendous reputation among the racers.

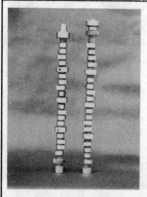

Chrysler's Direct Connection has many valvetrain parts in their new performance catalog. These two cams are based on the famous Street Hemi grind and they call them "bracket racer cams."

Clifford Research specializes in high-performance equipment for inline 6-cylinder engines. Among the many items offered are several excellent performance/racing cams.

Competition Cams is another new name in the field but they have worked with many top pro engine builders to widen the range of designs available.

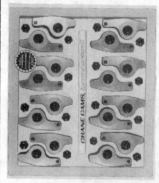

Crane Cams is well-known for their line of computer-designed camshaft profiles. Their catalog offers an incredible array of equipment, including such goodies as roller-tip, needle-bearing rockerarms, cam kits, valves and modified cylinder heads. They almost assuredly have something for every need and they provide one of the most extensive customer assistance services existant.

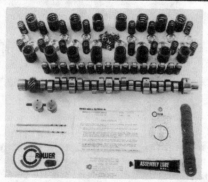

Crower Cams makes some of the finest hard-core racing parts (fuel-injections and roller cams) available but they also have a full line of torque/mileage cams for hi-po street engines.

Engle Racing Cams has profiles to suit most street and racing needs, such as this complete valvetrain kit for smallblock Fords that includes lifters, pushrods, cam, springs and retainers, locks and break-in lube.

Ford Motor Company dealers still have a few of their original muscle parts left on the books, such as this complete valvetrain kit for the Boss 351 (Cleveland) engine.

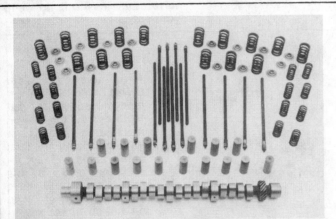

Howard Cams can fit you with a racing roller cam for a blown Hemi or just as easily supply you with the inexpensive street cam you need.

Interpart, the marketplace for import performance, has cams and kits for Datsuns. This one for the 510 includes the cam, dual-coil valve springs, rockers (followers), keepers and aluminum spring retainers.

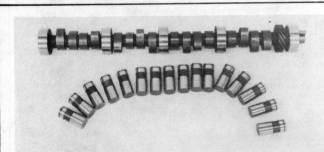

Lunati Cams first gained their reputation with some excellent drag-racing cam grinds. They have recently expanded to include track racing and RV cams. And, they have an excellent customer service department.

Holley markets more than just their famous carburetors. Their M/T line of custom equipment includes such valvetrain items as these polished aluminum valve covers. Cast valve covers seal better than stock ones and they look a whole lot better.

IECO, the small-car specialists, not only offer cam and valve gear for the Vega and Corvair, they also offer a full-modified Vega cylinder head that has been ported to increase flow 30%.

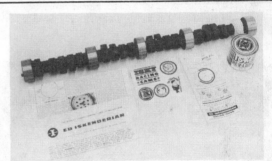

Iskenderian is without a doubt the most famous name in valvetrains. And deservedly so, their catalog lists about everything the racer or hot rodder needs for the performance engine building—camshafts, kits, gear drives, break-in lubes, tools, and a thorough description of valvetrain dynamics.

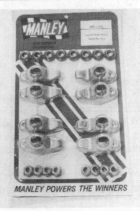

Manley manufactures a complete range of bolt-on performance parts that include many valvetrain items such as cams, pushrods, rockerarms, pushrod guide plates, rocker balls, lifters, and screw-in rocker studs.

Moon Equipment Company manufactures more than just aluminum fuel tanks, they also sell a line of camshaft designs developed from their own dyno research.

Mullen & Company are specialists in cylinder head work such as porting and special machine work, but they also offer a number of special valves for racing and serious street work, including stainless steel and exotic high-dollar titanium valves that they will finish to your specs.

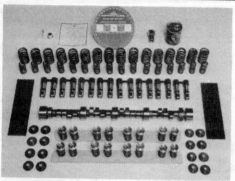

Norris Cams was one of the first companies to offer steel roller-tipped rockerarms but they also have a complete range of valvetrain gear. This is one of their racing roller-lifter cam kits but they also have many street profiles.

Pete Jackson Gear Drives markets a performance gear drive that features a simple bolt-on installation procedure. While a little noisier than stock chains, they reportedly give reliable cam timing and have successfully been used on full-on street machines.

Pro/Stock specializes in intake manifolds for popular Ford, Chevrolet and Chrysler engines, but they also offer the hot rodder these aluminum valve covers with satin fins and black wrinkle-finish paint.

Racer Brown has been grinding cams almost since before they were called cams. He is one of the sources for hot Chrysler grinds and his catalog is loaded with many unique valvetrain items and a cornucopia of hints and information.

Racer Walsh specializes in the Ford four-cylinder engines found in many Pintos and Mustang II's. Some of the valvetrain goodies they have for the 2000-2300cc engines include roller-tip rockerarms, special cams, and an adjustable cam sprocket.

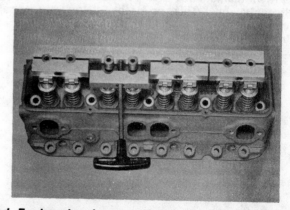

Reed Engineering is one of the big hitters in circle-track engineering. In addition to their respected cams they also have several valvetrain accessories like this stud tie-bar.

Sig Erson Cams has a full catalog of performance camshafts for you to choose from, including street, drag race, and oval-track profiles, with the coordinated kits to match.

Speed Pro is one of the big hitters in performance parts marketing and though they are best known for their pistons and rings, they also have an excellent line of street performance cams.

TRW has one of the largest selections of special performance equipment to be found anywhere. Their performance parts catalog includes many excellent high output cams and they have a full line of heavy-duty lifters, pushrods and rockerarms.

Schneider Racing Cams makes a line of street-performance camshafts and kits, called the "Lightning Street Pro" series, to complement their highly respected racing cams.

Varicam manufactures this unique cam timing product, a cam drive gear with an automatic, variable cam advance feature that is adjustable. It is said to deliver better low end and yet retain good top end performance.

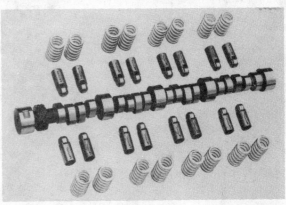

Weber Cams has been around for many years manufacturing performance valvetrain parts for race cars, VW's and other minicars, and street cams for the most popular Detroit engines.

Wolverine Gear & Parts Company manufactures a number of engine bolt-on parts, such as camshafts and kits like this one complete with lifters, pushrods, springs and aluminum retainers.

Champion Muffler offer the Pinto owner a special valvetrain service. They sell, on an exchange basis, a ported and polished, CC'd and milled head for the Pinto four with an Isky camshaft and followers installed. They also can install bigger valves.

CLUTCH & DRIVELINE

Traditionally, the young hot rodder pays little attention to his vehicle's driveline until something breaks. It's the unglamorous nature of the dirty and greasy components lurking underneath a car that keeps them out of the limelight, while attention is usually focused on more visible components such as chrome goodies, big wheels and tires, or custom body parts. But if you've "warmed over" your engine already and expect to deliver the new-found power to the rear tires without breaking something every time you put your foot down, there's a lot you can do to fortify the driveline. It's like preventive medicine, a little forethought goes a long way toward "happy motoring."

Twixt Engine and Four-Speed

The manual-shift transmission, particularly the four-speed variety, has become one of the ubiquitous marks of the performance car, both with home-built hot rods and factory supercars (back when you could still buy one). The stick shift transmission allows the driver to keep the engine rpm level wherever he wants, especial-

Well-designed driveline modifications will noticeably improve driving "feel" and increase reliability as well. Most chassis-related bolt-on equipment is designed to efficiently deliver engine power (hopefully, higher-than-stock power) to the tires.

ly important with a highly-modified engine that works best in the upper rpm ranges. Proper delivery of the engine power to the transmission, however, involves another set of parts that needs special attention to survive repeated applications of higher-than-stock horsepower.

Between your modified engine and your four-speed transmission reside the flywheel, clutch disc and pressure plate. These pieces must be rugged, dependable, and designed for high performance. There are quite a few specialty companies making nothing but special versions of these components, so obviously there are a lot of enthusiasts (their customers) who consider these parts important. Like most other speed equipment, performance driveline parts must be carefully selected for compatibility with extant and projected modifications.

A key element in this assembly is one not often considered by the beginner, the flywheel. Most factory flywheels are heavy cast-iron monsters, and this may come as a shock to those of you who like to "race" with stock parts, these flywheels are just not suitable for performance driving in the

The stick-shift lover has to rely upon good coordination (and occasionally a bit of luck) to the get the best high-rpm shifting performance. The application of horsepower to the rear end can be improved greatly by adding a performance clutch and flywheel, perferably of the explosion-proof variety.

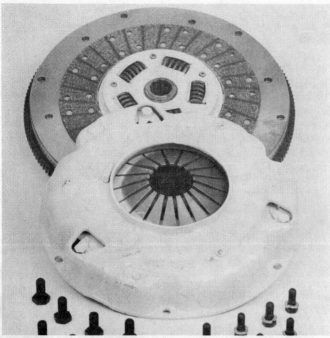

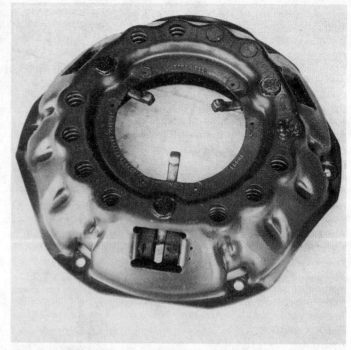

The high-pressure diaphragm clutch has become the most popular selection for many street applications. It is noted for clean release and excellent holding power without excessive pedal pressure. At one time diaphragm pressure plates had a reputation for "hanging up" at high engine speeds but current designs have eliminated this problem.

The Borg & Beck-style pressure plate offers strong holding pressure and positive disc release at any rpm, but they can be tiring to your leg in traffic! The B&B style is often found on Chrysler engines but similar pressure plates are available from Schiefer to fit nearly any engine/trans combination.

over-5000 rpm ranges. Because the safety regulations for organized drag racing events are so tough, you may never have the chance to see a clutch or flywheel explosion. It's not a pretty sight. When they let go, it can be like having a grenade blow up beneath the floorboards.

The specialty manufacturers, in response to sanctioning-body regulations, have developed special "explosion-proof" driveline components to supply both the racing and street markets. While no clutch or flywheel can be labeled totally explosion-proof, these products have an enviable safety record in all but the most brutal top fuel dragsters. The performance flywheel is designed for high-rpm safety and has several features not found in stock units: precision machining, perfect balance, special facings for better friction. They're also machined from high-strength steel, not castings of soft iron.

You have basically two choices when it comes to flywheel material, aluminum or steel. The specialty clutch companies make both, but the steel units are most often recommended for street use. Installing a light flywheel, such as one made of aluminum, has been a traditional rodding ploy because the lighter flywheel allows the engine to rev faster, creating super throttle response. However, the steel flywheel can store a lot more energy (inertia)

and this is considered more important for street use, where high-rpm "power shifts" aren't necessary. Whether aluminum or steel, a good number of specialty flywheels have a special frictional facing on the clutch side, usually a bronze and copper composition either riveted on or attached permanently by hot metal-spraying. In the end, the final criteria for the proper choice of a clutch and flywheel is the recommendation of the manufacturer (some facings are "race-only" whereas others are suitable only for street use).

The other critical components of the clutch are the disc and the pressure plate. The flywheel and these two parts make up a frictional sandwich, with the flywheel and pressure plate being the "driving" parts, and the disc (floating in between the two) being the "driven" piece, which turns the transmission input shaft.

The clutch disc is a combination of a splined hub, an outer ring, and the frictional material, or lining. The mating splines of the transmission input shaft connect the disc (by the hub) to the remainder of the powertrain. These splines are of many different configurations and you must be careful that the right spline (usually determined by the number of teeth and the outside diameter at the tip of the spline) is chosen for the trans you are using. Stock clutch discs have "organic" friction material, generally an

asbestos composition (due to the heat-absorbing qualities of asbestos). The outer ring (or rings) is made of thin spring steel and the frictional material is bonded or riveted to this ring. The thin steel of the ring is not completely flat when the lining is attached. It is wavy or "wafered" so it acts like a spring to cushion some of the blow when the clutch pedal is released and the disc is squeezed quickly between the pressure plate and flywheel. Also cushioning this shock load is the hub, which on street and stock clutches is attached to the outer rings by a plate holding five or six small coil springs. These springs are arranged in such a way that when the clutch is engaged the transfer of torque from the outer frictional material to the splined hub is dampened by the compression of the springs.

The racing clutch disc has very little in common with the ordinary street disc. It has special hard frictional materials made from powdered metals and sintered bronze. It does not have springs in the hub to dampen the shock load (known in racing terms as a "solid hub"). And there is little or no wafering in the outer rings. When you let one of these clutches out, it sends a stiff shock through the entire driveline! Not only are the racing units not recommended for street use because of the non-cushioning quality, but also because the frictional material can wear excessively.

As we have seen in other chapters, there are a number of traditional pitfalls awaiting the young high-performance "engineer," and in the driveline area it must be the pressure plate. Too often the "bigger is better" philosophy leads our erring hot rod hero to install a heavier-than-necessary pressure plate and wind up with a muscle-bound left leg!

The higher the pressure contained in the springs of a pressure plate, the better that plate's ability to firmly hold the clutch disc without slippage, even under the strain of high-rpm horsepower. Unfortunately, there is a direct correlation between increased plate pressure and increased clutch pedal pressure. Most stock pressure plates have a peak pressure (pressure with the pedal out and clutch engaged) around 2400-2500 pounds, and high-performance units generally have a higher range of around 2800-3200 pounds. Using any more than about 2800 pounds for a street pressure plate isn't recommended because it just isn't necessary and can be a bear to live with in stop-and-go traffic. Also, the heavier the clutch pressure, the quicker the wear on all of your clutch *linkage* parts, such as the cross-shaft and throw-out bearing. We know of one street machine that had an annoying habit of dropping the clutch pedal to the floor in traffic, because the heavy clutch would wear out the pedal bushings and the pedal retaining pin would shear! Quality in a clutch is more important than high pressure numbers, so stick with a brand-name product for reliable, long service.

There are several types of pressure plates that utilize spring pressure with varying degrees of effectiveness. They are the Borg and Beck, the Long, and the diaphragm type; the most traditional design is the Borg and Beck. The Borg and Beck in addition to the Long—the Long is a variation of the standard three-finger release design—is a semi-centrifugal (pressure increases with engine speed), single, dry-disc, coil-spring clutch. This type will often have heavy pedal pressure, at times exceeding 2800 pounds, but release is positive, and the life expectancy is very good. The diaphragm clutch replaces the coil springs with a dish-shaped "spring" that is much easier to depress (disengage). Early diaphragm clutches worked well at low speeds, but at high rpm they had the habit of sticking to the floor, turning a speed shift into a real show! Present-day diaphragms are virtually cured of this, and since they have the decided advantage of a comfortably light pedal, they are becoming a more common choice for the street. All things considered, however, the final choice of a clutch for your car should be made based on the manufacturer's recommendation and the specific application.

Whether you're going full tilt for the complete specialty flywheel, clutch, and pressure plate, or sticking to high-performance stock-type units, safety should be your paramount consideration. By all means, even if you can't afford the top quality explosion-proof parts, at least install a proven *steel* scattershield in place of your stock cast iron or aluminum bellhousing. The scattershield could be a literal lifesaver if your stock clutch or flywheel should decide to disintegrate at high rpm due to unseen, accumulated heat cracks or flaws.

In addition to this protection, your between-engine-and-trans assemblage should be installed properly. By this we mean that the flywheel and pressure plate should both be bolted in place with the correct torque, applied in proper sequence to prevent warping, and with *new* high-strength fasteners. Flywheel-to-crank bolts and pressure plate-to-flywheel kits are available in speed shops in plastic bags with a full set of high-strength fasteners and lock washers. A little bit of Loctite applied to the new bolts before use is extra insurance that they won't back out under sustained vibration.

If the pressure plate you've installed is a heavy-duty type, then you should also install a new, heavy-duty throw-out bearing at the same time. In fact, a new throw-out bearing should be installed any time a new or re-surfaced pressure plate and/or clutch disc is installed. And don't overlook the pilot bushing (small bushing located in the rear of the crankshaft); it's cheap, and replacing it when it's accessible will insure maximum clutch life with minimum future maintenance.

Finally, before your super clutch is put into service, make sure that all adjustments and clearance checks have been made, especially pressure-plate air gap. Air gap is the clearance between the disc and the flywheel (or pressure plate) when the pedal is depressed. Insufficient clearance here will allow the disc to drag against the driven members during shifts, causing hard shifting and excessive disc wear. Depending on the type of clutch you have chosen, you may have to modify some of the linkage (usually the cross-shaft) if the air gap is too small. Freeplay in the pedal is another "vital." The throwout bearing should not be allowed to contact the clutch fingers when released, because this can cause not only premature bearing

A steel bellhousing (often called, aptly, a scattershield) is definitely recommended for any 4-speed high-performance street machine. It's good insurance on the street and most drag strips won't allow you to run without one. This is a one-piece hydroformed model complete with a block plate.

A new throwout bearing should be installed whenever you put in a new clutch. Heavy-duty replacements are always recommended, but make sure you get exactly the right one for your clutch. These bearings have different flange-to-flange heights, and installing the wrong one could mean your clutch wouldn't release or wouldn't fully engage.

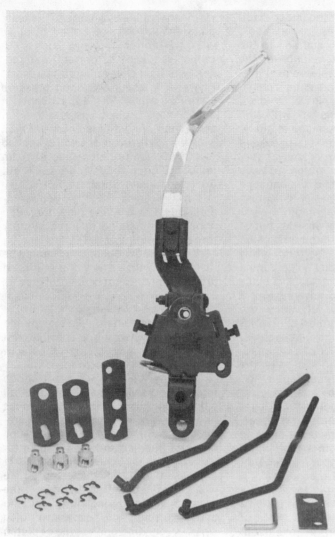

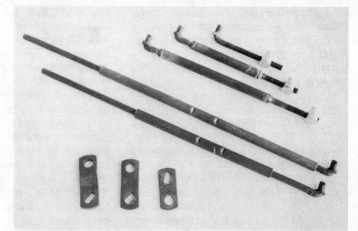

The Hurst Super Shifter is favored by many racers because of the unique mounting position that allows the shift rods to be straight. This eliminates flexing and provides a super-positive shift, even at extreme rpm.

Given the imprecision of almost all factory shifters, Hurst's famous super-precise shifters should be around for a long time. They are legendary for improving four-speed (and three-speed) shifting quickness and control.

A noted feature on all Hurst shifters is the adjustable length shift rods. Once the shifter body is installed, the rod length can be set to exact requirements and may even be varied, as desired, to suit the racer's specific shifting technique.

wear (both throw-out and crank-thrust), but also high-speed slippage and disc failure. A general rule of one-inch freeplay, measured at the pedal, is a good place to start. Freeplay is usually adjusted by lengthening or shortening the clutch-fork pushrod.

Shifters

The term "shifter" is usually taken to mean a gear changer for a manual transmission, but just as often this refers to an automatic shifter. In either case, there are many specialty equipment manufacturers that produce very nicely designed linkage systems to replace the factory setup. There is a need for these pieces because the factory must always be cost conscious in the design of components, more so than building them for high-performance use, and the typical result of using factory shifters with "overenthusiasm" is broken parts, bent linkage, or at least missed shifts.

The specialty shifter was designed for several purposes: to satisfy the individual that wants to buy dress-up items, to improve convenience and/or driveability, and to fulfill the need for a reliable, race-oriented gear changer that will withstand very hard use. Further, shifters function very differently depending on the manufacturer and the intended use; manual shifters can be had in the usual "H" type gate or in the more "racy" inline designs, with shift rods bent to clear the chassis and flooring or with straight reinforced rods for competition. Automatic shifters are also available in street and race configurations with the difference being the stiffness of the linkage and the overall quality of construction.

As we have mentioned, there are many brands that you can choose from, however, the market contains at least a few "well knowns," such as Hurst and Mr. Gasket. The lesser known units should be carefully evaluated for strength and rigidity,

since it makes little sense to buy a shifter that does a poor or less than precise job of shifting. Look for units that are constructed from quality steel and stay away from shifters that use "pot metal" castings. All included hardware should be grade 5 or better (have three or more lines on the bolt head), and those shifters that include self-locking nuts, lockwashers, and/or Loctite are usually of better design, since vibration is a major consideration if reliability is important. The stronger and harder (higher heat treat) the shift rods are, the more precise the shifter will select gears, and the use of metal (rather than plastic) bushings are often preferred by racers, as they are less prone to breaking and falling out. Steel bushings are suitable for the street, although a slight increase in vibration may be transferred to the shift handles.

Proper adjustment of both automatic and manual shifters is paramount to proper operation. Most man-

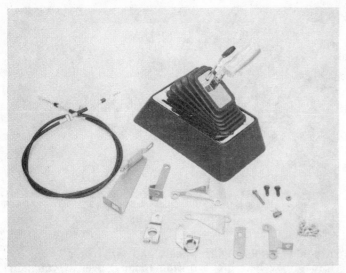

Automatic owners need not be without precise shift control. B&M has several street and competition shifters for automatics, including the brand new Star-Shifter shown here (complete with a reverse lock-out handle).

Modified converters can give some cars better off-the-line performance by allowing the engine to rev higher. But the higher the stall speed, the more slippage there is, and the less efficient the engine will be at slower speeds.

ual units come with an alignment pin that is inserted in the shifter assembly to lock the mechanism in neutral, after which the shift rods are adjusted in length to freely slide in the trans shift arms when they too are in the neutral position. This adjustment will remain intact as long as the shifter, mounting adapter—if any, and all hardware remain solid. If any movement occurs, the adjustment is lost and it will become difficult, if not impossible, to shift the trans properly. Automatic shifters can use either a cable (usually preferred) or linkage rod to move the shift arm on the side of the trans. Inside the automatic, this arm is connected to a hydraulic valve that, for most "autos," *must* be in the precisely correct position for proper operation. Poorly adjusted automatics will shift weakly or may suffer internal damage, so it becomes obvious that a well built shifter with precise indexing is very important.

Beefing Automatic Transmissions

Don't think that just because your particular street machine doesn't have a clutch there aren't any driveline improvements needed. The automatic transmission has come a long way since the days when the hot rodder derisively referred to it as a "slush box." We now take for granted reliable, sure-shifting three-speed automatics like the Ford C-4, and C-6, Chrysler Torque flites and GM Turbo-Hydramatics. With modern torque converters that actually multiply off-the-line torque, a street machine may even be *better* off with an automatic than a four-speed. And there are many ways to improve an automatic-equip-

ped driveline when high performance is desired.

If there is any disadvantage to the automatic, it is the available "stall speed" built into the torque converter. This is the engine rpm at which the torque converter fluid drive "locks up" and delivers full torque to the transmission with the minimum amount of slippage. The "stall" part of the term means that, if the brakes are kept applied, this is the maximum rpm the engine will turn with the throttle wide open (the converter "locks up" and prevents the engine from increasing in speed when the car is not moving). Stall speed is really another way of indicating how much "slippage" the converter will allow before hooking up, which gives us a clue as to why "high-stall" converters aren't suitable for street use.

For drag racing use, where maximum off-the-line acceleration is desired to really "launch" the car, special converters are used that are modified for extra stall speed. Some all-out

converters have as much as a 5500 rpm stall speed, while most stock automobiles get by with as little as 1200-1500 rpm stall speeds. The higher the stall speed before the converter hooks up, the more slippage. This means more heat is built up in the transmission parts and in the fluid (oil) that drives and cools them, and this shortens transmission life. An increase in transmission temperature of just 10% can halve the expected life of an automatic transmission!

Most of the specialty automatic transmission companies offer "street converters" that have only about 500 rpm more stall speed than stock. This is enough to make a noticeable difference, but these street converters are said to have little effect on gas mileage. They are sometimes smaller in diameter than stock units, say an 11-inch unit to replace a stock one of 12-inch diameter, and are considerably cheaper than the racing type. They may be the perfect adjunct to the mildly modified street engine.

One of the simplest ways to help dissipate heat from the trans fluid is to increase the size of the pan. These B&M deep pans bolt directly in place of the stock-type pan, allowing an extra quart of fluid to be carried in the trans. These pans, when used with a trans cooler, will provide the ultimate in heat rejection.

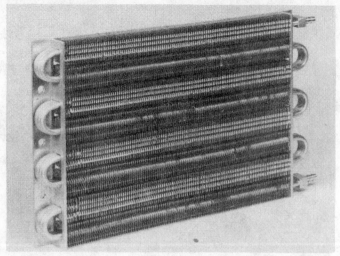

If your vehicle uses an automatic transmission, even if you make no other driveline changes, at least install an accessory transmission fluid cooler. In addition to extending transmission life, there are combination coolers that cool both transmission oil and engine oil.

If you're running wide wheels and large tires, front end forces may be increased dramatically, even if you don't realize it because of power assist. Though not a common modification, the owner of this slick street machine added a small cooler on the fenderwall to help cool the power steering fluid (right).

The subject of heat buildup in automatic transmission fluid is one some rodders neglect until it is too late. It is hard to fully realize how important that fluid or "turkey blood" is to an automatic. It is both the cooling and lubricating system and it is the working fluid for hydraulic action within the valve body (activates shift clutches). Keeping the fluid cool and clean will not only make the transmission last longer, it should also accelerate the car better. In most stock configurations the automatic fluid is pumped up to a small tank in the bottom of the engine radiator, where it gives up excess heat. When a high-stall converter is used or when the trans is used at high engine speeds for long periods, the stock arrangement may not dissipate enough heat.

Two ways to combat the killer heat is with an auxiliary fluid cooler and a deep-sump transmission pan. Deep-sump pans are available in chromed steel or cast-aluminum from most of the transmission specialty companies. They increase the total oil capacity a quart or two, they look trick, and they may stave off fluid "burning" from high heat during a long traffic jam.

Adding an accessory cooler is the most common automatic transmission modification. Like a small radiator or air-conditioning condenser, these coolers are available in a wide variety of sizes and configurations to suit every need from trailer-towing RV to street-and-strip hot dog. Basically, a collection of tubing running through heat-dissipating fins (identical in operation to the engine radiator), the coolers can be mounted to work in conjunction with the stock radiator cooler or in place of the stock cooler. It's best to pick the largest cooler you can and eliminate the stock cooler, since it only adds extra heat to the engine radiator and if the accessory cooler is *large enough and properly mounted* it should be all the cooler needed. An exception to this might be very cold climates, where plumbing the trans fluid through the stock radiator cooler will help the transmission reach operating temperature sooner. However, both hookup techniques work well, and we know of no instance where engine overheating occurred because of the heat added to the cooling system by trans oil.

Your new cooler, regardless of its plumbing, should be mounted where it gets a steady stream of air flowing through it. Often they are installed underneath the car next to the transmission, but this provides little cooling when the car is in traffic and isn't moving, and this is when you need it most! A more suitable location would be in the engine compartment, between the fan and the radiator core. Here at least the fan can pull air through the cooler even while idling, but this air has already been heated by the radiator. The best location is in front of the radiator. Here it gets cooling air at all times, even when stopped in traffic, and the cooler gets the air before the radiator.

A very popular type of transmission modification is to "reprogram" the shifting characteristics. As you no doubt have gathered so far, most of the components on your car have been designed as compromises, and automatic transmission shifting is one of those compromises. The transmission engineers strive for the most efficient use of the torque converter and gearing, but somewhere down the line there's a "control engineer" who tells them "Boys, it shifts too hard, make it really *soft*." So to please the buying public, who want luxury instead of performance, the engineers make the shifts smooth and easy instead of firm and positive. They accomplish this in several ways, but all methods make the transmission slip. When the transmission is shifting from first to second and from second to third, there is a short period in which both gears

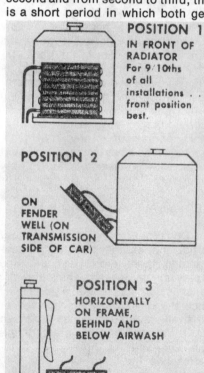

POSITION 1
IN FRONT OF RADIATOR
For 9/10ths of all installations . . . front position best.

POSITION 2
ON FENDER WELL (ON TRANSMISSION SIDE OF CAR)

POSITION 3
HORIZONTALLY ON FRAME, BEHIND AND BELOW AIRWASH

Unless you have an air-conditioning condenser out in front of your radiator, you should be able to mount a trans cooler there, where it will get the maximum airflow (and give the most cooling) under all conditions.

If the auxiliary cooler provides sufficient heat dissipation the stock trans cooler in the bottom radiator tank can be by-passed completely. This may improve engine cooling, but if you consider such a system, make certain to install a temp gauge in the trans pan to insure that the fluid temperature is within the recommended range.

A lot can be done to improve the shifting of any stock auto trans. This kit is designed for those with a vacuum-modulated shift mechanism. By "dialing in" the amount of vacuum applied to the modulator, the shift timing can be controlled by the driver.

are engaged at the same time. The transmission slips in both gears to effect a soft "overlap" between the gears. Most modern automatics shift so smoothly, you hardly notice a change at all unless you have your foot in it. The drawback to this method of shift control is that all that slippage during the shifts causes additional clutch wear and heat buildup in the transmission fluid, heat that shortens transmission life considerably as we explained earlier.

The specialty performance people have been modifying and beefing automatic transmissions for high performance and racing for almost 20 years now, and they have many cures for soft shifting. While there are complete performance transmissions available that are able to withstand severe horsepower and shift like a power-shifted four-speed, these complete transmissions are expensive and usually not suited for street use. What these manufacturers can offer you is modified valve bodies or simple kits to "reprogram" the shifting of your present trans. The kits generally cost under $50 and are easily-installed, while the valve bodies are over $100. By increasing the fluid pressure and modifying the shift timing, these "re-taught brains" reduce the overlap in the shifts, and can give you positive shifting at all times. These modifications are also said to actually lengthen transmission fluid life because the trans runs cooler (less overlap and less slippage reduce heat buildup).

These kits come in different strengths or stages of shift firmness, depending on the intended application. There are kits for street-and-strip cars with very stiff shift action, there are the milder ones for average street machines, and even special RV kits designed to help improve transmission life under towing conditions. These two latter types are the ones you'll be interested in, but by all means, go by the recommendations of the kit manufacturer as to which of his kits is best for your machine. Installation can usually be accomplished in a few hours with simple tools and an electric drill (for redrilling some of the holes in the valve body separator plate), all you need is the kit and a quantity of new fluid.

There are also special modifications (or kits) that convert the automatic shift feature to fully manual. This is best used by a drag car that must shift at precise engine rpm to minimize quarter-mile time and to maximize consistency. Manual-shift "autos" are not recommended for the street because often first-gear and

TransGo invented the "reprogramming" kit concept to reduce shifting overlap. By reducing the time during upshift when the trans clutch-apply cycle engages two gears at the same time, trans efficiency is increased and wear is reduced.

Shift kits are available in a variety of "strengths," from firm-shifting RV kits to teeth-jarring race kits. Some also require full-manual gear selection. Know what you want before you buy.

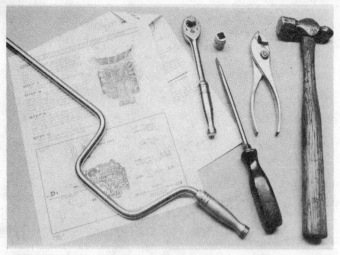

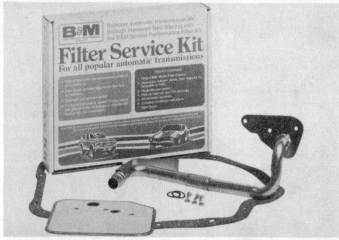

Most of the shift-improver kits come with complete instructions and require only basic tools to install (no torque wrenches needed). The step-by-step example in the next section shows a typical installation.

Turbo-hydro 400 owners may be interested in this B&M kit that has everything you need to change your transmission fluid and filters. It also has a unique O-ring sealed pickup tube designed to eliminate aeration of the fluid (a problem that can lead to overheating and trans failure).

sometimes first-and-second-gear braking are sacrificed (because of internal hydraulic re-routing). This will lead to additional brake-lining wear, and can be a real hazard when towing a trailer.

Even if you don't install a kit, you should change your trans fluid at regular intervals. While it doesn't get black with carbon residue like oil, it does get "burned" by excessive heat and can shorten transmission life when used for too many miles, by building up deposits of varnish on seal surfaces. Most cars should have the fluid and transmission filter changed once a year. If you opt for one of the specialty deep-sump pans, they usually come with a convenient drain plug for changing fluid, something the factory engineers didn't bother with. If you're using a stock pan, you can purchase a drain plug conversion kit that bolts into the pan, or if you install a transmission oil temperature gauge on your dash, the new sending unit you fit to the pan can be used as a drain plug. The transmission oil temperature gauge is especially desirable for

Some auto trans pans do not have removeable drain plugs. Adding this drain plug kit to the pan will make draining the pan a lot easier.

the trailer-towing vehicle. They're not expensive, but the transmission pan usually has to be removed and a threaded adapter welded into the pan to accept the sending unit. It's cheap insurance against losing an important element of your driveline.

Driveshafts and U-joints

The driveshaft is not commonly thought of as a performance part, but poor maintenance in this area can cause annoying, if not serious, problems for the "street machiner." Since the U-joints are out of sight and never need much attention, most motorists never concern themselves with driveline maintenance until telltale clanking sounds appear when the car is put in gear.

Lubrication is, of course, paramount to long driveline life, but even at most gas stations where lube jobs are performed, the U-joints seldom are remembered. From the factory, U-joints on most modern cars have no grease fitting, they are "permanently-lubricated" at the factory and sealed. Once the stock set has given up the ghost, replacement time offers some choices. This might be a good time to consider replacing the worn U-joints with one of the heavy-duty types offered by the specialty companies like TRW and Lakewood. Almost all the replacement U-joints do have good ol' Zerk grease fittings for periodic lubrication.

Just remember, when installing any U-joint that has Zerks, to install the yoke in such a way that the grease fitting won't be shrouded. They should be installed so that the fitting points out on the most accessible side of the assembly for greasing later. To

grease them after assembly, you'll probably need a "needle-nose" adapter for your grease gun. Also, install the yoke in such a way that the grease fitting part of the yoke will be under compression instead of tension when torque is applied to the driveshaft. Otherwise, the hole for the fitting could be considered a potential weak spot in a high-horsepower car.

If a driveshaft is straight and in balance and has good joints, it won't require your closest supervision. Generally, stock driveshafts are in good enough balance to not vibrate under normal conditions. But when hot rodders start shortening and lengthening them to fit various engine swaps, problems can arise. There is only one correct way to shorten a driveshaft, by cutting it in a lathe. The weld on the front of the tube is machined away until the yoke can be slipped out of the tube. The driveshaft is cut (again in the lathe) to the correct length and the yoke reinserted and rewelded (arc or heli-arc welded). This assures you of having the yoke in straight and the modified shaft will be fairly vibration free. Ideally, after welding, it should be professionally balanced.

Accidents can happen even with a good shaft and U-joints, and most major racing associations demand that you have a driveshaft safety loop installed, even on automatic-transmission cars. This is cheap insurance also for the muscular street machine you're building. You can imagine the results if your car was accelerating hard and all of a sudden the front U-joint failed and dropped the front of the driveshaft down to the pavement! Fast-moving cars have "jack-knifed" over a dropped driveshaft when not equipped with a

U-joints are the most overlooked part of the drivetrain. You shouldn't have much trouble unless you are making over 450 horses, enjoy "dumping" the clutch, or are rebuilding an older car. It's best to replace them with heavy-duty ones if you have any doubt. An unexpected failure is a very dangerous (and expensive) happening.

Selecting the type of ring gear carrier to be used is a basic decision when you are upgrading the rear end. The range of choices reaches from an open-type differential (left) through the posi-locking type (center) and the racing spool (right).

safety loop. They can also "whip" through the sheetmetal floorboards, which is why a good loop should go 360°, otherwise, you may be sharing the front seat with a violently-rotating piece of metal. A well-designed strap will encircle the driveshaft completely (very specific construction techniques are required if the car is to be raced at a sanctioned track; contact the respective association for details).

The End of the Line

Our discussion of a heavy-duty driveline would be incomplete if we failed to "bring up the rear," so to speak. The rear axle must bear the brunt of all the engine torque and it's called on to handle a pretty tough load at times. Depending on the car you have, the final gear ratio it has, your driving habits, and how much power your street motor is putting out, your stock rear end may or may not be adequate for high-performance use.

You have two choices. While the drag racer must have the best of everything that bundles of money can buy, you can choose between either beefing up the stock rear end in your car or swapping to one more durable. We'll quickly survey the most favored rear ends for heavy-duty work, and then tell you what can be done to improve a stock rear end's chances of surviving to a ripe old mileage.

The trio of superheros in rear ends are the Dana 60, GM 12-bolt, and the nine-inch Ford rear end. The Dana 60 was installed in four-speed versions of some of Chrysler's Hemi-powered muscle cars, but you'll have better luck in your wrecking-yard scrounging if you look for one under a medium-duty pickup truck (either Ford, Chevy, or Mopar). The Mopar 8¾-inch (diameter of ring gear) rear, although not an equal to the Dana 60, is certainly a suitable high-performance rear for all but the most serious "gear crashers." Look for the housing that has a casting

number that ends in "742" (cast steel instead of cast iron), and a posi-type differential that uses four planet gears with clutches instead of two gears and cones. The GM 12-bolt (this designation refers to both the number of bolts holding the rear cover on and the number holding the ring gear to the carrier) is found in most late-model, big-block-powered cars, with other GM cars using the weaker 10-bolt. The nine-inch Ford unit (refers to the diameter of the ring gear in this truly beefy differential) is found under station wagons and other full-size cars from the early 1960's and later.

In as-found form the above four rear axles should be able to take the torque of any normal street machine, but if you can't get one of them for a swap, there are modifications you can make to your present rear end for improved reliability. However, in the case of the Mopar 7¼ or 7¾ rear end, replacement is the *only* way to go. Since the precise assembly and

To professionally set up new rear end gears, they need to be coated with white lead to read the contact pattern. It takes some patience to gain a proper pattern because you have to adjust both the pinion bearings and side-thrust (carrier) bearings (arrows).

The "locking" or posi-traction type differential is a popular performance street selection. Normally, this type of carrier has some sort of clutching arrangement that transfers all the torque to the other wheel when one begins to spin (through the clutching arrangement).

This "posi-traction" rear end has been fitted with a steel-billet left cap (the one that receives the major amount of the load) retained by aircraft Allen bolts. High-strength Allen bolts are also used to hold the two halves of the posi case together. Definitely race quality stuff.

Few driveline changes can make as much difference in performance as changing the rear gears. Seek some pro advice if it's your first time. A ratio of about 3.50-3.90:1 is reasonable for a street machine.

adjustment of a differential is beyond the scope of what we'd call "bolt-on equipment," you should contact someone in your area who does rear end work professionally, or maybe you could get one of the more knowledgeable local drag racers to help you. At any rate, if you're going to be changing to a different gear ratio in the rear end, it has to come apart. While you have it apart, you might as well make the "right moves."

All of the bolt holes in the differential assembly should be chamfered to remove burrs, taps run through to clean all the threads, and everything should be fitted with aircraft-quality bolts or Allen (socket-head) bolts for strength. These should be used for the case bolts, ring-gear bolts (Allen bolts may not clear the housing in this application), and to retain the left-side bearing cap, where most of the torque will be felt. As a general rule, have the gears set up with .004-inch backlash clearance (.006-inch for used gears) and for other than just drag-only cars, fill the assembled rear axle with 140-weight lubricant. Most factory lube is 90 weight, but the 140 weight has a stronger film strength.

We mentioned that you may want to practice the above steps of preventive maintenance on your rear axle if it is going to be down anyway for installation of different gears. While not strictly a driveway bolt-on operation, installing a performance gear ratio can be one of the most cost-effective changes you can make to a street machine. In fact, during the past five years, the gear ratios of production cars have followed the compression ratios away from high-performance. For lower emission and better fuel economy, cars today have high gear ratios like 3.00 and even 2.73, and on the highway your engine is just loafing. This makes it difficult for the engine to rev enough to produce ready horsepower when you want to pass someone or come off the line hard from a stop.

Installing a set of 3.23 or 3.55 gears can really bring your modified engine to life! Unfortunately, the stiffer (higher numerically, but lower in ratio) you go with gearing, the more

Rear end specialists who build racing assemblies often recommend that nodular iron or steel caps be used to hold the carrier to the housing. This is good, inexpensive advice for a strong street runner, especially with a four speed.

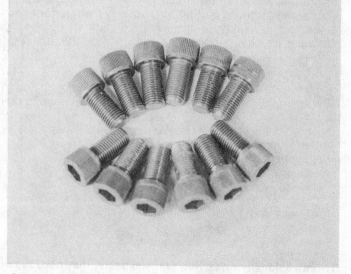

Another pro tip is to substitute grade-eight fasteners for all of the stock rear end bolts. Good bolts withstand greater strain than the stockers and they are, in effect, cheap insurance.

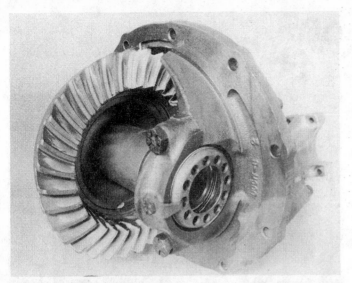

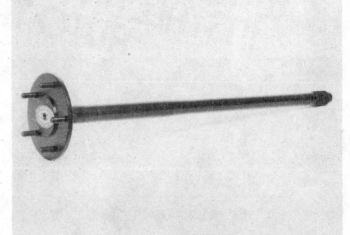

Most all-out racers are fitted with spool-type carriers. They are strong but do not provide true differentiating action between the inside and outside rear wheels as the car goes around a corner. Leave this sort of "magic" to the racers.

If you're making enough power with your street machine to twist or break a rear axle, you're probably reading this in a jail cell. Again, this is all-out racing esoterica. There must be about a million better places to spend your money.

fuel you'll use and the more wear your engine will get at the same vehicle speeds, but this is a sacrifice you have to make sometimes to get the performance you want. Even stiffer gearing like 4.11's and 4.56's used to be popular, but these really keep the engine revving even at 55 mph, and aren't recommended for cars used for transportation as well as fun. Just going up to a ratio like 3.23 or 3.55 in a smog-era machine can make as much difference in acceleration as improved cam timing and carburetion.

Whether you change gears or not, the driveline should be considered an area not to overlook in your quest for a "bulletproof" street machine.

Driveline Installation Hints

1) Never get "overenthusiatic" with a stock cast-iron flywheel. A clutch explosion can cost you your life! If you plan on any high-rpm shifts, ALWAYS install a SEMA-approved steel flywheel FIRST.

2) As a rule of thumb, a same-weight or heaver-than-stock fly-wheel will be the best choice for stop-and-start street driving, while the lighter wheel will allow faster revving and is more suited to road racing.

3) When you order a flywheel, it is often necessary to specify the diameter and the starter-ring-gear tooth count, and a disc must be ordered by diameter and the number of input shaft spline. Since optional engines and transmissions often use a unique clutch design—diameter, spline, and pressure plate tension, make sure of what you're buying before you attempt to bolt it on.

4) Clutch covers (pressure plates) are usually designed for a specific application, i.e. stock use, street/strip, or race only. Some of the super-high-performance units can be a real nightmare when it comes to hooking up the clutch linkage (and depressing the pedal without your eyes bugging out!). Stay with a pressure plate rated under 2800 pounds for the street and make sure that it is designed to install in your car without the need of linkage modification.

5) If you are replacing the throwout bearing as part of your clutch job (it's the best time to do it), carefully compare it with your old bearing—it should be identical. Any differences in length, inside diameter, finger contact surface, or clutch-fork-groove shape should not be tolerated. There may be exceptions to this in racing applications.

6) Because of the wide variety of design differences in driveline components, parts selection for clutch, transmission, drive-shaft/U-joints, and rear end modifications should be made with an extra measure of care. Pieces that don't seem quite right, probably aren't.

7) The use of Loctite or a similar liquid "lock washer" is greatly recommended in areas of high vibration. Specifically these are: trans shifter arm nuts, the shifter adapter bolts, clutch cover and flywheel bolts, and in cars with solid engine mounts just about *everything*.

8) Most posi-type rear ends must use a special "sure-grip" lube that allows the differential to lock up when needed. If regular "90 weight" is used, the posi unit can be completely disabled, although normal operation will usually be restored when the lube is replaced with the correct type.

9) U-joints that use two small metal straps to attach to the rear end yolk retain these straps by two small (usually ¼-inch) bolts. These bolts are a high grade material—grade 8 or better—and the use of "hardware quality" fasteners in this application means instant death on the first all-out pass.

10) And, finally, transmission oil coolers are a real plus in extending trans life, and engine oil coolers can at least help extend engine oil life, while reducing wear of internal parts. But all this is "for naught" if less than a proper job of plumbing is allowed. Neither the trans nor the engine will fare well if a hose or hose fitting leaks all the lubricant out on the ground.

HOW TO INSTALL AN AUTO TRANS SHIFT KIT

Installing a transmission reprogramming kit is a job anyone can tackle. To show how it's done with a Trans-Go kit on a 400 Turbo-Hydro, we shot the following sequence with the experts at Art Carr Transmission, in Fountain Valley, Calif. To start, disconnect the rod that runs up to the steering wheel lock (if your vehicle is so equipped).

Most transmissions do not have a drain plug, so taking the pan loose is the only way to drain them. Therefore, you may want to do this job when the fluid is cool. Hold the pan up with one hand when you get to the last bolt.

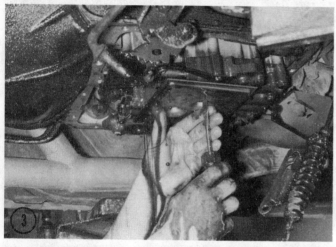

Wear your old clothes, because even after the pan is off, there'll be more fluid pouring down when you take off the transmission oil filter.

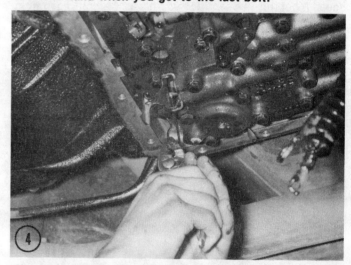

Use pliers to remove the pin holding the kick-down arm connection at the valve body.

Use a screwdriver to push down on the clip that holds the manual lever arm (forward-left corner of the valve body), then remove with your fingers.

Now you can pull the manual lever off to the side, then remove the little "S-clip" that holds the manual valve to the manual lever.

Use your speedwrench and socket to take down the bolt holding the detent roller and spring assembly in place and pull it free.

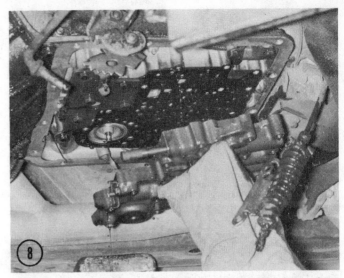

Remove all the bolts that hold the valve body to the transmission. As the last few bolts come out, more fluid will leak out, so be ready.

At the left-front corner, you'll find this spacer support plate which must be removed.

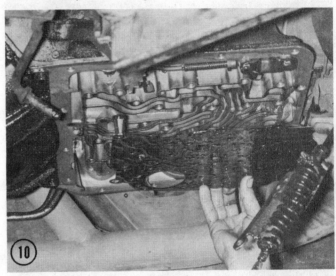

Now the valve body separator plate is ready to come down, but be ready to catch the check balls that will come out with the separator.

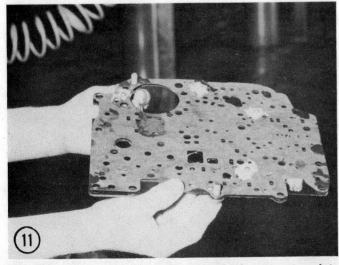

Here we have the new Trans-Go valve body separator plate with new gasket and the check balls held in place with white lithium grease. Use a few bolts to hold the gasket and plate in alignment (read instructions).

Being careful not to tilt the plate (the check balls may roll out of position if you do), put the separator plate carefully in place and use two or three bolts to hold it against the trans case.

The Trans-Go kit includes a new gasket for the spacer support plate. When it's bolted up, you can take out the separator plate bolts.

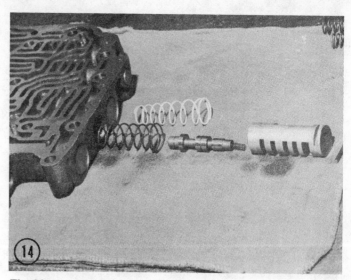

The kit comes with four special springs for the spool valves inside the valve body. This spool-valve assembly will have a new spring (the white one) when installed.

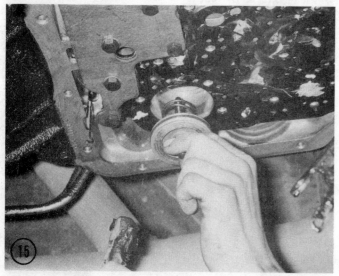

If the intermediate servo piston happens to fall out, reinstall it by coating it with thick wheel bearing grease to hold it in place. The grease will dissolve in the trans fluid.

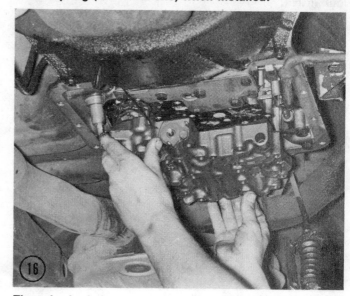

The valve body is now ready to be reinstalled and bolted in place.

Following the instructions packed with the kit, tighten the valve body bolts to the proper torque and in the correct sequence.

The S-clip, which connects the manual shift valve to the external linkage arm, can now be reinstalled. The linkage will slide to one side to allow the clip to be put in place.

The screwdriver indicates the clip that had to be pried off during the disassembly. Now you can reinstall it on the arm.

At one end of the detent roller and spring, the tab (1) must go into the hole, and the roller (2) must engage the range selector inner lever.

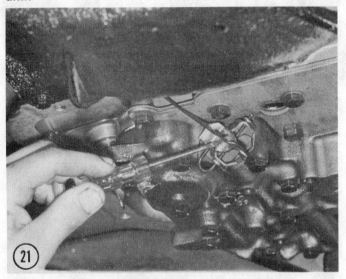

Reinstall the kick-down control arm using the same techniques as used for removal. Remember to reinsert the retaining clip removed earlier.

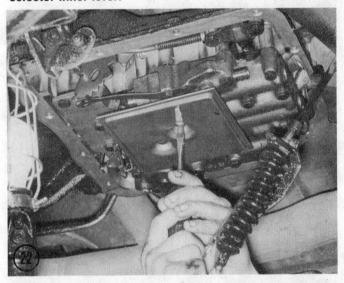

The filter can now be put back in place. Clean it thoroughly if you are reusing the stocker, but this would be an ideal time to add a new filter.

Clean the pan and case gasket surfaces and reinstall the pan on the transmission. Don't overtighten the bolts. This could cause the pan sealing surface to bend, leading to fluid leaks.

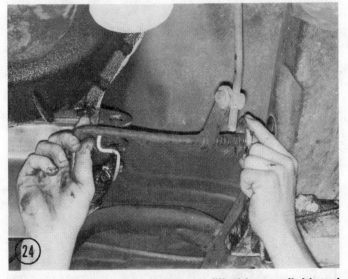

Reconnect the column-lock linkage, fill with trans fluid, and you're ready for some real high-performance automatic transmission shifting!

135

CHASSIS TUNING

Older hot rodders may remember the time when a discussion of "handling" was wasted on the average performance enthusiast. Only the "tea-baggers" in jaunty caps and driving gloves cared about whether their cars would negotiate corners quickly. The hot rodder was simply interested in going fast. Perhaps it was the burgeoning interest in Trans-Am racing in the late 1960's that got the average American performance enthusiast to start thinking about handling power. This was probably the first time large numbers of American cars were raced on road courses. The interest in handling has even spread to Detroit. Today it is not uncommon to find "special handling packages" on manufacturer option listings.

In the past the drive-in crowd often preferred to emulate their favorite quarter-mile drag racing heros with their own cars, at times jacking their suspensions up (as was the drag racing fad at that time) and installing straight-axle front ends, enormous slicks and very skinny front tires to capture the 1320 spirit. But somewhere along the line, about the beginning of the '70's, this trend began to die out, leaving only the nostalgia buffs with jacked-up chassis. (The drag racing crowd had already advanced in their own chassis designs, but the street hot rodders always seem to be a few years behind the hardcore racing fraternity). Whatever the reasons, whether it was the influence of the Trans-Am or not, street enthusiasts switched their styling emphasis towards a lower-profile vehicle in which, for the first time, the hot rodder was concerned with handling as well as straight-line performance.

This is really the key difference between the average street rodder and the reader of this chapter, we're all interested in performance, in going fast, but the enthusiast who's into handling likes going fast around corners. To him, a lonely, winding country road on a clear day is as much of a joy to negotiate as Main Street or the local dragstrip. As you probably know if you've driven one, those little foreign sports cars don't have an excess of horsepower, but what makes them fun to drive is that they have the handling to make full use of what limited power they have. When you're talking about driving in other than a straight line, whether country road or road-race track, it isn't always the car

with the biggest engine that gets to the finish line first.

Handling Elements

Being able to "go fast" around corners plays a large part in handling quality, but there are other factors. For example, braking is just as important to a good-handling car, as are steering, highway road feel, high-speed stability and even safety. Many books have been written about what handling is and how to get it, but we'll boil down some of the fancy technical terms you may have heard. Once you understand the factors that make up this complex subject, we'll get down to the nuts and bolts of what it takes to make your chassis "get down and boogie!"

Chances are, if you read road tests in automotive magazines, you've heard a lot of handling jargon, terms like understeer and oversteer, skid pad times, roll axis, etc. Most of these terms describe the various attitudes of a car negotiating a corner, how it reacts and what it does versus what you wanted it to do. *Oversteer* and *understeer* are two of the most common handling terms used. They both refer to how the car maneuvers through a turn in comparison to the input you give the steering wheel. With oversteer, the *rear* of the car swings outward on a turn due to centrifugal forces, which results in the car making a sharper turn than you intended with the steering wheel. This is more common to vehicles with a lot of weight in the rear, such as VW's,

Porsches, Corvairs and other rear-engined cars. Centrifugal force has more mass to act on at the rear than the front in such cases, so that end tends to get thrown to the outside of a curve. Most front-engined conventional cars exhibit understeer, in which the *front end* tries to drift to the outside of the curve. This causes the car to make *less* of a sharp turn than you intended. *Neutral steer* is the happy condition wherein a car goes just where you point it, no more and no less. The whole car will tend to swing to the outside of a turn, the so-called "four-wheel drift" that is conspicuous by its rarity, at least on street-driven cars.

The three conditions we've just outlined all occur near the traction limits of the car, so they aren't characteristics you'll discover while turning out of your driveway. Most drivers never know whether their car understeers or oversteers, having never pushed that hard in a corner, and they would probably consider either of the conditions as unavoidable sins caused by "driving too fast." For those who do care, Roland De Marcellus, engineer and handling expert of the ADDCO sway bar company, recommends a very simple test for determining basic handling traits with regard to steering. He suggests you find a large empty parking lot and (after attaining the owner's permission) drive a complete circle with the steering wheel held at a specific amount of turn, say half a turn, and at a specific speed such as five or ten mph. Mark the start/finish spot,

It is an unfortunate fact of life that most rodders spend far too little time getting the chassis in shape. Tons of horsepower is nice but a slick handling chassis is a pure joy to drive. Once you've experienced a proper setup you'll never be happy with a Detroit sled.

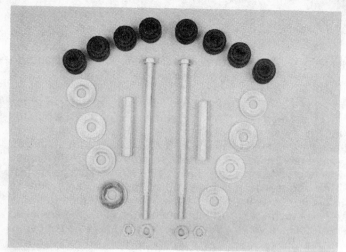

The use of worn front-end components will seriously affect handling. The replacement of worn parts is an essential first step in improving handling, and this TRW rebuild kit for the sway-bar link is just one of their many HD components.

These rebuild kits are for a '69 Camaro, which was one of the best handling cars ever offered. The addition of these TRW kits will restore the original handling qualities and prevent excessive tire wear (which can also improve gas mileage).

and try again several times, increasing the speed by five or ten more mph each time. Understeer would make your car take a larger circle, and if you kept making a *smaller* circle as you went faster, then you would be oversteering.

The importance of understanding these basic handling traits should be obvious even to the average driver. Just take one look at the outside curbing on a sharp turn or freeway off-ramp and check the number of black tire marks left by malhandling cars.

Your Stock Suspension

Unless you're driving an imported car, sports car or one of the new breed of minicars, you have the suspension design of the typical American sedan, which is to say, a chassis designed more for smooth riding than good handling. Chances are you have an unequal-length A-arm, independent front end, a solid rear axle suspended

by coil or leaf springs, and 60% or more of the total vehicle weight is carried by the front end. Given the forward weight bias, large amount of body overhang behind the rear axle and the typically mushy Detroit suspension, we'd guess your car falls easily into the understeer category. When you round a corner hard at higher speeds, the inside wheels unload and the outside wheels carry the extra load as the car leans heavily to the outside of the turn. More than likely, your tires will be screaming while your front end slides to the outside, an unpleasant condition roundy-round racers refer to as "pushing."

A few factors that influence cornering characteristics are the roll axis, center of gravity, and weight distribution. The roll axis is a theoretical line through the car, about which the car "rotates" as it leans in a corner. You may have heard the terms front and rear "roll centers," these are the points where the roll axis intersects

the projected planes of the front and rear spindles or axles. The front roll center is usually lower than the rear, falling somewhere between the engine and the ground on the average car, while the rear roll center is usually just above the rear axle. This forward slope of the roll axis creates extra body lean for the front of the car on cornering, because weight is transferring forward (as well as outward). This may aggravate an understeer condition by making the front end even more likely to slide, and this is particularly evident on cars of smaller wheel bases.

The center of gravity should be self-explanatory, it is the imaginary point within the vehicle where the balance of weight is the same in all three planes; fore and aft, side to side, and top to bottom. It should be your concern to lower the C.G., as this reduces the amount of body lean. When the C.G. is substantially higher than the roll axis, it means you have a considerable force working about that

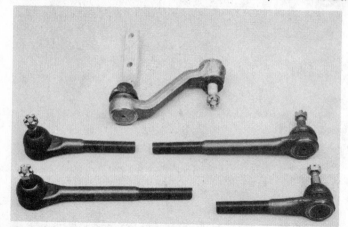

Precise steering is a joy to know. Once again TRW has a deal you can hardly pass up. New idler arm and steering rod ends will often eliminate the "mushy" steering feel. Mario Andretti, move over.

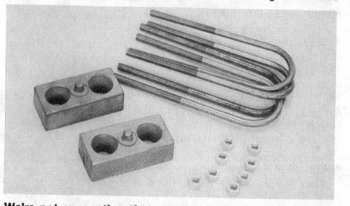

We're not suggesting that you get into the low-rider type modifications, but lowering the center of gravity of your car to a safe level and with safe devices can vastly improve cornering and road-holding. These are Genuine Suspension lowering blocks for leaf-sprung rear axles. They fit between the rear axle and the rear springs.

axis, leverage that works against any suspension aids you may employ. This is one of the reasons the "jacked-up" look faded away from the street scene.

Weight distribution plays an important role, too. The more weight there is at either end of the car, that end could be the one to slide first in a corner (within limits—an excessively light axle can also slide). Getting a conventional car to have the majority of sprung weight over the rear driving wheels is not easy and, as a consequence, we have typical understeer. A balanced 50-50 weight distribution in a passenger car is something even true sports cars seldom achieve.

Performance Tires and Wheels

You might expect this section to be concerned solely with a lot of suspension part numbers and math about theoretical chassis designs, but the plain truth is, the *most important* changes you can affect for handling are very basic and simple—tires and wheels. The addition of wider, better-handling tires and corresponding wheels can make more difference in street machine handling than any manner of trick shocks and anti-sway bars.

Several pages could be written about selecting tires for high-performance cars, but we'll try to give you the basics before you get "tired out." Tires represent the final contact between the car and the road surface; acceleration, braking and cornering power are affected seriously by the type and size of tires you select. Some enthusiasts run out to a tire and wheel shop to purchase the absolutely largest tires and wheels they can fit under their car, even to the point of virtually destroying the suspension to gain necessary tire clearance. While they may be under the impression that the larger tires give a better "grip," most such tires are purchased simply on the basis of looks. They look "mean." Race cars have huge tires, so why shouldn't street machines? Actually, unless you lower the air pressure or make the car heavier, the amount of rubber on the road will remain almost the same, although the contact patch with wider tires will be wider (although shorter, so the area remains nearly the same). The wider tires do, however, have the advantages of a wider vehicle track for better handling, less instability on road irregularities, less sidewall flexing and tread heat.

There is a lot of talk going around about the differences between standard tires, belted tires, and radials. Basically, the standard tire has biased plies, plies that run forward and back around the circumference of the tire, with succeeding plies (layers of cord) running at shallow angles to each other. The radial-ply tire has the cords running at right angles to each other. The popular belted tires have plies (usually two) that run straight around the circumference of the tire, with conventional angled plies underneath and on the sidewalls. In this respect they are a compromise between the bias-ply and radial-ply tires. With this extra stiffening in the tread area, the belted tires are better for handling than conventional bias-ply tires, but perhaps not quite as good as radials, and not as expensive either. Radials are said to give the best handling because they have a flexible sidewall that allows the tread to remain in contact with the road longer, but they also do not give you as much of a warning when they are ready to lose traction in a corner. Still, the radial design is the top choice of sports car manufacturers the world over.

With regard to size, this will depend partly on the rims you can use. You can't fit a tire that is much wider than stock on a stock rim. You should use the widest tire you can fit under your fenderwells without uncomfortably increasing the steering effort, but this will surely mean buying a set of wider wheels to mount them on. Luckily, there is not a lack of companies that will be glad to sell you a set of special wheels.

Actually, there are a number of good reasons for using a set of "mag" wheels. They improve handling by their reduced weight compared to steel wheels of the same size. A lighter vehicle is easier to accelerate and brake, and lighter wheels reduce "unsprung" weight. The weight advantage (at least in those wheels which are really made of magnesium or cast aluminum and not a steel rim with aluminum centers) may be partially offset by the increased weight of the

Trick wheels are a sure way to add some class but they can also aid handling. If you find some wheels that are lighter than the stock ones, you can decrease "unsprung" weight. This increases the efficiency of the springs and shock absorbers.

Few performance improvements can beat the addition of a set of wider tires and suitable rims for increased cornering power as well as improved appearance. These steel-belted radials and lightweight rims reduce unsprung weight and the tires could last as long as 40,000-50,000 miles.

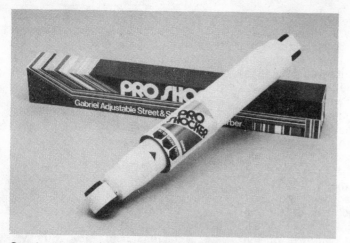

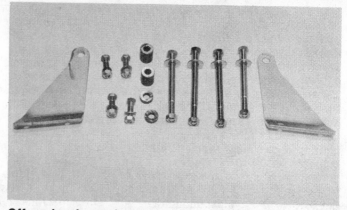

Stock shock absorbers just don't do the job when you need increased cornering power or better performance at the drag strip. Gabriel's new Pro Shocker is perfect for the weekend bracket car because it is adjustable for both street and strip valving.

Off-road racing and travel has become popular all over the country and many people are finding that a stock suspension just doesn't cut it in the rough going. To avoid overworking and overheating the stock shocks, Advance Adapters makes this simple bolt-on kit for Chevy pickups that allows installation of dual shocks at each front wheel for more control.

larger tires but overall weight should still be down a little.

The wider wheels and tires improve handling, but they have the drawback of possibly creating accelerated wheel bearing wear if the extra rim width is offset to the outside of the vehicle. *Ideally*, the new wheels should center the new tires right where the stock tire centerline was, with the extra width equally divided on either side of the inner and outer wheel bearings.

Don't buy your new wheels based solely on price, either. You want safe wheels above all, so look for those wheels that are marked as having passed the rigid SEMA specs (Specialty Equipment Manufacturers Assoc.). It's probably true that the majority of custom wheels and tires are purchased for looks alone, but you won't go wrong if, in addition to pleasing looks, you buy your wheels based on weight, safety and proper size for the tire and vehicle.

Suspension Modifications

If you have more than 30,000 miles on your car, you probably need new shock absorbers, and now is the perfect time to upgrade to shocks more suited to your handling needs. Movement of your wheels is controlled by your springs, but the action of the springs is tempered or dampened by the shock absorbers, which contain fluid that travels through internal orifices to change the amount of dampening depending on the speed and amount of wheel travel. In other words, the shocks exert a specific resistance to the springs at a given rate of wheel deflection on a bump or corner, and a faster movement (a more severe bump or rut) creates more resistance.

With larger wheels and tires, you'll need heavier shocks to keep control over the heavier wheel momentum. However, you can go too stiff on shocks, because a truly stiff suspension will corner worse. Hitting a bump in a corner will make a stiff rear suspension bounce away from the pavement, creating oversteer and loss of traction. The heavy-duty shocks found in discount stores and auto parts stores are fine for the average car, but they won't be handling "cure-alls."

If you're really serious about making your machine a cornering king, investigate some of the special performance/racing shocks, such as the adjustable and the triple-valved shocks. Adjustable shocks allow you to dial in the stiffness of "valving" that you desire for the street, and even gain more stiffness for rallying or gymkhana competition. The so-called triple-valved shocks have sets of compression and rebound valves that control initial, intermediate, and high-speed movement. By segmenting the range of valving, the shock engineer can arrange better control of bumps, cornering forces, and high-speed driving jounce (where ills of lower speed are magnified). When higher vehicle speeds or wheel travel speeds are encountered, the pressure built up inside the triple-valve shock releases a spring-loaded secondary orifice which has a different level of control, and at even higher speeds a third valve may be opened. The idea is to reduce the rate of roll angle increase and thereby reduce understeer. (The roll angle is that angle between the ground and a line drawn parallel to the plane of

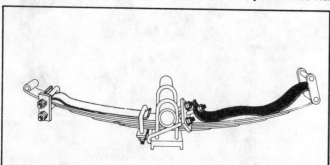

Trucks, especially those that haul a trailer or a camper to the races, need extra spring control to compensate for the added weight, and sometimes a set of overload spring leaves like these (Hellwig) do it.

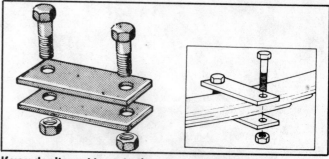

If you don't want to go to the expense of adding traction bars and need a temporary solution to spring "wrap-up" during acceleration, you can bolt these spring clamps along your leaf springs to stiffen them. This should increase axle control without seriously affecting ride comfort.

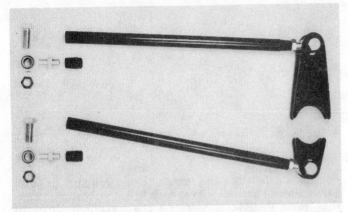

Rigid traction bars like these Harwood pieces look good and work great on race cars but have virtually no ride cushioning and so increase ride stiffness considerably. They aren't recommended for street unless you are willing to sacrifice some ride comfort.

Bolt-on traction bars like these from Lakewood will help reduce wheel shudder on leaf-sprung clutch-equipped cars and will not substantially reduce ride quality. A better, but more expensive, solution is a stiffer set of springs.

your bumpers.) Reduced roll angle means less lean on corners, but heavier-duty shocks carry with them an inevitable penalty in ride comfort. The stiffer the shocks are in reacting to bumps and quick cornering forces (weight transfer from side to side), the harsher they will also be in overall riding quality, so don't go too heavy.

Rear shock action can be improved even without buying new shocks, simply by applying a little Detroit musclecar engineering. Chevrolet started the trend with the early Z-28 Camaros by staggering the rear shocks, that is, mounting one shock (the right shock) ahead of the rear axle, and one shock behind. This results in better resistance to the twisting tendency of the rear axle under acceleration and braking, almost like a traction bar. You'll probably have to make new upper and lower shock mounts to do this (although some specialty traction bars are designed with staggered mounts), so this is usually not an easy "bolt-on" modifica-

tion, but it is something to consider if you are willing to do some fabricating.

This brings us to the subject of traction bars. If you're going to do some serious weekend drag racing, then by all means you'll have to have a set of these to control wheel hop on leaf-sprung cars (although some leaf suspensions, including most Mopar cars, and most coil-sprung rear ends need no extra traction bars at least for street or dual-purpose use). What the traction bars do is limit the amount of spring "wrap-up" that can take place during hard acceleration and braking. This is murder on springs and causes a loss of traction. There are other ways of stiffening the springs to handle this problem, such as attaching a number of clamps along the leaves or adding extra spring leaves, but these really stiffen the ride considerably. You may have need of the spring-stiffening only once in a while, but the harsh ride will always be there.

The best types of traction bars available today are those that bolt on

either under or in place of your stock spring plates. They run forward underneath the spring leaves and end with a rubber snubber that contacts the front spring eye under acceleration, limiting axle "twist." There may also be a clamp between the forward part of the spring and the traction bar, which would help some on braking traction, but such clamps will harshen your ride. Whatever design you choose, whether the old-fashioned weld-to-the-chassis type or the bolt-on variety, the front pivot point or snubber should not be any further forward than your front spring eye, and preferably just the same length, so that the spring and traction bar pivot at the same point and don't fight each other.

If there is one kind of suspension modification which carries less of a penalty in ride quality for its contribution to handling, it is the addition of heavy-duty anti-sway bars. Next to adding the proper tires and wheels, anti-sway bars can probably do the most for cornering power. A front

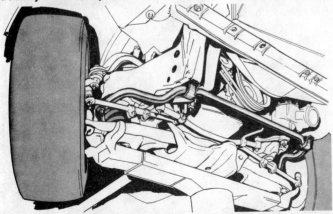

On most conventional chassis the front anti-sway bar is the only component that will counter body lean in a corner. A larger diameter, stiffer bar will reduce roll compliance but will also increase oversteer unless the rear roll stiffness is also increased by adding a rear sway bar or by increasing the stiffness of the factory installed rear bar.

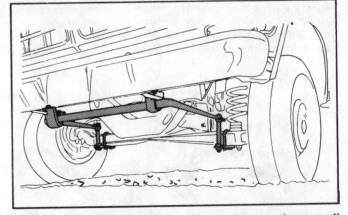

Finding the proper balance between front and rear roll stiffness can be a little difficult for the novice. Several companies offer anti-sway bars in various sizes (stiffness). The best way to determine what you need is to find a large empty parking lot and test the chassis for understeer or oversteer.

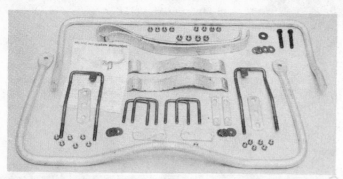

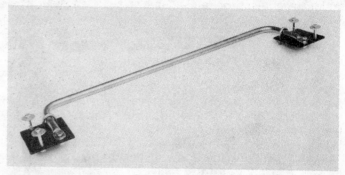

Vans and trucks may also benefit from chassis modifications and many handling kits are available to take some of the body sway and instability out of these top-heavy machines. This is one of Hellwig's complete van suspension kits.

For many cars with solid rear axles and coil springs, sway bars are made to fit solidly to each lower control arm, where they exert their twist force on the arms instead of the chassis. This is the style of most optional factory rear sway bars.

anti-sway bar is basically just a torsion bar connecting the front suspension members on one side of the car to those on the other side. The anti-sway bar allows both wheels to move when subjected to the same bump or force, but when just one wheel tries to move, the movement is resisted, and this resistance is fed to the other wheel (in a corner, body lean is reduced by attempting to lift the inside wheel). They will not stiffen your suspension when encountering a force that is equal for both wheels, such as crossing a frost heave or railroad tracks, but on small bumps there might be a sacrifice in ride quality. Most cars today have at least a front anti-sway bar, and many of the performance models or heavy-duty suspension packages include a rear bar, too.

Since our objective is to reduce the understeer caused by our forward weight bias, a stiff front anti-sway bar is not exactly a cure-all, since it can contribute to the oversteer itself and overload the outside tire even though body lean is reduced. If the car already has a front anti-sway bar, a technique to improve handling and cut understeer would be to improve the rear suspension with a rear anti-sway bar. Many performance enthusiasts add a thicker-than-stock (thus stiffer)

anti-sway bar up front, which should definitely be coupled with a new rear bar. If your car doesn't have front or rear bars, the addition of mild aftermarket bars on both ends should make a dramatic difference in handling! You'll notice after driving your car hard with anti-roll bars installed that the tires don't squeal nearly as much as they used to, and the steering will seem more responsive.

Anti-sway bars (incorrectly called roll bars or sway bars by some) come in varying diameters and stiffness rates, and it is best for the beginner to go by the manufacturer's recommendations as to which is specifically suited for the type of driving intended. If you do only occasional "sports car driving" you won't need as stiff bars as you would for a car being set up for rallies or slalom competition. And don't make the mistake of just going by the bar diameter in determining stiffness. Since the middle of the bar is attached (in rubber bushings) to the chassis and the outer ends to the wheels, the length of the bar that is between these mounts (the part that actually gets twisted) and the length of the arms that go to the wheels also have an effect on stiffness. How far our towards the tire the end of the bar is attached to the wheel suspension will also affect sway stiffness.

If there is one chassis facet that is generally overlooked as a contribution to handling, it is the brakes. We tend to think of the brakes as one of those systems that either works or doesn't work, with little room for improvement, and worse yet, little understanding of the need for improvement. After all, your car stops, doesn't it? But having really good braking capability can easily be likened in its psychological effect on the driver to improved steering response, roll control and high-speed directional stability. No one has to tell a race car driver how important brakes are, he knows that better brakes allow him to drive deeper into a corner, secure in the knowledge that he can depend on his brakes to help him through the turn. In this sense, braking efficiency and reliability has been the winner of almost as many sports-car or road races as high-horsepower engines.

But what can I do to give my car more braking power, you may be asking? There are several avenues available. Assuming that your car has drum brakes all around, we might suggest investigating the possibility of adding disc brakes up front. This can often be done by swapping spindles with another model in the same car line, such as GTO discs on a Tempest

Good brakes are every bit as important to handling as wide tires and special shocks. One of the best improvements you make with drum brakes is to add a set of metallic linings. These powered-metal linings require more pedal pressure (especially when cold) but they are rugged and won't fade.

If you've added a healthy front sway bar you should have a moderate rear bar to balance out the car. Most rear sway bars bolt on to the lower control arms or clamp to the rear axle and have separate links to connect with the chassis.

or Mustang discs on a Fairlane or Falcon, etc. There's a lot of interchangeability between the early muscle cars and similar production models. On some cars the swap can be made strictly as a bolt-on proposition. By the same token, larger drum brakes can also be fitted to your car, from one of the larger and heavier cars in the same line, such as Lincoln brakes for a Mustang, full-size Chevy brakes on a Nova, or Charger spindles and drums for the "A" body cars. In the case of the drum brake swaps, this is usually a simple job, and a natural swap if the stock brakes are due for a replacement anyway. Not only will the larger brakes give you better stopping power, they will also go a lot longer on a set of shoes, since they are being used on a car that is lighter than their original design intended. However, if larger brakes are installed on the front only, the disproportionate braking effort may require the use of a proportioning valve—an excellent adjustable unit that is used on Corvettes is available from GM.

If you already have sufficient brakes on your machine, or don't want the possible hassles of a swap, then you might investigate using metallic brake linings in your current brakes. These are available for both drum and disc systems, and instead of the "organic" lining compositions of asbestos found in standard linings and pads (that, by the way, is known to cause cancer and lung disease if the dust is inhaled), these have material composed of fused metallic powders. Several specialty companies market these linings for popular applications, and if yours is an oddball, there may be a local brake reliner in your area who can install such material on your existing shoes or pads. Except for having your drums ground for a very fine finish, there is no difference in installation of these metallic brakes from any other kind of linings. The metallic linings may cause some acceleration of drum wear, but the linings seem to last almost forever (we've seen sets go longer than 70,000 miles!) and they exhibit virtually no

fading under harsh conditions. Basically, the hotter the metallic brakes get, the better they stop, just the opposite of stock linings. Trailer-towing and mountain driving are perfect for these brakes, they accept the challenge without a whimper or squeal. If there is a drawback to the metallic brakes, it is that they do take greater pedal effort (not a problem if you have a power booster), just as disc brakes take more effort, and they need a few stops in the morning before they warm up and reach full effectiveness.

Chassis improvements, like changes made to the driveline, may not be as glamorous as adding a hood scoop or chromed valve covers, but they nevertheless pay dividends in improved safety and performance. Once you've experienced driving your car, or any car, with superior handling capabilities, you'll discover a whole new world of driving. All those twisty back roads you previously avoided will now seem like they were expressly designed for the enjoyment of handling-minded drivers and their reponsive machines!

Chassis Tuning Hints

1) Rear end "high rise" packages will, in fact, raise the rear of the car so that it may look like a streamlined rocket sled, but it sure won't handle like it is on rails. Raising the rear end transfers more weight to an already front-heavy distribution, making the vehicle much more likely to suffer from excessive oversteer.

2) The front anti-sway bar, a very important part of a good handling machine, will function at its optimum only if the mounts are in the best of condition. The chassis mounts should be solidly bolted to the frame and the rubber bushings like new. The suspension ends will often benefit from "solid" nylon-type bushings, but, in any case, should transfer as much wheel motion as possible to the bar ends.

3) The selection of high-performance tires designed to exhibit good handling characteristics is the single most effective modification that you can make to your chassis/suspension. But long tread life and optimum road performance is possible only when the suspension bushings, ball joints and alignment are "right on."

4) The installation of "heavy-duty" or "extended-life" front end components (a complete set for most

applications is offered by TRW) is an excellent investment, because the relatively high cost of installation (working on front ends isn't cheap) is amortized over a longer life. Also, the amount of time that the suspension remains in "right-on" shape is extended.

5) Above all else, when involved with front-end work your main concern should be *safety!* Don't take short cuts by eliminating cotter pins or lock washers. These practices can be fatal, but don't let us scare you off either. Taking a little extra time to *make sure* all is done right (or having it checked over by an experienced individual) is never a waste of time.

6) If you must turn your steering wheel more than 3½ turns to go from lock to lock (from full left to full right turn), you can improve road "feel" by adding a quicker ratio steering box. Depending on the kind of car you have, there are manual steering boxes down to about two turns lock to lock, and in power to about one and one-half turns (and that's plenty quick!).

7) A more drastic modification to improve handling is changing the front and rear spring rate. With a coil sprung car, this is usually no easy project, although if the

car uses front torsion bars, the chore can be much reduced. In either case, the vehicle will ride a good deal stiffer and can generally be considered less steerable, although this really depends on what you want and how you define "steerable."

8) Adjustable shock absorbers, much easier to install than stiffer springs, are a good second-choice modification (and not a bad first-choice "mod" either). Most adjustables have three positions that govern the installed stiffness. Generally speaking, the "lowest" setting is just about stock, the next is firm, and the last is often teeth-jarring stiff.

9) As safety should be foremost in your mind, the braking system is not to be overloaded. *At least*, the entire system should be fully operational and leak free. Just as much a part of "high-performance" as the engine, the brakes can benefit from the installation of specialty equipment that can improve life and functionalism.

10) The most effective modification that can be made to drum brakes is to *replace* them with disc brakes. Discs offer longer pad life, better high-speed braking, are less affected by water, and don't require periodic adjustment. The ultimate setup is disc brakes on all four wheels.

HOW TO INSTALL AIR SHOCKS

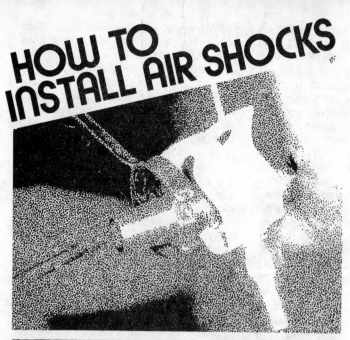

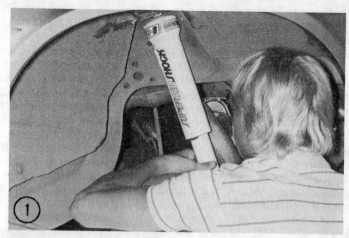

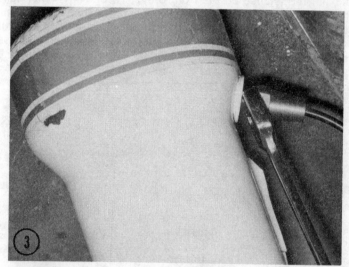

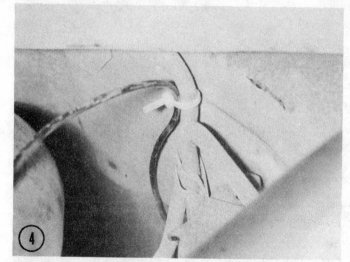

Except for the routing of the air lines, installation of a set of air shocks is no more difficult than in changing stock shocks. Hurst Super Airshocks were chosen for this Camaro. At the top of the inner fenderwall, you can see scrape marks made by the tires before the Hurst shocks were installed.

Extend the shocks by hand and slip the upper mounting stud through the hole in the body, then install the lower mounting bolts. From inside the trunk or under the back seat cushion you can reach the upper mounting nut. Use a small wrench to hold the square end of the shock stud, tighten the nut down and install the locknut.

With both shocks installed, angle each one so that the air fittings point inward. Hook a new fitting, ferrule and line to each shock, with a short line on one and a long one on the other.

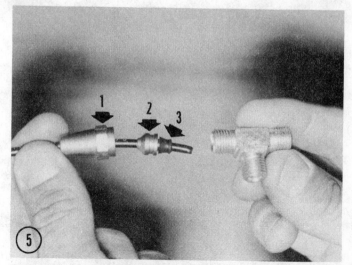

Route the long line from one shock to the opposite side of the car, over the rear axle. Use the plastic ties supplied to fasten the air line to a fuel or brake line to keep it away from the rear axle and exhaust pipes.

Tight and clean connections must be made if you don't want the shocks to leak air. Each connection is made with the plastic hose sticking through the brass nut (1), the tapered compression fitting (2), and the rubber ferrule (3).

144

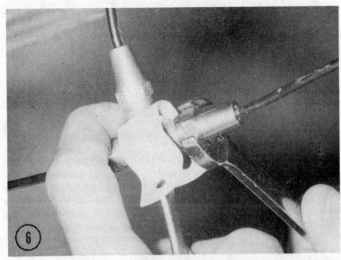

The air lines from each shock are joined with a brass T-fitting. Use a wrench to hold the fitting while you tighten each nut. The third line is the one that will run to the rear of the car for the filler valve.

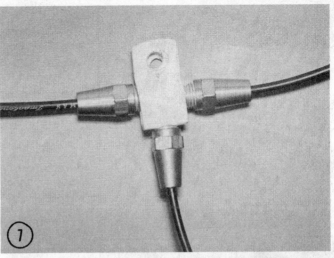

A plastic clamp is supplied with the Hurst shocks and is slipped over the T-fitting before assembly. This allows for mounting the fitting to the car with one of the self-tapping screws.

The T-fitting was mounted on the left side of the Camaro underbody, away from the exhaust. One line leads to the right shock, another to the left shock (short line) and one goes rearward toward the gravel pan.

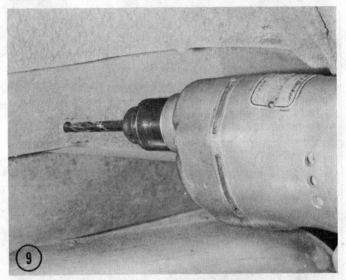

Going rearward along the underbody, there were no convenient lines to which the air hose could be clipped, so holes had to be drilled for press-in clips.

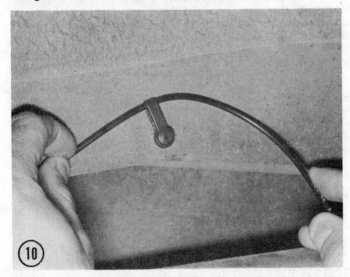

Leave sufficient length in the hoses so that you can route them without kinks. The plastic clips supplied will snap into the holes you drilled, keeping things sanitary.

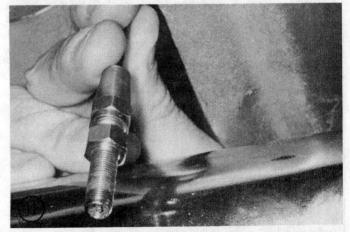

At the rear gravel pan, a hole is drilled for mounting the filler valve. For street use a common filler is used for both shocks. For drag racing a separate filler could be used for each shock, allowing the right shock to be pressurized more than the left. This is a neat way to "tune" the chassis so the car will leave the line straight.

CHASSIS & DRIVELINE BUYERS GUIDE

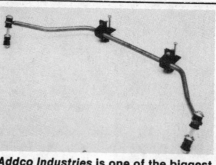

Addco Industries is one of the biggest names in specialty sway-bar kits. In addition to their quality add-on front and rear sway-bar kits, they also offer a very informative and valuable booklet on suspension.

Advance Adapters are specialists in the four-wheel drive and truck market. Among their many goodies is this "leveling block" kit which, when mounted on those trucks with the springs mounted above the axle, becomes a suspension raising kit.

B&B Performance Products markets dozens of helpful products for the racer or hot rodder, with some chassis and suspension goodies among them.

B&M Performance Products is a well known name in automatic transmission performance. They not only sell many complete transmissions for racing and street use, but also coolers, shifters, and other trans items.

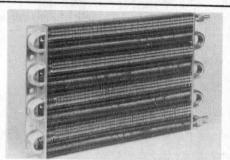

Cheshire Manufacturing markets a complete line of automatic transmission coolers for street and RV use. Models are available to fit every application, including dual engine/transmission oil coolers.

Chrysler Direct Connection dealers have a number of items that could be of interest to the chassis/driveline shopper, including this package of parts they call the "shift improver." It fits only Torqueflites, naturally.

Gabriel Division of Maremont Corp. is the name behind this famous line of shock absorbers, which ranges from simple and heavy-duty replacement shocks to handling shocks, street and strip models.

Harbor Industries are experts in triple-chrome-plating and among the items their catalog lists are chromed heavy-steel rear end covers for the popular 10-bolt, 12-bolt and Dana rears.

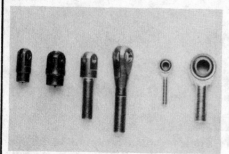

Harwood Performance Sales is one of the leading manufacturers of race car hardware, particularly in the area of chassis parts for traction, handling, and rear axle control.

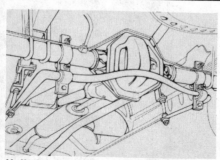

Hellwig Products are specialists in heavy-duty suspensions. Their catalog of accessory sway bars, overload springs and steering stabilizers concentrates on the truck and van market.

Hurst is the biggest name in shifters and their reputation is well earned. They also offer performance shock absorbers.

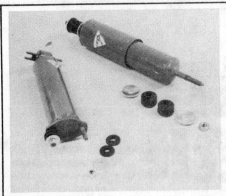

Kensington Products is the U.S. distributor for the famous Koni shocks made in Europe. They are expensive, but ruggedly built, fully adjustable and many Koni models are rebuildable.

Lakewood Industries is known for their entire line of chassis/driveline performance parts, such as traction bars, snubbers, wedges, bushings, heavy-duty U-joints, motor mounts, metallic brakes, and their famous hydro-formed bellhousings.

Maier Racing is the source for Ford performance engine and chassis parts. Their inventory includes not only the many special parts that they manufacture for Mustangs and Shelbys, but also many original high-performance Ford parts that may not be available from Ford dealers anymore.

Racer Walsh Company specializes in Pinto equipment, with a complete line of high-performance and racing parts from engine equipment to suspension goodies for street or slalom.

Rocket Racing Products manufactures a wide range of products for high performance, many of them in the chassis/driveline area, such as this cast-aluminum 12-bolt rear end cover, finned for heat dissipation.

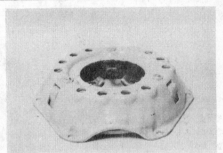

Schiefer is one of the oldest names in performance clutches. They provide extensive assistance to racers but they have super-duty clutches and flywheels for street, too.

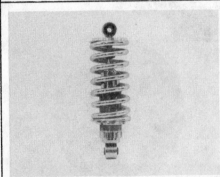

Carrera Shock Absorbers specializes in asphalt and dirt circle track suspension equipment. They have the parts and the advice to help any serious racer.

Thermo-Chem Corporation is one of the leading manufacturers of coolers for automatic transmissions, with a line of engine coolers as well, and complete combination units.

Trans-Go has over the years built a considerable reputation for their line of transmission reprogramming kits, a term they coined.

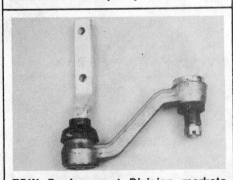

TRW Replacement Division markets their stock and heavy-duty parts for engines, chassis and drivelines. They have an excellent line of replacement front end and steering components.

Turbo Action builds a complete line of automatic transmission products, including converters, shift kits (like this one) and complete transmissions built up for racing, street, or RV use.

Weber Performance Products builds a diversified line of items including camshafts, high-torque starter motors, and performance clutches, discs and flywheels. This is their "combination pressure plate", a B&B style unit with an exclusive 360° cover design.

147

INSTRUMENTS & ACCESSORIES

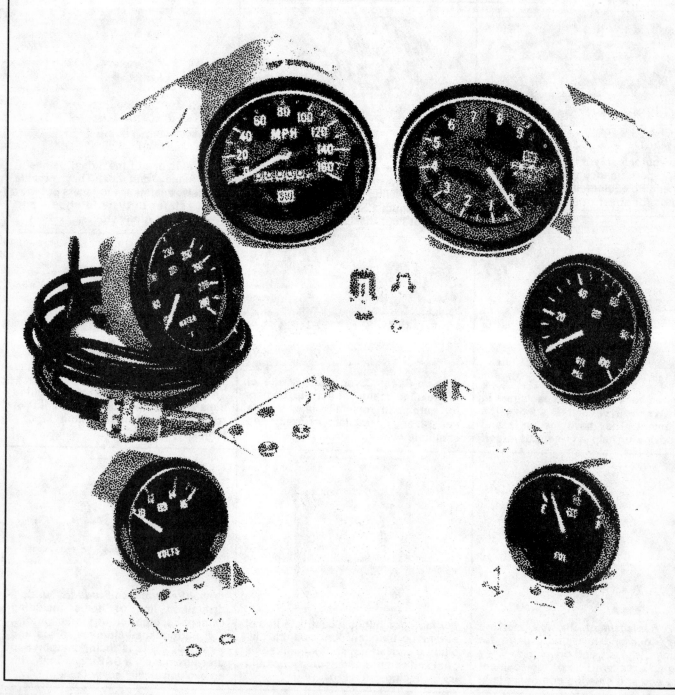

Although we have chosen to spend our last chapter looking at accessories and instruments, this is one of the most important and usually one of the first areas of interest for the neophyte hot rodder. Chrome accessories add sparkle and eye appeal to any performance engine. They also have functional advantages in some cases, as we will soon see. Engine instruments, on the other hand, are almost totally considered as functional improvements, in that they help the rodder keep track of how his engine is operating. Every performance engine, no matter how little it is modified, should be fitted with the basic monitoring gauges. These instruments will give early warning if a slight malfunction occurs. Often this will prevent a costly engine failure, a likely occurrence if a small problem is permitted to grow into a large problem.

Chrome Accessories

The range of accessories for a performance engine runs from chrome air cleaners to special manifold bolts. The full spectrum of possibilities is unbelievable! No matter what you can imagine, somewhere, someplace, someone makes it. There is, in fact, so much available that it's often difficult to decide what to buy. Unless you have an unlimited budget, you're going to have to be selective about these things. It would take hundreds of pages to explore all of the possibilities but we'll take a shot at some of the more important items.

Previously in the carburetor chapter we talked about air cleaners. It's

worth going over the subject again. This is one area where many newcomers make mistakes. A bright, shiny chrome air cleaner looks great sitting on top of your new Holley carb. But, remember one thing - if that carb has a maximum flow capacity of 700 cubic feet of air-per-minute, the air cleaner has to have at least equal flow.

It is difficult to look at an air cleaner/filter and tell exactly how much flow capacity it has, but we can learn a little from past experience. In the late 60's and early 70's when the Detroit engineers were into performance they studied the problem with their sophisticated computers. They developed some excellent air cleaners that were designed specifically to provide enough clean air to feed high-performance carburetors with flow capacities as high as 800 cfm. If you want to be sure your new engine is not choked by the air cleaner, look at what these engineers developed and buy something similar.

There are two important things to note. These factory-designed cleaners were usually large in diameter, often measuring 12-16 inches across. They were also usually pretty tall. Often the filter element was 3-4 inches thick. The filter element was also very special. Usually they were made of a special porous paper, folded several times around the perimeter of the element. All of this accomplished one important thing. It provided a *large area of filter!* So, even if the filter eventually became partially clogged by dust (as it surely will unless you change the element every week), there was still enough area of filter to allow sufficient air flow for the carburetor/ engine needs.

Fortunately, in recent years the performance manufacturers have been making suitable large-capacity air

cleaners. Excellent models are now available from Moroso and K&N filters. Hooker headers also distributes the excellent line of oil-wetted foam filters previously sold by Filtron.

One last piece of advice, don't attempt to run a performance engine on the street without an air cleaner. The engine will ingest an enormous amount of dust (you have no idea how much dust and dirt flies around under the hood of a typical car, even while the driving slowly down a paved street). All of this junk winds up inside the cylinders and leads to dirty oil, scored cylinder walls, increased ring wear and bearing problems. If you really care about performance, buy a large-diameter, high-capacity air filter and change the filter element often.

Valve covers—this is another big area of interest. When you first begin modifying an engine for performance, it's going to be a temptation to buy some fancy chrome or aluminum valve covers. There's really nothing wrong with the idea. This adds a touch of "class" to the engine and may even serve a valuable function. The stock engine valve covers are often stamped from thin metal and can easily be bent or warped if the hold-down bolts are tightened too much. If you have the covers off the engine often to adjust the valves, it is very easy to inadvertently bend the metal around the hold-down bolt if you lean on the wrench a little too much. This leads to leaks and grimy oil all over the side of your new engine. A good quality cast aluminum valve cover will greatly reduce this problem.

The gasket flange around a cast aluminum valve cover is much stiffer than on a stamped steel (or stamped aluminum) cover. If you glue the valve cover gasket to the flange on the cast aluminum cover and tighten the

One of the most popular and most essential add-on accessories is the performance air cleaner. Swapping carbs may require a new air cleaner. Look for a large diameter, tall filter element.

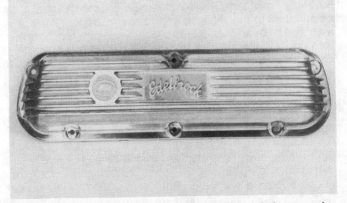

Every hi-po engine has to have a pair of fancy valve covers. Stamped metal covers bend easily. Cast aluminum covers will usually provide a better oil-tight seal without distortion along the gasket rail.

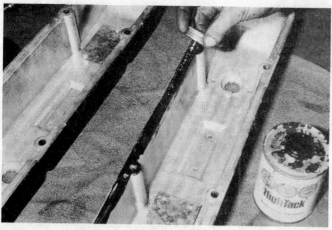

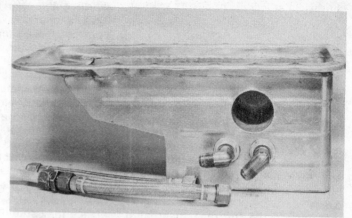

If you must remove the covers often to adjust valve running clearance, it is a good idea to glue the cover gasket directly to the flange. Use cork gaskets and don't over-tighten the holddown bolts.

Oil pans have become the latest glamour item. If you use a specialty pan make sure it fits your chassis/engine combination and will work with your oil pump pickup. It is often necessary to fabricate an extended pickup to insure against aeration and starvation on hard acceleration.

hold-down bolts evenly, such a cover will provide excellent leak-proof sealing for quite a long time.

There are several stamped metal covers currently being sold for racers who use stud tie-bars. These covers are taller than the stock covers and allow extra clearance for the tie-bars, which usually are quite a bit taller than stock or posi-lock type adjusters. These are fine for racing and can be suitably used for street engines as long as you tighten the hold-down bolts carefully. These stamped covers are usually quite thin (supposedly to save weight) and will bend even easier than stock covers. Recently, some companies have been making tall covers out of cast aluminum. If weight is not a major factor (after all, how much can a valve cover weigh), these would be an excellent choice as they would clear the stud tie-bar and still allow an oil-proof seal on a daily-driven engine.

Before you spend the money on any specialty valve cover, make certain it has all of the holes, plugs or access caps you will need. If you have a street engine with smog equipment, you will probably have some hoses that must be plumbed to the valve cover and you may have to add oil to the engine through an access cap in the valve cover. Make certain your new fancy chrome covers will "function" just like the old ones. You have a big problem if you bolt on those new beauties and then you don't have any way to put oil into the engine!

On the bottom of the engine sits a ubiquitous piece of stamped metal called the oil pan. It is about as glamorous as a dirt clod. But, never fear, the relentless marketeers have another way of prying open your wallet. Just as valve covers and air cleaners have become big eye-appeal items, the oil pan has recently been "glamorized." Racers spend a great deal of time and effort controlling the oil inside the pan. Road racers and drag racers want to make certain that the engine has a steady flow of reasonably cool oil. This is stored inside the pan and is drawn out by the pickup of the oil pump. If you spend a lot of time going around corners at 100 mph or you have a street Pro Stocker capable of accelerating from 0-100 in six or seven seconds, then you may need a highly engineered oil pan. If not, a stock pan will probably do just fine. Some manufacturers have completely stock pans that have been chrome plated. If you like to spend time laying under the car polishing your oil pan, one of these should make you very happy.

Certain manufacturers, most notably Moroso and Milodon, have many special pans built for street high-performance use. These feature simplified baffle and swinging-gate systems to help control the oil but are less elaborate than the all-out racing pans. One of these could be a wise investment if you can unquestionably detect an oil supply problem. So, how do you know if you have an oil supply problem? In the next section we will discuss gauges in greater detail. Here we will only say that with a good gauge you can read the oil pressure, and as long as you don't see the needle drop dangerously low under your normal driving conditions, you probably don't need a "fancy" oil pan (which may also require a special pump/pickup and a greater drain on your wallet).

Besides the basic engine accessories mentioned above there are many hundreds of additional add-on pieces available. Many are worthwhile and a small percentage are unnecessary or even possible sources of trouble. Our best advice when considering such items is to go carefully. Inspect the item to see if it will fit correctly and try to determine if it has a functional benefit or, at least, if it is purely a glamour item, that it fits or "functions" as well as the item it is replacing. Any engine is a complex arrangement of several hundred parts. They must all work correctly and fit properly or problems will occur. It is easy to get discouraged when you have problems, so we recommend that you make all decisions with careful consideration. Don't make any more trouble for yourself than necessary — keep it simple.

Instruments

A good set of engine monitoring instruments is certainly among the best investments any performance buff can ever expect to make. It's just not very smart to build a high-performance engine and not take special steps to make certain it is operating at peak efficiency all the time. The only way to check this is to have a good set of engine gauges.

The primary engine gauges usually considered as essential are: an oil pressure gauge, a water temperature gauge and a voltmeter or ammeter. Obviously each of these gauges has a specific use, but there are other gauges which can augment these basics. We will look at the auxiliary gauges later, but for now let's look at the three primary monitors.

The oil pressure gauge, of course, monitors oil pressure when the engine is operating. Oil is like the lifeblood of an engine. If the main bearings, the valvetrain and all of the other high-friction interfaces of the engine are not supplied with a constant source of clean, relatively cool oil, friction and heat increase and before long a major failure will surely occur. Every engine should be fitted with an accurate, reliable oil pressure gauge.

The water temperature gauge, sometimes merely referred to as the "temperature" gauge, is the second most important monitor. This gauge is important to make certain that the cooling system is carrying off sufficient residual heat from the cylinder block and heads to prevent dangerously high heat levels that reduce oil effectiveness. Undue heat may also lead to metal fatigue and all kinds of other calamities. Today street engines are restricted to relatively low compression ratios (because of the lousy gasoline available), so overheating is not as prevalent as in the past. (High compression creates more heat in the engine, and thus more power, and creates a greater strain on the cooling system.) However, most modern engines operate with very lean fuel-air mixtures. This can also lead to overheating and is an equally important reason for using a temperature gauge to make certain that the water pump and radiator are in good working order at all times.

The voltmeter and ammeter are less critical gauges but they each serve an important function. These two gauges are primarily for monitoring the condition of the electrical system. And, though an electrical failure is usually less critical than an oil or cooling malfunction, it can still be very irksome. Each of these gauges monitors the electrical system and though many rodders prefer either one or the other, most knowledgeable car buffs will use both gauges. The ammeter monitors the functioning of the alternator or generator, as the case may be. It determines that the alternator/generator is charging the battery as

necessary to replace the energy consumed by the car. The voltmeter continuously monitors the battery, no matter if the engine is running or not (an ammeter works only when the alternator or generator operates). Some mechanics feel, therefore, that a voltmeter is somewhat more useful because it gives an immediate reading of the electrical system condition, even before the engine is started. On the other hand, modern storage batteries are very reliable, and, in recent years, the ammeter has become very popular (most Detroit cars are equipped with some sort of ammeter, even if the information is displayed only on a warning light).

Beyond these basic gauges there are other useful monitors: The vacuum gauge, the cylinder head temperature gauge, oil temperature gauge and even the exhaust temperature gauge. These are somewhat more specialized than is generally considered useful for a street-driven engine. Their functioning is pretty much self-explanatory and they are usually reserved for special racing or supercharging applications.

Tachometers

The last, and perhaps the most important, gauge we will discuss is the tachometer. There's probably not a single high-performance engine in the entire country worth it's salt that doesn't have an accurate tachometer hooked to it. A tachometer (sometimes called a rev counter) tells you so much about the condition of the engine that it must be considered as mandatory, It is important for shifting, for checking on the idle speed, for watching cruise speed and for tuning the engine. It is virtually the heartbeat of the engine.

Electric vs Mechanical

Before closing, we should explain the difference between electrical and mechanical gauges. This is pretty simple. A mechanical gauge uses a direct monitoring device to read out the essential information. For example, a mechanical tachometer has a long flex cable that attaches between the distributor and the gauge. A gear mechanism at the distributor causes the cable core to rotate. The rotation is sensed by another gear mechanism inside the tachometer and the gauge needle is hooked directly to the gearing, giving a "direct" readout.

In the other case, an electrical gauge gives a readout through an electrical impulse system. Some sort of electrical sensor is used at the source to convert the mechanical action into an electric potential. The potential is sent through a wire to the gauge. At the gauge the electrical potential is converted back into a mechanical action to control the position of the needle or pointer on the gauge face.

In general, mechanical gauges are considered to be somewhat more rugged and reliable than electric type gauges. However, modern advances in electronics have largely negated this advantage. Furthermore, electric gauges are much easier to install. There are no long cables or tubes which must be routed from the engine to the gauge. It is generally much simpler to route a wire up to the dash-mounted gauge. We have talked to hundreds of rodders who have used each kind of gauge with success and each has a personal preference that they swear is the best. You can't go wrong with either type, so use whichever you like.

Engine monitoring gauges are an absolute must on every performance engine. Oil pressure, water temp and ammeter are the most popular types. Shown are Autometer electrical (upper) and mechanical (lower) models.

"Mechanical" gauges use a direct-reading sensing device inside the gauge. Electrical gauges use a remote sensing device that converts the info to electrical potential that is sent to the gauge by wires.

HOW TO INSTALL A CUSTOM GAUGE PANEL

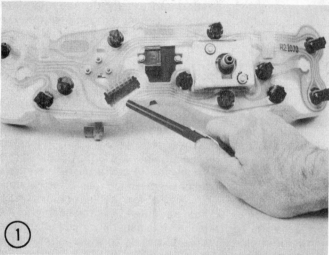

(1)

Most modern cars have a printed circuit behind the dash instead of wires, which can make the installation of accessory gauges difficult. Indicated here is the opening where a plug connects the panel with the wiring.

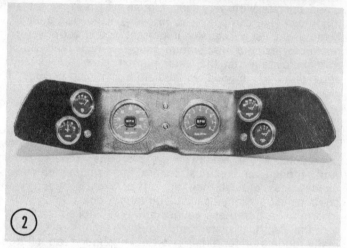

(2)

Here's a custom dash panel made of aluminum covered with vinyl. Ro-Lan Sales will be making these in fiberglass for late-model Camaros. This one is fitted with turn signal indicators, brake warning light, high-beam indicator, and six instruments by Autometer.

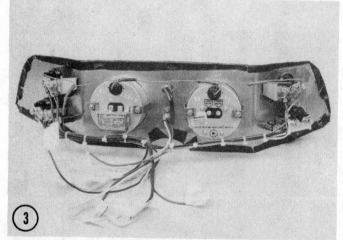

(3)

The same panel from the rear shows most of the wiring completed and put neatly into bundles with Ty-Wraps. All of the gauge lights can be hooked together, as can the ground and hot lead wires for most of the gauges (except for the ammeter). Number code or tag all new wires.

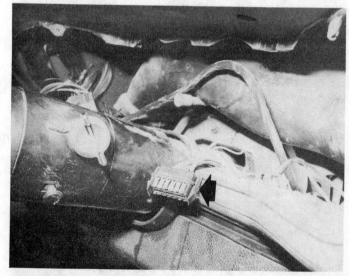

Hanging over the edge of the stock instrument panel cavity in this '70 Camaro is the stock plug that goes to the back of the printed circuit.

Since the stock plug is simply a bundle of copper contact strips, the wires needed for this gauge setup were clipped off, to be fitted instead with solderless terminals.

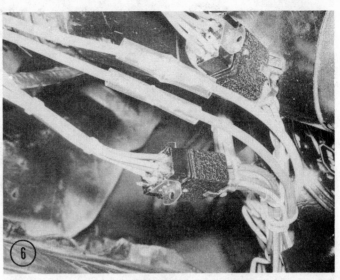

This view shows the male end of a quick-disconnect plug with pigtails which are attached to the wires cut from the stock plug with butt connectors.

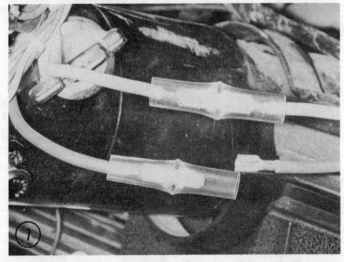

Installed as it is between the alternator and the battery, an ammeter handles a lot of juice, so 10-gauge wires are necessary, here fitted with snap-in connectors for dash removal.

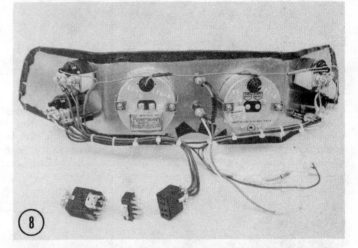

Here's the custom panel with some of the gauge wires soldered to half of a quick-disconnect plug. The other half was soldered to the wires cut from the stock plug. These take-apart connectors have numbered terminals and only snap together one way.

Here's the quick-disconnect plug from the custom gauge panel hooked up to some of the wires cut from the stock plug (arrow). Solderless butt connectors are used for the connections.

Installed in the '70 Camaro, this custom panel looks clean and functional, with real gauges as opposed to "idiot lights" and a black vinyl covering to match the accessory steering wheel. The use of precision gauges enables you to keep tabs on your modified street engine.

Accutronic, as their name implies, makes accurate electronic instruments and test equipment, including this 4-inch mechanical race tachometer with telltale and rev counter.

Autohaus manufactures a variety of specialty products designed for VW's and VW-powered vehicles, such as a cylinder head temperature gauge with bolt-on sending unit.

Auto-Meter Products offers the performance enthusiast more than their well-known tachometers with insulated mounts. They also manufacture a full range of performance gauges.

Automotive Accessories markets the Astra-View sunroofs, designed with mirrored safety glass, positive locks, aluminum frame and closed-cell seal.

B&B Performance Products makes a great many items for the performance engine builder, such as aluminum harmonic dampeners, head bolt washers, high-strength head bolt kits and stud kits, dial indicator holders, ring compressors and piston/rod holders.

Cal Custom is a name famous for accessories since the early 1940's when customizing started, but today their products are strictly up-to-date, like this cast-aluminum, polished oil pan for smallblock Chevy engines.

Cole-Hersee isn't a household name but they make most of the special switches, lights and electrical components for all major car makers. Their catalog is loaded with stock and specialty electrical components.

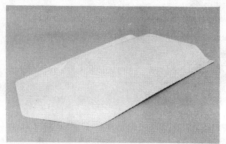

Harwood, Inc. manufactures performance chassis components and is one of the leading makers of "Borg Warner Cycloc" hood scoops (a non-plastic or fiberglass construction) that have smooth edges for easy finishing.

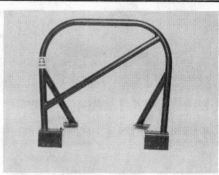

Hobrecht builds a variety of products from heavy-duty steel tubing, including brush guards and roll bars for trucks, vans, mini-trucks and cars.

Jones-Motrola is the major manufacturer of mechanical tachometers. Nearly all of the mechanical tachs sold by other "name" manufacturers are made by Jones.

Milodon Engineering, Inc. builds more than their famous "VII Litre" aluminum racing engine. They also make a line of HD oil pumps, pans and gear drives.

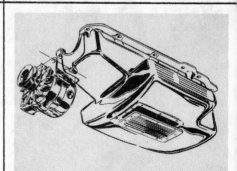

Moon Equipment Company has recently released these highly-polished, cast aluminum oil pans for the Chevrolet small and big-block engines.

Moroso has an endless selection of special parts for the perf/racer. They have tools, gauges, suspension, engine and body parts.

Rotiform Corporation manufactures this up-to-date digital speedometer that is accurate to within one mph and is calibration-adjustable with a screwdriver. Three warning lights alert the driver of high speed ranges.

Smittybuilt, Inc. manufacturers rollbars, cages and grille guards for trucks, vans, chopper VW's and this new cage for late pickups which is a bolt-on built of 2-inch steel.

Sun Electric Products markets a complete line of custom accessory gauges for your car or truck, but they are perhaps best known for their line of top quality tachometers.

Rite Autotronics Corporation has for many years marketed a fine line of gauges and accessories for every need. They also manufacture tuning aids and instrument panels.

R.P.I.* Inc. offer the hot rodder with a valuable car the means to protect his investment, the Autolarm burglar alarm. With an eight-second delay, it allows you to get in and out, but goes off if anyone else enters or tampers with CB or other accessories.

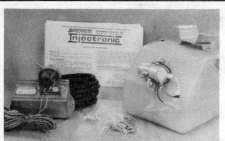

Spearco Performance Products, Inc. makes a lot of products aimed at the small-car crowd, but one item they have that applies to all engines is this electronic water injector.

TRW Replacement Division makes many products that the average enthusiast may not be familiar with. Besides their well-known engine parts, TRW also sells these under-dash gauges and panels.

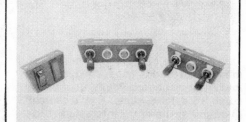

Ro-Lan Sales has made a specialty of supplying the hot rodder with the electrical and wiring accessories and tools he needs, including bulk wire, terminals of all kinds, switches, fuse panels, gauges and crimping tools.

Sears has a complete line of tools and tuneup instruments for the part-time or serious mechanic. This Penske inductive timing light is one of many useful items they offer.

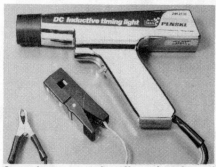

Stewart-Warner is one of the largest manufacturers of gauges, shop equipment and many other parts. Their catalog offers every conceivable type of custom instrument and gauge panel.

VDO Instruments has an impressive array of performance gauges in their catalog, which covers applications from automobiles to snowmobiles and cycles. These are their highly-rated "Cockpit" series gauges.

This list of major parts and equipment manufacturer addresses is included for reader convenience. Nearly all of these companies have sales and technical literature available to interested readers who seek further guidance. Normally this literature is available free of charge or for a nominal charge. If you have a specific problem or need detailed information about a particular piece of equipment, most of these people will be glad to help.

A

ACCEL
P.O. Box 142
Branford, Ct 06405
Ignitions

Accutronics
P.O. Box 142
Branford, Ct 06405
Instruments

Addco Industries
958 Watertower Rd.
Lake Park, Fl 33403
Sway bars

Advance Adapters
13629 Tale St.
Santa Fe Springs, Ca 90670
Engine/trans adapters

Allison Automotive
1267 Edna Pl.
Covina, Ca 91722
Ignitions

Appliance Industries
23920 S. Vermont
Harbor City, Ca 90710
Headers & Wheels

Autohaus
1338 W. 6th St.
Corona, Ca 91720
Accessories

Auto Meter Products
22 S. State St.
Elgin, Il 60120
Instruments

Automotive Accessories
2609 Woodland Dr.
Anaheim, Ca 92801
Accessories

Autotronic Controls Corp.
6908 Commerce St.
El Paso, Tx 79915
Ignitions

B

B&B Performance
25692 Taladro Circle
Mission Viejo, Ca 92675
Accessories

B&M Performance Products
9152 Independence
Chatsworth, Ca 91311
Auto Transmissions

Borg-Warner Corp.
11045 Gage Ave
Franklin Park, Il 60131
Trans Engine Driveline Parts

C

Cal Custom
23011 S. Wilmington
Carson, Ca 90745
Accessories

Cam Dynamics
3926 Runway Rd.
Memphis, Tn 38118
Cams

Cannon Industries
9073 Washington Blvd.
Culver City, Ca 90230
Cams, Accessories

Carrera Racing Shocks
203 Marray Drive
Atlanta, Ga 30341
Suspensions

Carter Carburetor Co.
9666 Olive St.
St Louis, Mo 63132
Carbs, Fuel Systems

Casler Headers
1031 W. Brooks St.
Ontario, Ca 91762
Headers

Champion Muffler
14426 Whittier Blvd.
Whittier, Ca 90605
Exhaust & Head Porting

Champion Spark Plug Co.
P.O. Box 910
Toledo, Oh 43661
Spark Plugs

Cheshire Manufacturing Co.
312 E. Johnson Ave.
Cheshire, Ct 06410
Coolers

Chrysler Performance Parts
P.O. Box 857
Detroit, Mi 48288
Cams, Headers, Ignitions

Clifford Research
1670 Sunflower Ave.
Costa Mesa, Ca 92626
Manifolds, Headers, Accessories

Cole-Hersee
20 Old Colony Ave.
South Boston, Ma 02127
Electrical

Competition Cams
2806 Hangar Rd.
Memphis, Tn 28118
Cams

Cragar
19007 S. Reyes Ave.
Compton, Ca 90221
Headers, Ignitions

Crane Cams
100 NW 9th Terrace
Hallandale, Fl 33009
Cams, Valvetrains

Crower Cams & Equipment
3333 Main St.
Chula Vista, Ca 92011
Cams, Valvetrains

Cyclone Automotive Products
7040 Lankershim Blvd.
N. Hollywood, Ca 91605
Headers, Exhaust Systems

D

Douglass Mfg.
5636 Shull St.
Bell Gardens, Ca 90201
Headers, Exhaust Systems

E

Eagle Specialty Products
8341 Canoga Ave.
Canoga Park, Ca 91304
Headers

Earl's Supply Co.
P.O. Box 265
Lawndale, Ca 90260
Plumbing

Edelbrock Equipment Co.
411 Coral Circle
El Segundo, Ca 90245
Manifolds

EELCO Mfg.
2601 S. Garnsey
Santa Ana, Ca 92707
Accessories

Engle Cams
1621 12th St.
Santa Monica, Ca 90404
Cams

Sig Erson Racing Cams
15881 Chemical Lane
Huntington Beach, Ca 92649
Cams, Valvetrains

G

Gabriel Shock Absorbers
200 E. Randolph Dr.
Chicago, Il 60601
Shock Absorbers

General Nucleonics/Speedatron
2811 Metropolitan Pl.
Pomona, Ca 91767
Ignitions

H

Harbor Industries
13025 Halldale Ave.
Gardena, Ca 90249
Accessories

Harwood Performance Sales
11501 Hillgaurd Rd.
Dallas, Tx 75243
Accessories

Hayden Trans Coolers
1531 Pomona Rd
Corona, Ca 91720
Trans Coolers

Hays Sales
15116 Adams St.
Midway City, Ca 92655
Ignitions

Headers by "Ed"
2710-16th Ave S.
Minneapolis, Mn 55407
Headers

Hedman Hedders
9599 W. Jefferson
Culver City, Ca 90230
Headers

Hellwig Products Co.
16237 Ave 296
Visalia, Ca 93277
Sway bars

Herbert Automotive
1933 South Manchester
Anaheim, Ca 92802
Cams

Hobrecht Enterprises
15662 Commerce Ln.
Huntington Beach, Ca 92649
Roll bars

Holley Carburetor Co.
11955 E. Nine Mile Rd.
Warren, Mi 48090
Carbs, Fuel Systems

Hooker Headers
P.O. Box 1010
Ontario, Ca 91762
Headers

Howard Cams
19122 South Main St.
Los Angeles, Ca 90003
Cams

Hurst
50 W. Street Rd.
Warminster, Pa 18974
Shifters

I

IECO Automotive Specialties
1431 Broadway
Santa Monica, Ca 90406
Accessories

Interpart Corp.
141 Oregon St.
El Segundo, Ca 90245
Cams, Headers, Accessories

Iskenderian Racing Cams
16020 S. Broadway
Gardena, Ca 90248
Cams, Valvetrains

J

Pete Jackson Gear Drives
1905 Victory Blvd. #9
Glendale, Ca 91201
Gear Drives

Jones-Motrola Instrument Corp.
432 Fairfield Ave.
Stamford, Ct 06904
Instruments

K

K&N Engineering
561 Iowa Ave.
Riverside, Ca 92507
Air Filters

Kensington Products Corp.
150-64 Green St.
Hackensack, NJ 07601
Koni Shock Absorbers

L

Lakewood Industries
4566 Spring Rd.
Cleveland, Oh 44131
Accessories

Lamb Components
1259 W. 9th St.
Upland, Ca 91786
Specialty Brake Systems

Lunati Camshaft Co.

3871 Watman Ave.
Memphis, Tn 38118
Cams

M

Maier Racing Enterprises
235 Laurel Ave.
Hayward, Ca 94541
Ford Specialties

Mallory Electric Corp.
1801 Oregon St.
Carson City, Nv 89701
Ignitions

Manley Performance Products
13 Race St.
Bloomfield, NJ 07003
Cams, Accessories

McCleod Industries
1125 N. Armando St.
Anaheim, Ca 92806
Clutches

Milodon Engineering
7711 Ventura Canyon
Van Nuys, Ca 91402
Accessories

Moroso Sales
737 Canal St., Bldg 23
Stamford, Ct 06902
Accessories

Moon Equipment Co.
10820 S. Norwalk Blvd.
Santa Fe Springs, Ca 90670
Cams, Accessories

Motorola Automotive Products
9401 W. Grand Ave.
Franklin Park, Il 60131
Ignitions

Mullen & Co.
340-C East Carson St.
Carson, Ca 90745
Valves, Head Preparation

N

Nelson-Dunn, Inc.
940 So. Vail Ave.
Montebello, Ca 90640
Aeroquip Hose, Fittings

Norris Performance Products
14762 Calvert St.
Van Nuys, Ca 91401
Cams, Valvetrains

O

Offenhauser Sales Corp.
5232 Alhambra Ave.
Los Angeles, Ca 90032
Manifolds

P

Pacer Performance Products
5345 San Fernando Rd. W.
Los Angeles, Ca 90039
Manifolds, Headers, Accessories

R

Race Car Parts
22628 S. Normandie
Torrance, Ca 90502
Plumbing, Accessories

Racer Brown, Inc.
9270 Borden Ave.
Sun Valley, Ca 91352
Cams, Valvetrains

Racer Walsh
11 Washington Ave.
Suffern, NY 10901
Cams, Accessories

Reed Engineering Co.
126-130 New St.
Decatur, Ga 30030
Cams

Ridgeway Racing Associates
P.O. Box 281
Stafford Springs, Ct 06076
Accessories

Rite Autotronics Corp.
3485 S. La Cienega Blvd.
Los Angeles, Ca 90016
Instruments

Rocket Racing Products
9935 Beverly Blvd.
Pico Rivera, Ca 90660
Accessories

Ro-Lan Sales
1031 S. Laramie St.
Anaheim, Ca 92806
Electrical Supplies

Rotiform Corporation
5140 W. 106th St.
Inglewood, Ca 90304
Instruments

R.P.I. Inc.
13740 Midway Rd., Suite 509
Dallas, Tx 75240
Burglar Alarms

S

Savage Industries
810 W. Collins Ave.
Orange, Ca 92667
Clutches

Schiefer Clutches
50 W. Street Rd.

Warminster, Pa 18974
Clutches, Gears

Schneider Racing Cams
1235 Cushman Ave.
San Diego, Ca 92110
Cams

Sears, Roebuck & Co.
Sears Tower
Chicago, Il 60607
Accessories, Instruments

Smittybilt, Inc.
2124 N. Lee Ave.
S. El Monte, Ca 91733
Exhaust Systems

Sorensen Mfg. Co.
1115 Cleveland Ave.
Glasgow, Ky 42141
Ignition Wiring

Spearco Performance Products
2054 Broadway
Santa Monica, Ca 90404
Accessories

Speed Pro/Sealed Power
2001 Sanford St.
Muskegon, Mi 49443
Cams, Engine Parts

Stahl Headers
1515 Mt. Rose Ave.
York, Pa 17403
Headers

Stewart-Warner Corp.
1826 Diversey Pkwy.
Chicago, Il 60614
Instruments

Sun Electric Corp.
3011 E. Rte. 176
Crystal Lake, Il 60014
Instruments

T

Taylor Cable Products
301 Highgrove Rd.
Grandview, Mo 64030
Ignition Wiring

Team G
P.O. Box 65977
Los Angeles, Ca 90065
Manifolds

Thermo-Chem
10516 E. Pine
Tulsa, Ok 74116
Coolers

Doug Thorley Headers
7403 Telegraph Rd.
Los Angeles, Ca 90040
Headers, Exhaust Systems

Thrush Performance Products
22 Iron St.
Rexdale, Ontario, Canada M9W 5E2
Exhaust Systems

Tom's Differentials
15547 Paramount Blvd.
Paramount, Ca 90723
Custom Rear End Assembly

Trans-Dapt
P.O. Box 4157
Compton, Ca 90224
Trans/Engine Adapters

Trans-Go
2621 Merced Ave.
El Monte, Ca 91733
Auto Trans Shift Kits

TRW Performance Parts
8001 East Pleasant Valley Rd.
Cleveland, Oh 44131
Cams, Engine Parts

Turbo Action
P.O. Box 5581
Jacksonville, Fl 32207
Auto Trans Shift Kits

V

VDO Instruments
116 Vistor Ave.
Detroit, Mi 48203
Instruments

W

Weber Cams
1663 Superior Ave.
Costa Mesa, Ca 92627
Cams

Weber Clutches
P.O. Box 142
Branford, Ct 06405
Clutches

Weiand Automotive Ind.
P.O. Box 65977
Los Angeles, Ca 90065

Weiand Automotive Ind.
P.O. Box 65977
Los Angeles, Ca 90065
Manifolds

Wolverine Gear & Part Co.
2 So. Birdlake Rd.
Osseo, Mi 49266
Cams, Gears

Z

Zoom
Dovesville Hwy
Darlington, SC 29352
Gears

We're interested in your opinion

In an effort to make our publications more interesting and informative (and because it's fun), we would like you to give us your opinion. Please answer the following questions and return this portion of the page (or a copy) to the publisher as indicated on the reverse side. Thank you very much.

How did you find out about this book?
☐ Saw it on the counter   ☐ From a magazine ad
☐ From a friend   ☐ Other

What part of this book did you find most interesting?
☐ Photos and captions   ☐ Text

Was this book difficult to locate?
☐ Yes   ☐ No

How did we cover the subjects?
☐ Covered well   ☐ Adequate   ☐ Poorly done

Where did you buy this book?
☐ Speed Shop   ☐ Auto Parts Store   ☐ Book Store
☐ Military PX   ☐ Other

On a scale of one to ten, I would rate this book:
☐ 1 to 3   ☐ 4 to 6   ☐ 7 to 9   ☐ 10

The Best In High-Performance Books

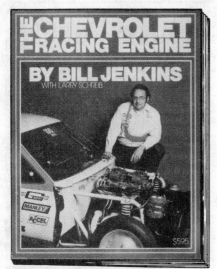

THE CHEVROLET RACING ENGINE is the sum of twenty years of racing, winning, and experience. Bill Jenkins, in this once-in-a-lifetime book, has written a thorough, in-depth study of race preparing the smallblock Chevrolet engine. This fine publication contains 160 pages, over 300 illustrations, and the best Chevy racing information ever published. By Bill Jenkins with Larry Schrieb. Cover price $6.95.

SUPERPOWER provides practical bolt-on information on today's hottest performance subjects. A separate chapter for each simply describes how the systems work, evaluates the good and bad points, supplies do-it-yourself instructions and a source list of available kits and suppliers. The 160 pages and over 320 photos were authored by Pat Ganahl, Larry Atherton, and Jim McFarland. Cover price $6.95.

MOPAR PERFORMANCE is the best single source for the latest smallblock and big-block performance information. Totally up-to-date and complete, this guide can help both the beginner and advanced engine builder. Two distinct sections separate the "A" and "B" material, however, duplication is avoided providing a thoroughly informative book cover to cover. Over 110 pages and 200 photos. Cover price $6.95.

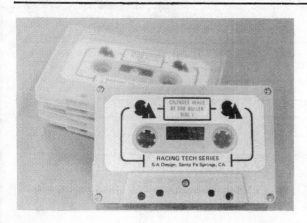

THE DESIGN AND MODIFICATION OF RACING CYLINDER HEADS BY BOB MULLEN

Technical information presented on cassette has previously suffered from lack of quality and content. But today, S-A Design Publishing has produced an in-depth study of cylinder-head theory and practical modification with the nation's leading racing-head expert Bob Mullen of Mullen and Company. Bob's unique knowledge in the field is explored through the discussion of separate and specific questions. Air-flow testing, dyno development, valve weight and design, valve springs, a unique method of intake gasket matching, and many other subjects are explained in terms all can understand. Tapes are available in cassette only, no 8-track, etc. By using the coupon on the reverse side, you can order this super tech tape at the special price of $4.95. Order Now!

What subject(s) do you enjoy reading about?
- ☐ High-performance engine building
- ☐ Carburetion and induction systems
- ☐ Strip performance
- ☐ Street performance
- ☐ Suspension (street, strip and road race)
- ☐ Cylinder head modifications
- ☐ Economy
- ☐ Vans
- ☐ RV's
- ☐ Nascar
- ☐ Other_____

Please mail this questionare to:

S-A Design Publishing Company
11801 East Slauson, Bldg. E
Santa Fe Springs, CA 90670

Would you like us to put your name on our mailing list for information on new tech books? ☐ Yes   ☐ No

Name _____

Street _____

City _____

State _____ Zip _____

4

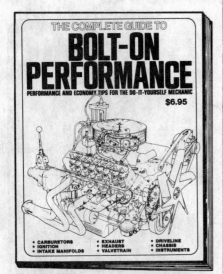